Beyond the
Punitive Society

Beyond the Punitive Society

OPERANT CONDITIONING:
SOCIAL AND POLITICAL ASPECTS

edited by Harvey Wheeler

CENTER FOR THE STUDY OF DEMOCRATIC INSTITUTIONS

W. H. FREEMAN AND COMPANY
San Francisco

Library of Congress Cataloging in Publication Data

Wheeler, John Harvey.
    Beyond the punitive society.

    Papers presented at a symposium organized by J. H.
Wheeler and sponsored by the Center for the Study of
Democratic institutions, held in Santa Barbara, Calif.
    1. Operant conditioning—Congresses. 2. Human
behavior—Congresses. 3. Behaviorism (Psychology)—
Congresses. 4. Skinner, Burrhus Frederic, 1904-
I. Center for the Study of Democratic Institutions.
II. Title.
BF319.5.06W47   301.15   73-1269
ISBN 0-7167-0785-3

Printed in the United States of America

1 2 3 4 5 6 7 8 9

Preface

Operant conditioning is one of the most important contributions to psychology and the social sciences in the past fifty years. Although it had always been surrounded by controversy, the storm of controversy that erupted following the publication of *Beyond Freedom and Dignity* forced a consideration of its merits, limitations, and social implications upon thinking persons throughout the world. The purpose of this book is to present an overview of operant conditioning, a critical evaluation of Skinner's ideas together with responses to his critics. The chapters of this book were commissioned by the Center for a symposium in Santa Barbara at which Skinner was present. A final purpose is to prepare for a technological assessment of operant conditioning. We are familiar with assessments of technologies deriving from the physical sciences; in the future, we shall have to make such assessments for social technologies as well. With operant conditioning serving as a model, this book explores some of the approaches that may be useful in doing so.

February, 1973   *Harvey Wheeler*

Contents

Beyond the
Punitive Society

1

Introduction:
A Nonpunitive World?

Harvey Wheeler

Harvey Wheeler, a senior fellow at the Center for the Study of
Democratic Institutions, is coauthor (with the late Eugene Burdick) of
Fail-Safe *and author of* Democracy in a Revolutionary Era *and*
The Politics of Revolution. *Wheeler commissioned the chapters and*
organized the Center conference upon which this book is based.
His introduction provides a background discussion of operant
conditioning and the related issues that form the substance of this book.

B. F. Skinner's Book *Beyond Freedom and Dignity* discusses some of the
social and philosophical implications of behavior modification through
operant conditioning. Of course, behavior modification did not start
with modern behavioral psychology. One of the functions of politics has
always been to modify behavior. Plato stated this as his leading goal in
writing *The Republic.* Our educational practices are devoted to behavior
modification. Each time we draft a new law we have in mind the modification of behavior to conform with the provisions of the law. The aim
of modifying behavior is not new, but recently the techniques for modifying certain types of behavior have developed a high degree of sophistication. The most familiar include such examples as the behavioral drugs,
tranquilizers, and energizers. Moreover, we are told that the world's

leading nations are engaging in large, secret research projects in behavioral drugs: drugs that can be sprayed over large population centers
to render their inhabitants docile or disoriented and easy for an invading
army to manipulate.

Many fear that such drugs may be used for other purposes: to quell
a riot or to calm angry commuters caught in traffic jams and subway
failures. If they can be used for this, they can also be used for more
general, dictatorial purposes. A modern Hitler, for example, might use
behavioral drugs rather than concentration camps.

Electronics combined with brain research provides another technique
of behavior control. Electrodes implanted in the brain can stimulate
pleasure centers so effectively that the subject abandons all other needs
and functions in favor of pressing the pleasure button over and over
again. Already, these stimuli can be activated by remote, wireless
control. Perhaps some day it will no longer be necessary to actually
implant electrodes in the brain in order to achieve similar results.

Molecular biologists seem to be on the verge of understanding the
way in which the DNA–RNA replication process works. When they do,
genetic engineering may become a reality. Many good things can be
done: genetic surgery can correct congenital defects in the newly born.
But these are all partial and discrete applications. Skinner goes beyond
this. He believes his psychological principles can provide the foundation
for a new social system. The mere suggestion is enough to frighten us
with specters of *Brave New World* and *1984*. Yet our own world, the
one Skinner and his followers want to supplant, is in good measure the
result of the work of an eighteenth-century behavioral psychologist,
Jeremy Bentham. In his time, Bentham was attacked and derided and
his social prescriptions were feared, much as is the case with Skinner
today. The parallel between Skinner and Bentham is of special interest
because, despite the similarities in their work, it is precisely Bentham
whom Skinner wishes to dethrone. Or rather, it is the laws and institutions that resulted from Bentham's theories that Skinner wishes to
supplant with new ones based on his own theories.

Jeremy Bentham and his utilitarian followers were behaviorists and
their political philosophy was based upon Bentham's pleasure–pain
psychology: man, he said, seeks pleasure and avoids pain. Although
the Benthamites were empiricists, this was not an empirical proposition.
It was a postulate rather than a scientifically verified proposition. But
the pleasure–pain hypothesis accorded well enough with common-sense
observations to seem generally acceptable. Once the proposition was
accepted, it was possible to derive from it a complete system of political
theory. This is what the early "liberals"—Bentham, James, John Stuart
Mills, and their followers—did. The completed edifice was known as

liberalism, a philosophy as well as a prescription for the construction of a practicable political system. Jeremy Bentham was one of the most influential men who ever lived. Within fifty years of his death, nearly every theoretical proposition he had ever announced had become written into the laws of the "liberal" democracies.

Bentham's *Theory of Legislation* was especially useful. The pleasure–pain principle, he reasoned, could be used for the control of social behavior in a way that would be effective and, at the same time, maximize the amount of liberty in society. (He also defined liberty in a common-sense way: the absence of restraint.) The formula was simple. To maximize liberty meant to minimize restraints. The problem of government was to prevent restraining behavior, both by individuals and by political authorities. One prevented unwanted behavior by punishing it. In theory, one could calculate the amount of pleasure the restrainer derived from his restraining behavior and then write a law prohibiting that behavior, affixing a punishment in such a way that the punishment just overweighed the pleasure. The undesired behavior would no longer bring pleasure to its perpetrator and, hence, would be suppressed. The punishment would, *a la* Gilbert and Sullivan, fit the crime. If the system worked, crime would be banished and liberty would flourish.

The system did not work, at least not according to plan. But Benthamism, if not liberty, *did* flourish. Criminal law throughout the western world followed the principles of Benthamite pleasure–pain psychology. Punitive laws and punitive modes of thought dominated legislatures and courts. The catalogue of crimes was subjected to an intensive bookkeeping analysis. Each was weighted with its appropriate punishment according to the pleasure–pain calculus: so much money to be taken from somebody who committed an unwanted civil act; so much freedom to be forfeited in prison for the commission of crimes. Norval Morris claims that general reliance on imprisonment for crimes was, like Benthamism, an innovation of the eighteenth-century. It rested upon the alleged correlation between time and crime. Prior to the mid-eighteenth century, criminals were often simply executed. The contemporary social institution we know as the prison was the direct result of the liberal, behaviorist pleasure–pain principles that became dominant in western thinking after Bentham.

Today, the validity of the prison as an institution is being questioned. Though doubtless it was an improvement over what went before, now it, in its turn, seems to have become obsolete. Punishments, despite the claims for Bentham's pleasure–pain calculus, no longer deter crimes. Prisoners do not expiate their crimes and they are not rehabilitated. Thrown together with other criminals, they learn chiefly how to be more intrepid, if not more skillful, criminals. We attack the prison system, yet we have no idea of how to cope with undesired behavior except through punishment and imprisonment, which maintains the tie between time and crime that is our legacy from Jeremy Bentham and the eighteenth-century liberals.

We cannot imagine how a nonpunishing world would work, even though it is clear that the punishing world we have does not work. That is, *most* of us cannot imagine what a nonpunishing world would be like. A minority among us can, however. Its members are adherents of a new behaviorism with a new non-Benthamite psychology, one that claims to rest upon solid scientific foundations rather than merely superficial common-sense postulates. This is the psychology of operant conditioning, invented (discovered) by B. F. Skinner. Its adherents are multiplying throughout the world just as the adherents of pleasure–pain psychology did earlier. The new ideas seem strange and threatening. They draw cherished beliefs into question. They promise a new world of tranquility and creativity, but only if we first give up tenets of freedom and dignity that have been at the core of our liberal heritage.

The Benthamites, who started the process that led to the enshrinement of these beliefs, met with fear and hostility when they began. They won, even without having hard scientific evidence on their side. If, as is conceivable, Skinner were to receive a Nobel Prize for his work on operant conditioning, the fright and apprehensiveness provoked in many of us by his theories will magnify and, at the same time, the corps of dedicated operant conditioners will expand.

Clearly, we must all inform ourselves about operant conditioning. Indeed, we must do more. We must analyze and assess it. It is a science with distinct technological implications, just as physics is. Today, as we look at the recent advances in the physical and biological sciences, we have growing concerns about where they may lead us. We speak of the need for "technological assessment" of their novel implications. Nobody yet knows how to make such technological assessments accurately. We know even less about making accurate technological assessments for a behavioral science such as operant conditioning. Yet it is imperative that we try. In fact, Skinner himself, in one sense, has come to the same conclusion. *Beyond Freedom and Dignity* might be called a technological assessment of the social implications of putting operant conditioning into practice throughout society. If we want to assess the implications of this new technology, the best place to start is with Skinner's book. This is what we have tried to do in this collection of essays. This collection is by no means a definite assessment; it merely inaugurates a process that should be continued and expanded. Much more needs to be done—by universities, research institutes, and citizens groups.

What, then, is operant conditioning? Perhaps the best way to find out is to read two early books by Skinner, *Contingencies of Reinforcement* and *Science and Human Behavior*. Even then, however, many doubts and questions will remain unanswered. Although the scientific demonstrations on which operant conditioning rests are very simple, its new way of thinking and of expressing things is devilishly complex. Indeed, it may not be far off the mark to say that operant conditioning presents us with a Copernican revolution in our ways of thinking. Just as Copernicus told us that the apparent reality of a physical world in which the sun revolves around the earth is illusory, so Skinner tells us that the apparent reality of a behavioral world in which organisms respond to stimuli is almost as illusory. Skinner is to Pavlov, then, as Copernicus was to Ptolemy. But this may be a gross overstatement. Many distinguished people, among them Noam Chomsky, think it is. This is one of the questions readers of this book will want to judge for themselves when they have finished.

Let us look back again at the earlier behaviorists, the Benthamites. Their critics immediately pointed out defects in the pleasure–pain hypothesis: what was pleasure for one person was pain to another; each man to his own taste. What to do, for example, about the masochist? Moreover, degrees of intensity of pleasure and pain vary among individuals. Finally, how does one add up pleasures and pains? Can the pleasures of a few persons outweigh one person's pain? Now we see that Benthamism's foundation was not scientifically valid and the calculus was impossible to apply. The main reason for restating this is to emphasize a point made earlier: our present society operates on certain assumptions about the alleged efficacy of punishment, and these assumptions have proved to be false. They are false whether or not Skinner and the operant conditioners are right. However, the operant conditioners make a further point. Punishment *can* work. It works differently from the way the Benthamites thought it would, but it does work. Punishment effectively suppresses undesired behavior, even though it may, in the process, also suppress other highly desirable behavior.

Indeed, suppression (punishment) is the primary way all previous social systems have controlled unwanted behavior. Up to a point in social development, prior to the time social interrelationships became extremely complex, the benefits of suppression may have outweighed its defects; that is, the generalized system of suppression did not produce intolerable side effects. That point, say the avant-garde operant conditioners, has long since passed by. Just as prisons teach criminals how to be criminals, not how to be good citizens, so punishment teaches persons how to punish; how to punish themselves by haranguing themselves with guilt feelings, as well as how to punish others retributively. When interrelations are complex, each punishment may have a multiplier effect. The result is a society characterized by punishing; repressive behavior produces a suppressive society. Such a society is dysfunctional; no species can survive in such an environment. The human being, marvelously subtle and resourceful creature that he is, has been able to accommodate much more suppression than can other living things, but even he can take only so much.

Innovative operant conditioners believe that punishment control systems are technologies and that they produce "pollution" just as do other technologies. Automobiles produce noxious gasses, but as long as the density of population is low and there are but few automobiles, the pollution dissipates and the benefits from the technology outweigh the evils. When concentrations of people and automobiles increase, the situation changes. The evils from the polluting side effects outweigh the benefits of the technology. It is the same with punishment systems, according to operant conditioners. In simple societies in which personal contacts are few and not densely intertwined, the evil effects of punishment techniques are dissipated; but under complex conditions, they produce a noxious form of social pollution. They produce Vietnam-type wars; rootless, disillusioned youth; anomic, suicidal adults; disaffected ethnic minorities; cynical, manipulative leaders; presidential assassins; and Manson families. Fortunately, so the argument runs, behavior can be controlled in a better way, in a way that produces expressive rather than suppressed individuals, a way that is rewarding and reinforcing rather than punishing. Nearly everything that can be done by punishment can be done better and with fewer bad side effects through reinforcements. Moreover, everybody will be happier. How do operant conditioners know this?

The answer is that they do not yet know it. This is another reason operant conditioning must be subjected to an intensive technological assessment. The claim is that human societies can be improved if we follow lessons that were learned in the laboratory from experiments involving primarily (but not exclusively) pigeons and rats. Many successful human applications have already been made—for example, operant-conditioning teaching programs. If such programs are designed by talented technicians, they are more effective for most students than are traditional methods. Moreover, the results are duplicable. The programmer need not be present in person, he need only draw up the original program. Once that is done, the program can be used anywhere with anybody.

Certain intractable situations, such as the care of institutionalized autistic children and "back ward" psychotics, can be improved beyond anything previously possible. Many organizational and administrative problems become solvable. Certain behavioral diseases or disorders, such as alcoholism and drug addiction, seem to respond better to operant conditioning than to traditional treatments. A prison can be transformed into a relatively tolerable environment with a considerable reduction in disciplinary problems. Such successes are increasing, but they have so far applied only in marginal situations; the case is far from being demonstrated. Should the evidence become much more persuasive in the near future, we can expect the movement, which is already expanding rapidly, to take on an exponential growth rate. This was what happened with Benthamism, and it had absolutely no laboratory or experimental verification behind it. If, for example, the behavior-modification program with which Vitali Rozynko and his colleagues are associated (see page 71) turns out to produce dramatic results in dealing with alcoholics, psychiatric wards all over the country will introduce similar operant-conditioning programs. In his essay "Skinner's New Broom" (page 190), Alex Comfort predicts that, if operant conditioning proves successful in mental hospitals, it will spread inexorably throughout the rest of society.

Suppose this happens: Will we be ready for it? Will the proper technicians be available? Will the punitive teacher, recognizing the trend, go home one night as his accustomed self and emerge the next morning as a self-proclaimed operant conditioner? These and many other possibilities lie ahead if the movement takes hold. We may be confronted with problems due not only to operant conditioning's inherent flaws but also to its over-hasty and inept adoption. This is what has happened in the past to many technologies: the computer, thalidomide, the automobile. A major public commitment to the technological assessment of operant conditioning should be mounted immediately, not only to determine its validity, but also, in the event it is found valid, to establish conditions and standards under which it may be introduced more widely throughout society.

Suppose we now enter, ever so tentatively, the world of operant conditioning. What does it look like? What is different? At first, nothing is different, and the reason is that the world has always been an operant-conditioning world. If it had not been, operant conditioning could not have been discovered in the first place: The world always was and always will be (so the doctrine holds) an operant-conditioning world; but operant conditioning's special contribution, the reduction of punishment in the environment, was not possible before the mainsprings of behavior were discovered. The world was a Newtonian world before Newton, an Einsteinian world before Einstein, and so on. I use these illustrious names as illustrations, not as comparisons. A better example has to do with the behavioral faculty known as language. All human beings throughout all time have possessed language. In every natural language there is an implicit grammar, even though few societies using language have ever discovered grammar. In grammar there is an implicit logic and in logic there is an implicit mathematics. The world, we now say, is a mathematical world. It always was a mathematical world, even before there was mathematics. Mathematics was implicit in human behavior once the first *Homo sapiens* began to use the first rudimentary language. Operant conditioning is to behavior in general as mathematics is to natural language. It was always implicit in behavior, it simply took a long time—far too long, many think—to be made explicit. How was it made explicit?

This part of the story goes back to the famous Pavlov, the man who described stimulus and response and trained a dog to salivate at the ringing of a dinner bell, as if the bell were actual food. This stimulus–response chain was consistent with certain experiments on autonomic nervous systems: prick the muscle of a frog and his leg will contract: stimulus produces response. All behavior, so the behaviorists of the early twentieth century believed, was stimulus–response behavior. This is what John B. Watson meant by behaviorism. Freud derived the "dynamic" aspect of psychoanalytic theory from the Pavlovian reflex arc.[1] It was a picture consistent with nineteenth-century mechanics: energy was fed into one end of the system and work was produced at the other. Skinner was well along into his own research before he realized something else was going on. The important discovery came about as the result of an argument with two European psychologists. They had responded to one of his published articles by claiming to have earlier discovered and published very similar findings. In defending his own work, Skinner was led to ponder Edward Thorndike's thesis about the educational process. Why he was led to Thorndike is not clear. One must not discount the possibility that a predisposition toward pragmatism was at work. The crucial role of consequences in both pragmatism and operant conditioning seems more than accidental. Thorndike had emphasized the potent role of consequences: learning is enhanced if the student is rewarded for achievements. Looking back over his own laboratory findings, Skinner perceived that he had *not* been observing a stimulus and then a response pattern but, rather, behavior that was shaped in an orderly pattern by its *subsequent* reinforcement. This innocent-appearing modification led to the elaboration of the entire

---

[1]Otto Fenichel (1945) states this as follows: "The basic pattern which is useful for the understanding of mental phenomena is the reflex arc. Stimuli from the outside world, or from the body, initiate a state of tension that seeks for motor or secretory discharge, bringing about relaxation. However, between stimulus and discharge, forces are at work opposing the discharge tendency. The study of these inhibiting forces, their origin and their effect on the discharge tendency, is the immediate subject of psychology."

operant-conditioning system. Stimulus-response leads us to concentrate on prior conditions; operant conditioning leads us to concentrate on what happens after behavior occurs. Stimulus and response reactions are not disproved, specifically not the reflex actions of the autonomic nervous system. However, the environmental contingencies within which behavior takes place become crucial. Behavior operates on and within these contingencies and is conditioned for the future according to the results experienced. Behavior is *reinforced* when the consequences increase the probability it will recur when similar circumstances arise in the future.[2] Now *probability* is used here in a special sense. Usually, it refers to a measure of frequency distributions. In operant conditioning, probability is quite a different notion, reminiscent of its use in Percy Bridgman's operationalism. Different types of reinforcement schedules produce differently shaped curves of behavior. However, whatever increases probabilities is a positive reinforcer. The subject "reveals" what his positive reinforcers are by the way they shape his behavior. Food and sex are common positive reinforcers, not because we are told they are "liked," not because they are said to give "pleasure," and not because they are called "good." It is the other way around. We report that we "like" them and we call them "good" because they positively reinforce behavior associated with them. We know this not from expressed opinions but from shaped behavior: when a positive reinforcer is added to the environment, it increases behavior rates.

Behavior in a subject can also be affected by removing certain things from his environment, or by removing him from the environment containing them. We escape from the consequences of a fire either by fleeing it or by putting it out. The consequence, relief from heat, shapes our subsequent behavior. The beneficial result of our negative action reinforces the escape behavior just as food does with positive behavior. The reinforcement is produced by a negative act, rather than a positive one, and it is the negative act that is reinforced. Behavior, assuming we put out the fire, was increased (reinforced) by taking something *out* of the environment. The thing that was taken away was a *negative reinforcer*, because the action consisted of eliminating from, rather than adding to, the environment. Reinforc*ement* is produced both by positive and by negative reinforc*ers*.

---

[2]Pavlov's *a priori* formula was in accord with classical mechanics: stimulus produces response. Skinner defines behavior *a posteriori*: responses are shaped by consequences. This is biological rather than mechanical. It is reminiscent of the concept of tropism and of C. H. Waddington's (1967) notion of the "chreods," the necessary pathways of organisms. It is interesting to speculate on what changes might be produced in psychoanalytic theory if the principles of operant conditioning were to be substituted for those derived from Pavlov. The result might well bear a close resemblance to Eric Berne's transactional analysis.

Behavior can be suppressed as well as reinforced. This is done by adding something aversive to the environment when escape is impossible. This is what is commonly called punishment. In operant terms, it is an *aversive stimulus*. We detect its presence by observing that the behavior associated with it is suppressed. Skinner once believed aversion to be a less effective behavior modifier than reinforcement, but this has since proved to be false: the stability of the curves associated with the suppression of behavior through aversion and those for eliciting behavior through reinforcement turn out to be roughly similar. However, one may elicit desired behavior both ways: it is possible to specifically reinforce the desired behavior or to aversively suppress everything *but* the desired behavior. Of the two methods, however, reinforcement wins hands down. It is more efficient because it is more precise. It is more effective because it has fewer side effects. It does not, as aversion does, needlessly suppress extra behavior in order to achieve the desired result. When stated abstractly, this conclusion seems obvious. Yet a great deal of human behavior is shaped the inefficient and ineffective way. A common example is the parent who wishes his child to come when called and punishes the child for doing anything other than that. A very high proportion of social interaction follows this pattern, even though most people who engage in it know better. A more difficult situation obtains when we attempt to discourage automobile drivers from speeding: We prohibit speeding by law, and whoever is caught violating the law is arrested. If they learn anything from being arrested, speeders learn to avoid getting caught (one of the ways to do this being to refrain from speeding). Despite its inherent ambiguity, aversion does work, and this fact raises a serious question for operant conditioning. When simple avoidance is what we wish to teach, reinforcement is very inefficient and aversion can be effective. In theory, it would be possible to reinforce drivers in such a way that they would always drive at the legal speed; traffic police would then be unnecessary. However, the effort would be enormously expensive and the process would be extremely arduous, two consequences with quite aversive effects.

This leads to the notion of deferred consequences. Candy may be immediately reinforcing but ultimately aversive, in that dental caries and excess weight may result from eating it. A law may be immediately aversive but ultimately reinforcing in similar fashion. We need methods for presenting future consequences as part of the present environment. When we wish to produce simple avoidance, or restraint, aversion may be the preferred device, especially when considered in the light of deferred consequences. During the early days of liberalism, from the eighteenth century until the mid-twentieth century, governments were suppose to do very little, and that little was to be directed primarily at preventing persons and groups from interfering with the liberty of individuals. This was the day of negative government. That government was thought best that governed least; anarchy plus the street constable was the stated ideal. So long as these conditions existed, aversive controls may have been ultimately reinforcing. They had one further advantage: People do not like aversive controls and try to avoid them. Aversive controls may even produce revolutionaries and, if so, they may be self-correcting. But this happens only if aversion has not become so widespread as to produce a suppressed population. In such cases, the people become lethargic and more withdrawn, rather than restive and rebellious. Such behavior is characteristic of slaves and of the subjects of totalitarian regimes. Terror, the control device of totalitarian regimes, is the constant distribution of aversion throughout the environment, keeping the people in a permanent state of apprehension and suppression.

Toward the middle of the twentieth century, the so-called liberal democracies began to develop into what we call the positive state. The state did more things, and it also required individuals to do more things. It introduced the controlled economy as well as a wide range of controls over general behavior. However, it tended to do this through its accustomed "liberal" mode of control, namely, aversive and punitive measures: the positive state was accomplished through the expansion of punitive and suppressive regulations. The tables were turned on the past. Now aversion was used to create immediate satisfactions—for example, more jobs—but at a fearsome deferred social cost through the increase in persons exhibiting suppressed behavior. Such, at least, is the argument of the operant conditioners.

The antidote? Dismantle the aversive control system; abandon the control theories of the early liberals. Substitute instead operant-conditioning devices to control behavior through (negative as well as positive) reinforcers. Society's work will get done and everybody will be happier. Some punitive laws will remain, but most tasks will be accomplished through positive reinforcement schedules. A few lawyers will still be required to frame old-fashioned punitive legislation, but most policies will be accomplished through the aid of skilled operant conditioners programming reinforcement schedules.

What is wrong with this? Nothing, obviously, if that is the only difference. However, the critics of operant conditioning believe there would be plenty of others. People, they believe, would be too happy and too smug and too comfortable. Moreover, they would not be aware of their controls. It is easy to see how a punishment controls behavior, but a reinforcer works insidiously. In fact, operant conditioning itself proves that we would all have a very difficult time altering behavior that had been shaped through reinforcements. A dictator, if he were really clever, would rule through operant conditioning and maintain his authority by keeping everybody happy all the time. In one light this may seem like a diabolically clever scheme, but would mankind suffer notably at the hands of rulers who ran society in the way a just God would run paradise?

The more persuasive reason for caution and skepticism is that we cannot estimate the deferred consequences. This is what a proper technological-assessment project might tell us. However, the task would be formidable. Operant conditioning is quite easy to understand, so long as we consider the behavior of one individual at a time; when interactions are visualized, it becomes much more difficult. *Science and Human Behavior* contains a chapter entitled "Social Behavior," but it is very thin, indeed. Moreover, though Skinner does not say so to the reader, he discusses nothing more complex than two-person behavior. Two-person behavior is indeed complicated, and it presents difficult problems for operant conditioning. The same behavior (for example, person *A* getting rid of person *B*) may be negatively reinforcing to one and aversive to the other. Adding a third person, or an "*n*th" person, enormously complicates the situation, so that it virtually defies analysis. Imagine a simple task to be accomplished by five persons in such a way that each is positively reinforced and nothing aversive occurs. Undoubtedly, game theory could be redefined according to operant-conditioning principles and then such problems could be worked out on computers. However, this would require a logic, or an axiology, of operant conditioning and so far none has been produced. L. A. Zadeh's essay, "A System-Theoretic View of Behavior Modification" (page 160), is a promising start, but much more is required before theoretical analysis will be possible. My own appendix to this chapter consists of a series of propositions that are intended to express the implicit logic of operant conditioning. Operant conditioning is an empirical science, not a theoretical one, and this is one of its major deficiencies. If it could be given authoritative theoretical expression, many of the disputes between Skinner and his opponents might be resolvable. At least, bystanders would be in a better position to judge between them.

Beyond Freedom and Dignity purports to present us with the philosophy of operant conditioning. It does no such thing. Instead, it tells us Fred Skinner's personal credo, with operant arguments attached, possibly in the hope of reinforcing the reader. With the general reader, it was partly successful. At least not all younger readers were put off by his attack on established notions of freedom and dignity, and they were often attracted by the prospect of a nonpunishing world. With the critics, however, the opposite occurred. Repelled by Skinner's own beliefs, they took his word for it that these were implicit in operant conditioning. Having disposed of his beliefs to their own satisfaction, they then assumed they had thereby disposed of operant conditioning, which, of course, they had by no means done. Operant conditioning, with its successes as well as its limitations, stands today exactly as it did before the publication of *Beyond Freedom and Dignity*, except that considerably more people are now misinformed about it. The reason for this traces to Skinner's own philosophy.

Skinner did not begin his professional career as a psychologist. In fact, he took no psychology courses at all as an undergraduate. Upon graduation from Hamilton College, he worked at being a novelist before deciding to take graduate work at Harvard.

He began as a Baconian pragmatist and an admirer of Bertrand Russell. Russell led him into John B. Watson's popular book on behaviorism. Only after this did he turn to more technical works and decide to do graduate study in psychology. Empiricism, positivism, behaviorism—these were Skinner's philosophic antecedents, and the precedence of philosophy over science is important. The precedence has persisted. Chafing under the attacks on *Beyond Freedom and Dignity*, Skinner now plans a new book, not on operant conditioning, but on the philosophy of behaviorism.

Skinner believes that, if one accepts the validity of his scientific accomplishments, one must also assent to his more general behaviorist philosophy. He tends to dispose of his critics, not by meeting their arguments head on, but by complaining that they could not have said the things they did if first they had either satisfied themselves about the truth of the science and the efficacy of the technology or, for the sake of the argument, had assumed their validity. The book does not discuss either the science or the technology, but it does give references permitting the skeptical reader to satisfy himself about their claims.

First off, it must be determined whether or not this perspective is a defensible one. I think it is not, and I think that, if the following propositions can be agreed upon both by Skinner and by his critics, much of the basis for their differences will disappear.

It is true, as Skinner suggests, that three topics are at issue; it is not true that they relate to each other in the binding way he suggests. The three topics are: the philosophy of behaviorism, the science relating to contingencies of reinforcement, and the technology of operant conditioning. The last two are intimately connected. The first has no necessary connection with the others at all.

As a confirmed empiricist, Skinner believes in what humanists call scientism, namely the view that the methods of the physical sciences can be applied to the study of human and social problems. He also believes in reductionism. As a physiological psychologist, he deals with individual organisms; that is all he sees. When he looks at society, he does not see structural forces, such as capitalism, or spiritual forces, such as the Protestant Ethic; he sees individual behavior. Skinner believes that all social problems can be reduced to individual problems. Scientism, reductionism, and behaviorism provide the basis for Skinner's ideological attack on freedom and dignity. Of these, behaviorism has occasioned the most discussion.

One can be a philosophical behaviorist without being either a contingencies-of-reinforcement scientist or an operant-conditioning technologist, and vice versa: One could be a Platonist, a Kantian, a Hegelian, a Husserlite—even a Chomskyite—and still accept the findings of operant conditioning just as one might accept the findings of any other empirical science. This is not a proposition Skinner can easily assent to because, in his own case, the science and the technology came after and, hence, positively reinforced the philosophy. A special problem occurs over Skinner's arguments (in the absence of empirical demonstrations) concerning verbal behavior, but that is a separate issue. Most of Skinner's critics are really critics of the philosophy of behaviorism rather than of operant conditioning. Behaviorism as a philosophy possesses several difficulties. Skinner's critics point these out with some acerbity, seldom bothering to take his science on its own terms or to discuss its political and philosophical implications.

The general theory of behaviorism that Skinner holds goes beyond what we are warranted in assuming by virtue of the scientifically valid propositions that derive from the theory of positive reinforcement. It also goes beyond what can be demonstrated by the technique of operant conditioning. Hence, we must make a distinction between the general theory of behaviorism, on the one hand, and, on the other, the special theory of positive reinforcement with its associated technology. In short, we are not warranted by the evidence in concluding that all behavior, including verbal behavior, is explicable within the terms of operant conditioning. If some behavior is not satisfactorily explained in this way, the universal claims extrapolated from the system cannot be accepted. Hence, we have the option, within the terms of operant conditioning, of giving it qualified acceptance. Suppose we do this: what then are the larger implications?

One implication is that we must adopt the same stance toward the theory of positive reinforcement that we do toward any other scientific proposition. That is, we value it because it can explain certain things about what is going on; it answers a set of "what" questions. It does not, however, answer any "why" questions. Specifically, it does not tell us why people respond in some situations more effectively to positive reinforcements than they do to punitive (aversive) measures. As Skinner has said, "One might be tempted to conclude that people do so because that is the way the brain is wired." But this would be no explanation; it would be going beyond the evidence, and it would not increase our understanding even if there were some evidence suggesting that it was indeed true. Skinner has stated that, in any case, this is the sort of thing that is investigated by neurophysiologists rather than by behavioral psychologists.

If "why" questions can be disposed of we avoid immediately some of the difficulties occasioned by a hasty reading of *Beyond Freedom and Dignity*; for in some parts, the book does seem to be addressing itself to "why" questions—to the discussion of overall purposes and their presence or absence—rather than merely to "what" questions. Specifically, we cannot say, within the terms of operant conditioning, "why" men invented liberty, dignity, responsibility, or any other of the classical moral and political virtues. At most, we can offer a behavior analysis of their functions. We cannot say which, if any, of these have survival value, because we cannot judge this without reliance upon criteria outside the scope of behavioral analysis. An example Skinner cites illustrates the point. Men evolved as organisms highly reinforced by sweets. We are not justified in suggesting exactly why this occurred merely from observing that it did occur. It may have been found that it was a useful survival trait at one time. In any case, it appears now to be a trait that reduces survival potentials. But this is something that could not have been known in the past when it appeared to possess survival potentials. The same difficulty arises over any other characteristic that may now be reinforcing, or of any other behavior that we may now decide to reinforce. In other words, in considering any significant behavior we may wish to adopt, the question whether or not it possesses survival value must be decided on criteria separate from the behavior of the organism.

All of this must not be taken to imply that Skinner's own conception of operant conditioning, either as an empirical science or as an applied technology, is the only (or even the preferred) one. Many important qualifications, divergences, and improvements have been made by those who have followed later. Karl Pribram, in Chapter 5, argues that Skinner's view of operant conditioning is not so much wrong as it is obsolete. This is reinforced by the work of William T. Powers, who has used the analogy of the closed feedback loop to explain behavior in a fashion that purports to resurrect purpose and, hence, "freedom." These, as well as the other qualifications found throughout the book, merely serve to reinforce the argument in favor of a rigorous technological assessment of operant conditioning.

Suppose we adopt this qualified view of the application of operant-conditioning techniques. What difference will it make? First off, it induces one important change in our world view. We accept the fact that behavior is, and always has been, strongly affected by environmental factors composed of both aversive and reinforcing elements and that, for certain types of performance, the most powerful conditioners are the positive reinforcers. Humans now live, and always have lived, in a world of positive reinforcement: that is the fact, and it is a fact with sound scientific underpinning. Therefore, there can be no question of deciding whether or not to *believe* in operant conditioning, or whether or not to introduce it, much as we may decide whether or not to introduce the computer or the SST.

Having recognized that operant conditioning is, in fact, one of the ways behavior is shaped, we then have the option of leaving things in the operant condition presently existing or taking advantage of this new awareness and adopting more widespread applications of operant-conditioning practices, substituting positive reinforcers for aversive stimuli in a number of cases.

What would be the effect of the latter choice? One of the first things we would have to decide would be the relative effectiveness of reinforcing and aversive controls in specific cases. Recall the example of traffic regulations. We could, conceivably, eliminate all policemen and all traffic signs and positively condition people to get to places correctly and at proper rates of speed. It is not likely we would decide to do so, because it appears that the costs in time, money, and other desirables would be prohibitive. That is, we would end up with a system that would be ultimately more punitive than is the more efficient, though characteristically aversive, mode of control we now apply. Hence, even within the assumptions of positive reinforcement, there may be overall characteristics of a set of positive reinforcements that, taken as a whole, are indirectly more aversive than would be alternative techniques for achieving the same goal through overtly aversive means. This does not mean that some qualified or partial applications would not be desirable, but it does mean that the choice for or against the practice would always be one in which the possible deferred aversive effects of positive reinforcers would have to be measured against the possibly amplified deferred reinforcements of immediate aversive means. Again, this is a case somewhat akin to that of the effects of sugar as a positive reinforcer.

Moreover, our choice must depend upon our ultimate goals, and these cannot be derived from within behavioral assumptions. For example, today we simply do not know what the correct ecological policies for safeguarding the environment should be. Soon, through the application of something like the Forrester–Meadows model, we may be able to calculate ecological effects more accurately and, thus, avoid what Forrester calls counterintuitive policies. But until something like this is possible, we have no way of knowing what ecological behavior ought now to be reinforced; on the other hand, we do know that much of what we actually adopt is ultimately aversive, in the counterintuitive sense. Thus, we need much more sophisticated goal-setting devices before we can accurately calculate the marginal reinforcement potentials of alternative policies.

Suppose this problem is solved and we begin to adopt positive-reinforcement techniques for a large range of social and political policies, how different would the new society be from the one we now have? Several suggestions can be made:

1) Punitive institutions will tend to give way to educational institutions (educational in the sense that persons can be taught how to avoid deferred aversive effects through operant conditioning).

2) The overall punitive, or legalistic, environment will be reduced and somewhat supplanted by positive-reinforcement practices, with a resulting decrease in repressive measures.

3) Management of people and direction of organizations will tend to become debureaucratized, for it will be possible to condition behavioral patterns in people rather than objectify them in organizational structures.

4) Organizations will themselves become smaller due to the reduction of formalistic superstructures.

5) Organizations will operate more along self-management lines, rather than authoritarian lines, which will result in an approximation of goals traditionally associated with anarchism.

6) The increase in technically qualified people in the field of operant conditioning may be similar to the previous increase in experts in accounting, economics, and other social technologies. It is difficult to visualize the role such experts would play. It is certain that professional standards must be established, and some safeguards against improper practices will be required. It is even possible that a central governmental agency for the survey of the possible applications of operant conditioning may be required, much as a central agency for economic forecasting is now required.

7) A separate issue arises because of the possibility that operant conditioning may work best through focusing initially upon verbal behavior. This is not established at present, but it may turn out that, when the problem is to change overall *normal* behavior in some significant way, the device will be through verbal behavior. (See the essay "Controlled Environments for Social Change," by Vitali Rozynko et al., on page 71.) In this event, something similar to the group mind-

changing practices pioneered in China may appear. This will obviously raise numerous issues, one of them relating to liberty.

8) The atmosphere of liberty is not likely to alter as sharply as is described in *Beyond Freedom and Dignity*, but the emphasis is likely to change. The role of negative liberty—liberty conceived as freedom from restraint—is certainly not going to disappear, for one of the effects of introducing positive reinforcement is to diminish restraints and, hence, to expand liberty. It is likely, however, that the positive idea of liberty—liberty interpreted as the freedom to do, or the ability to achieve, what one wants—is likely to take precedence over the more traditional idea of negative liberty that has been associated with the tradition of western liberalism. In this restricted sense, the society will, to some extent, have moved beyond liberty, if not dignity.

9) A special jurisprudential problem concerns the relation between law and planning. Plans are goals and they are also laws. But they are not laws in the traditional liberal sense because one cannot punish people for failure to achieve goals. To do so leads to distortions and falsifications of the sort familiar from the Russian experience in attempting to enforce compliance with planning goals. At the present time, there is no adequate jurisprudence applicable to the legal problems of a planned society. Operant conditioning may point toward the solution of this problem: a form of law in which achievement of goals is prescribed but failure to achieve them is not punished.

Freedom and dignity, as we know them, are largely the invention of modern western industrial man. True, these notions have been utilized by other civilizations, but not in the meanings Skinner gives them. The problem is to evaluate the costs and benefits attributable to them. It is a formidable task, but given the momentous consequences that might follow their abandonment, it is something that must be attempted before we can decide whether or not to eliminate them. For example, to what extent does an environment containing freedom and dignity achieve the ends we want more efficiently than might otherwise be possible? This raises a host of questions. There is the question of individualism and how its ravages of our national resources can be curbed. It raises questions relating to the findings of Kurt Lewin and his demonstrations that environments providing freedom and dignity are more productive than those that do not. But beyond this, it raises the question of the overall effects of the social environment. A society providing freedom and dignity amounts to a moral society. It teaches its members that they are autonomous moral agents who must choose between good and evil and act accordingly. Even if they choose to do evil or to violate the law, they are accorded the dignity of an autonomous person (and punished accordingly). To the extent that they have no choice—that is, to the extent that they behave compulsively, when "out of their minds" (from drugs or insanity) or under duress—they are absolved from responsibility. In such cases, they are accorded treatment (often hospitalization) rather than punishment. The first result of dispensing with freedom and dignity is the elimination of the assumption that men are responsible for their acts. Hence, the moral society will be supplanted by the "hospital society" or, as it has also been called, the "therapeutic society." This is not as fanciful as it might first appear; it is one way of describing contemporary China. China is one of the societies that never experienced such western values as freedom and dignity. This is not to say that freedom and dignity were unknown to traditional China, but only that the peculiarly western versions of them were never assimilated by the Chinese. Moreover, when China began industrialization, it adopted procedures much like those described in *Beyond Freedom and Dignity*. It often applied reinforcement rather than aversive methods to induce its people to accept the new behavioral environment. It then arranged its reward system so as to positively reinforce actions that were in conformity with the values of the new environment. Deviation was not so much punished as it was treated. Recalcitrant individuals were given group think treatments—called brain-washing—in which they were rewarded for expressing approved sentiments. China provides an example that can be useful in preparing a model for the technological assessment of operant conditioning.

We may raise a somewhat more subtle issue. Even assuming that the above difficulties can be resolved, what about the positive role that such notions as freedom and dignity may have played? Skinner argues they are bad because they stand in the way of full-fledged adoption of operant-conditioning principles in human affairs. He argues further that they are wrong because a behaviorist point of view reveals them to be myths. Suppose we agree that such concepts, formerly deemed ennobling, are, in fact, myths. May it not be true, even from a behaviorist point of view, that such ennobling myths are necessary positive reinforcers for a humane and decent society? If so, the role of behaviorism would be to induce a firm belief in the intrinsic validity of verbal behavior that it claims is no more valid than an archaic code of chivalry. This, in fact, is close to the conclusion of an earlier behavior modifier. Plato concluded that people in general could not be induced to engage in the normative behavior they ought to observe unless they could be made to believe in certain myths capable of inducing such behavior. This led Plato to his theory of the noble lie: a rule of behavior that is just, but whose justice is not suspectible to being perceived by the average person. Many of Skinner's critics have suggested that he is, in effect, a negative Plato, and that what he has presented us with is an ignoble lie.

My own conclusion is that this is an erroneous interpretation. I have many doubts about the political and social conclusions he draws from his work. The fact remains, however, that Skinner's work has resulted in the creation of a rapidly maturing technology of behavior modification. It is effective, and because it is effective it will be used. The political problem facing us is the same one that faces us when any powerful technology is developed: how to control it so that we can enjoy its benefits rather than suffer from its abuses. After the debate over the merits of the arguments in *Beyond Freedom and Dignity* has subsided, this problem will remain; a problem that would be posed to us by Skinner's scientific contributions even if he had never written *Walden II* or *Beyond Freedom and Dignity*.

Appendix: A Tentative Logic of Operant Conditioning

1) We begin with an organism responding in an eventful environment. The events of the environment include events taking place inside the nervous system.

2) There may be much in the environment to which the organism is neutral; no response occurs. Although we cannot say that an organism is *not* behaving, we can say that, inasmuch as it responds selectively with regard to the events in its environment, it may be neutral to many if not most of them. Specific events, or categories of events, may move in and out of neutral status.

3) Organisms exhibit tropisms and enantiotropisms; they develop toward (positive) and away from (negative) various things in their environment.

4) These are, to use C. H. Waddington's term, chreods (necessary pathways). There are positive and negative chreods.

5) The various chreods exhibited by an organism make up its repertoires.

6) Alterations in the environment alter the repertoires.

7) An organism acquires highly articulated repertoires when they increase in quantity, or frequency, or both.

8) The record of the interaction between an organism and those events to which it is not neutral is its response rate.

9) The interaction may result either in suppression or in reinforcement of the response.

10) Suppression reduces response rates; reinforcement augments response rates.

11) Both can be assigned operationalist probabilities denoting the likelihood with which they will tend to occur under similar conditions in the future.

12) Positive suppression is a decrease in the probability of the same response occurring in the future and is achieved with direct aversive stimuli.

13) A negative suppression is a decrease in the probability of a response occurring in the future and is achieved with reinforcement of behavior preclusive of that response.

14) A positive reinforcer is something *added* to the environment that increases the probability a given response will recur in the future.

15) A negative reinforcer is something *eliminated* from the environment that increases the probability a given response will recur in the future.

16) All reinforcement achieves negative suppression of responses contradictory to the one being reinforced.

17) Suppression and reinforcement are known through the responses of the individual organism; although most members of a species respond similarly, what is suppressive for one may be reinforcing for another.

18) This is true both relatively and reflexively.

19) Relatively, the same event may suppress a response in one organism but reinforce that response in another.

20) Reflexively, when an event incorporates the behavior of two or more organisms, the reinforcement experienced by one may induce suppression in another.

21) A relationship creates a corporate behavioral event.

22) Corporate events consist of reflexive responses.

23) Corporate events can be classified according to the reflexive effects of an event on the responses of each member.

24) Two extreme possibilities exist: the positive reinforcement of all members, and the positive suppression of all members.

25) Positive reinforcement on the corporate level would be an event in which all the reflexive responses of each member are positively reinforced.

26) It is possible to simulate an operant-conditioning model for corporate events in which positive reinforcement is optimized.

27) It would be possible to minimize the amount of punishment in society by applying the model to the shaping of actual corporate behavior.

2

The Skinnerian Revolution

John R. Platt

John R. Platt, research biophysicist and associate director of the Mental Health Research Institute at the University of Michigan, is the author of The Excitement of Science, The Step to Man, Perception and Change: Projections for the Future, *and other books.*

The first half of "The Skinnerian Revolution" is devoted to explicating what Platt calls Skinner's "revolutionary manifesto." Platt manages to clarify aspects of Skinner's approach that have puzzled many readers of Beyond Freedom and Dignity, *and his presentation is sufficiently comprehensive that those who have not yet read Skinner will be able to understand the balance of this book.*

In the last half of his article, Platt reviews Skinner's methods from a more existential viewpoint and comes to the conclusion that they "offer us the brightest hopes of any methods we now have for rapid restructuring of many of our obsolete and dangerous institutions, and for building, not merely a Skinnerian society, but any new society for the world ahead."

What Skinner Has Done

THE IMPACT ON PSYCHOLOGY

B. F. Skinner's new book, *Beyond Freedom and Dignity*, is a revolutionary manifesto. It proposes the design of a new society using our new methods for improving the behavior and the interactions of human beings. It has been roundly condemned, as all his earlier books have been, by humanist critics who at other times call for improved human interactions. In fact, from this point of view, Skinner may have had the worst press of any great scientist since Darwin.

In order to understand the important new philosophical ideas in *Beyond Freedom and Dignity*, I think it is essential to understand—as most of his critics have not understood—Skinner's basic discoveries about behavior, what they imply about human relations, and how they are already being applied to a multitude of problems today.

The comparison with Darwin is not inappropriate. Both men started from a small set of problems and forced a radical rethinking of everything else in the field. Both men displaced the old verbal explanations with an almost mechanical description of basic processes of life and man. Darwin's mechanism of the evolution of species is even closely parallel to Skinner's mechanism of the evolution of behavior in a single individual. Darwin, like Skinner, was accused of unjustified extrapolation from birds and dogs to man, and of treating man as a mere animal. And in both cases, in spite of the scientific clarification and the technical successes, there were loud protests from the defenders of humanism and morality.

There is no doubt that Skinner's approach is leading to a radical reprogramming of psychology. Until recently, psychology has seemed to be standing still for lack of a general organizing principle. Freud's formulations have been greatly discredited by recent experiments; Pearsonian measurements and correlations usually do not show us how to do anything; personality "traits" and even intelligence tests are under fire; the theories of "drives" could not even explain such compulsive behavior as gambling; the great learning theorists did not show us how to teach faster; the "classical conditioning" methods of the early behaviorists have been of little use in schools or child training, or even animal training; and the schools of loving responsiveness, group therapy, and "peak experiences" have been warm and inspiring but not very scientific.

Into this sea of ineffectiveness, Skinner has brought, over the last thirty-five years, a technique and theory of "operant conditioning" and behavior modification that has transformed every behavioral problem and approach. His method can speed up animal learning by 10 to 100 times (Skinner, 1959; Pryor, 1969), can be used to improve behavior in psychiatric wards (Ayllon and Azrin, 1968), cure problems such as bedwetting and stuttering that have resisted psychiatric treatment (Ulrich et al., 1966; Krassner and Ullmann, 1965), cure disruptive or delinquent behavior (Tharp and Wetzel, 1969), and can double the learning rate in schools from kindergarten through college (Skinner, 1968a; Whaley and Malott, 1971). It can be used for self-control of unwanted habits (Ulrich et al., 1966; Stuart and Davis, 1970; Whaley and Malott, 1971), and even for yoga-like voluntary control of heartbeat, blood pressure, and other autonomic functions that had been supposed to be beyond conscious control (DiCara and Miller, 1968; Miller, 1969).

It is evidently important for us—and for everyone—to understand just how such a powerful method works and what it implies about biology and human nature. Only then can we assess the real or imagined dangers feared by Skinner's opponents. In the end, I think we can show that a considerable reconciliation is possible between Skinner's approaches and those of his critics, when we see how their different contributions fit together into a total view of man and of man's self-determination of his society and his future.

THE PRINCIPLE OF CONTINGENT REINFORCEMENT

The basis of Skinner's methods of learning and behavior modification is his principle of contingent reinforcement, or "operant conditioning," which he first stated more than thirty years ago (Skinner, 1938). He showed that a three-term formulation is necessary to describe how an animal or human being is induced to change its behavior (Skinner, 1969). (This is why the usual one-term or two-term learning theories—such as learning-by-experience, learning-by-doing, trial-and-error, and stimulus-and-response, or, in computer language, input–output—are so ineffective.) Koestler confused Skinner's method with stimulus-and-response [p. 166].[1]

The three necessary terms are stimulus–behavior–reinforcement, and their relation can be symbolized by

$$B$$
$$S \quad R,$$

thought of as repeated:

$$B \qquad\quad B \qquad\quad B$$
$$S \quad R \ldots S \quad R \ldots S \quad R. \ldots$$

The lower line in each three-term unit represents the environment's actions on the organism, and the upper line represents the organism's actions on the environment. S is the preliminary stimulus or situation, B is some behavior the organism may then show or "emit," and R is then any change or "reinforcement" from the environment that is *immediate* and *contingent* on a particular B. (A particular behavior B

---

[1]Thoughout this paper, page numbers in square brackets refer to pages in Skinner's *Beyond Freedom and Dignity* (Alfred A. Knopf, 1971).

emitted by the organism is called an "operant," and when this is induced to be emitted regularly under a given S and R, the process is called "operant conditioning.")

Any R that is followed by an increase in the probability of B is called a positive reinforcer, or R^+. Any R that is followed by a decrease is called a negative or aversive reinforcer, or R^-. Some critics object to this as being a circular definition of reinforcement—as, for example, in the phrase "the enhancement of behavior by positive reinforcement"— but the problem is no more difficult than that of the useful Darwinian phrase "the survival of the fittest." In fact, reinforcers, unlike "fitness," can be fairly reliably predicted or extended to other situations and other species.

The R^+ and R^- differ from ordinary "rewards" and "punishments" in being more precisely defined. Ordinary "rewards" (food, for example) may become aversive (too much food), whereas "punishment" to a response-starved child may be positively reinforcing. Skinner also defines an R^0, called "time out" (removal of S), which plays a useful role in shaping behavior.

Skinner showed the importance of the immediacy and contingency of R in inducing a changed B. An immediate R—within one second or less—singles out the B that is being reinforced from all the other Bs of minutes or hours earlier. And for fast and accurate learning, R must come *only* after B has been emitted.

However, R does not have to follow a given B every time. In fact, the fastest method of changing behavior is to give R^+ every time after some initial B is emitted, and then withhold it until B fluctuates a little in the desired direction. An R^+ then reinforces this new B, and can be again repeated and again withheld, so proceeding on a "reinforcement schedule" step by step to reach the final desired behavior. In the later stages of learning, an intense and repeated B can be maintained by "stretching the ratio" and giving R^+ randomly and more and more rarely, as a slot-machine. This is the basic explanation of gambling, on the one hand, and of certain types of patience and perseverance on the other. By stretching the ratio a little at a time, pigeons have been induced to keep pecking for more than 10,000 times for a grain of corn, though wasting away steadily—like the gambler (Skinner, 1959).

In shaping behavior, the size of the reinforcer is much less important than its immediacy and contingency. An animal will work harder for a sequence of small bites of food than for a big dinner that would be satiating, and a gambler can be hooked by repeated small payoffs. And an animal or child will work at one task just to get to do another task that he likes better [this is known as the Premack principle (see Premack, 1959, 1962)]. Or animals will work when the reinforcer is nothing but a sharpening up or clarification of the stimulus situation (Skinner, 1959)—just as humans will work to get a better map or a clarification of their problems.

The role of "secondary reinforcers" is extremely important and useful. A positive reinforcer, R^+, can be replaced most of the time by some secondary reinforcer, $R_S^{(+)}$, that has been associated with it. Thus, a baby obtaining the primary reinforcer of milk also comes to be reinforced by secondary maternal responses and by adult voices and smiles, so that these come to serve as generalized social reinforcers throughout our lives. Harlow and Harlow (1962) have shown that baby monkeys, like children, who are given food but deprived of these other responses become antisocial and psychotic adults. And we all know that material secondary reinforcers, such as money or school-tokens that can be exchanged for primary reinforcers, are of the greatest importance for our own learning and efforts and social behavior.

Putting this all together, we find that any simple initial behavior B, such as a body movement, or an eyeblink, or a secretion or an intestinal contraction, can be increased or decreased in probability or intensity by the correct reinforcement schedule of Rs. Or it can be "shaped," step by step, into new forms, or compounded with other Bs into a complex chain of behaviors. (A chain, $B_1 - B_2 - \ldots - B_n$, is built up by working backwards from the last element so that each learned B is used as the reinforcer for the previous B). A larger repertoire of behaviors can thus be built up.

By having a reinforcement schedule that depends on S, any of these behaviors can then be "brought under the control of" some new S situation, or can come to be emitted with finer and finer discriminations between different Ss. We learn to respond to the green light, with R^+, and ignore the red light, with R^-. [In fact, the Terrace technique permits these discriminations to be transferred to another set of discriminations *without errors*! (See Skinner, 1968; Terrace, 1963a, 1963b.)]

These Bs can then be maintained indefinitely in full strength by a weak and intermittent R^+ or by a secondary reinforcer, $R_S^{(+)}$. Or a B may finally be "extinguished" and no longer emitted if it ceases to be followed by any R^+, or if the reinforcer continues to be given but is no longer contingent on B. In short, Skinner's central discovery is:

Immediate reinforcement contingencies—the schedule of Rs as related to S and B—are what shape successive behavior in all learning animals.

To change behavior, first change the reinforcing contingencies.

This is very far removed from Pavlov's 1910 discovery of the "conditioned reflex" and "classical conditioning," although this work of more than sixty years ago is still confused with Skinner's work by his critics—most recently in 1971 in the pages of *Science!* (See Holden, 1971; Semb and Nevin, 1971.) Pavlov rang a bell as he presented food to a dog, and then found that the dog would salivate to the bell alone. In this type of experiment, the experimenter does both things beforehand, not waiting for the animal's "operant" behavior; and the animal does nothing but "associate" them, so the method is useless for shaping new behavior. (The role of the third term, the R^+ of food, in maintaining the bell-induced salivation, remained to be recognized.)

In 1921, the other leading early behaviorist, J. B. Watson, actually used intense bangs to make a baby fear small animals (Ulrich et al., 1966), much as described by Huxley in *Brave New World*. (Again, Skinner's critics confuse his work with Watson's pairing, and confuse the methods in his behavioral utopia, *Walden Two* (1948), with the stereotyped behavior methods in *Brave New World*.) But Watson interpreted his shock treatment again as "association" or stimulus–response, neglecting the preshock behavior B, which he thus could not enlarge.

Today, by contrast, an animal can be taught by reinforcement methods —not in days but in a few minutes—to control autonomic behaviors like salivation or the blushing of one ear (DiCara and Miller, 1968; Miller, 1969), or even the pulses of individual brain cells (Fetz and Finocchio, 1971). Pigeons can be taught to dance a figure eight for the first time in just thirty minutes (Skinner, 1959). Pryor (1969) induced a porpoise to emit not a particular behavior but continual novelties of behavior. And Gardner and Gardner (1969) have taught a young chimpanzee to "talk" in deaf-and-dumb sign language with a vocabulary of more than 100 words.

These Skinnerian results go as far beyond Pavlov as the atomic bomb goes beyond dynamite.

CYBERNETIC AND EVOLUTIONARY PARALLELS

In spite of the time it took to straighten out the effects of reinforcement, the principle is not alien to other ways of formulating the organism–environment relationship. Thus, the parallel between reinforcement and the way we learn from the natural environment is obvious. An animal or baby is rewarded by food after it reaches for food, and so learns to reach more and more accurately. The reinforcement principle is also somewhat parallel to the older "transaction theory" of interpersonal relationship, where A maintains his behavior because of response by B, and vice-versa.

There is an even closer parallel to Wiener's theory of cybernetics, which describes the behavior of a goal-directed organism, or an automaton, such as an automatic gun-director. Such a goal-directed system can "track" a target and hit it accurately because there is an ongoing feedback-loop process, which consists of detecting the distance from the target (S), moving toward it (B), and then detecting the error or success (R), which serves, in turn, as the stimulus (S) for the next move (B), and so on.

Von Holst, and Held and his co-workers (Held and Hein, 1963; Held, 1965), have shown in a different way that this kind of feedback-loop relation holds between an animal or human and the environment. The organism's own motions lead to "reafferent stimulation" from the environment, and this is a necessary condition for all visual perception or adaptation. A kitten, for example, can only learn to see if, in the weeks after birth, its visual stimulation, S (afferent), can be followed by its own self-motions, B, which change in a natural way the new visual stimulation, R (reafferent).

These parallels with modern feedback theory make the three-term formulation of the completed reinforcement loop, S–B–R, appear to be a necessary natural formulation for describing the goal-directed behavior of any learning organism. In *Beyond Freedom and Dignity*, Skinner has now gone on to develop the larger parallel between the reinforcement principle and the Darwinian mechanism of natural selection. New behaviors in the individual are like variations or mutations in the species, which are not directed in advance but are selected afterwards by the environment, in the one case by reinforcement and in the other case by survival. As he says, "the environment does not push or pull, it *selects*" [p. 16]. So over the lifetime of an individual organism, numerous types of complex behavioral responses are built up and evolved by the long sequence of natural and social reinforcement contingencies from birth—just as, in the course of organic evolution, numerous species of animals have been evolved by the long sequence of evolutionary survival contingencies.

This is the reason why Skinner's theory and experiments, like Darwin's, are generalizable from pigeons to human beings, in spite of the enormous genetic and neurophysiological differences between such organisms. Learning by reinforcement may go back 500 million years or more, so it is primitive, even though not quite so primitive as the survival mechanism. Undoubtedly, some day we will discover far more sophisticated principles of higher brain response and capability to put on top of this. But at this stage it is only clear that we all need positive reinforcement, like lower animals, for shaping our behavior and happiness, just as surely as we need food. It is only surprising that the demonstration has taken so long and has been so resisted.

AGAINST PUNISHMENT

The reinforcement experiments have led to conclusions and applications that go far beyond animal training. One dramatic demonstration is the severe behavioral consequences associated with punishment or aversive reinforcement, R^-. Skinner discusses the consequences of punishment and the alternatives to punishment more systematically in *Beyond Freedom and Dignity* than in any previous books. It is true that punishment can stop unwanted behavior almost immediately. This, of course, reinforces the parent or punisher, leading him to do it again and again! But the experiments show that punishment is ineffective unless applied immediately every time (quite opposite to the situation with R^+ reinforcers), and the punished behavior always comes back, along with such additional behavior as attempts to escape, or to evade punishment, or to retaliate. Skinner says that this is why windows are broken in schools and not in drugstores.

There are also general behavioral effects. The punished animal or child cowers and loses his confidence and creativity, or else he becomes defiant; and the punished child acquires long-lasting anxiety and guilt feelings. It might be supposed that "not being punished" for being "good" would be equivalent to being "rewarded," but the behavioral effects are very different. (Changing from R^- to Not-R^- may be equivalent to changing from no reward to R^+ in mathematics or economics, but it is not the same in behavior. This profound discovery has not been appreciated by many critics. The notation and usage here, in which R^- is applied to punishment, is a change from strict Skinnerian usage, but is designed to bring out this difference. The present notation has been found useful in applying reinforcement to microeconomic bargaining and to two-person game theory.)

The most effective fast way to stop unwanted behavior without these severe additional effects is by R^0, or "time out." The machine simply stops working for the pigeon, who starts pecking madly in every direction to turn it back on so he can work for his corn; or the child is put in a bare room for exactly five minutes. The effect is to encourage return to the creative environment and exploration for positive reward, rather than to discourage it, as R^- does.

But the best long-run way to eliminate unwanted behavior is by completely eliminating the R^+ reinforcements that maintain it, so that it becomes extinguished, and working at the same time to displace it by providing R^+ reinforcements for wanted behavior that is incompatible with it. This is not immediately reinforcing for the parent or teacher, because it may take two weeks' more patience before the correction is seen, but it is more rewarding in the long run because it preserves the learning relation and does not generate the other behaviors of escape, defiance, or cowering. The displaced behavior can then be brought back in full strength later in other contexts in which it may be positively useful. So the energy of a disruptive child in class may be displaced during that time by positively reinforced study behavior, but it may be brought back later as a valuable asset to the tennis team.

The result is that the Skinnerian school, from the beginning, has come out strongly against punishment as a method of teaching either animals or human beings. (Some of his opponents do not seem to know this.) Yet, throughout human history, large parts of family life, education, law, and religion have been based on punishment methods of control. They produced damaged and constrained human beings, as all our literature testifies. The London schools have only now abolished caning, although the more vicious punishments of parents, schools, and jails have been greatly reduced by the enlightenment and more permissive child-rearing practices of the last 50 years.

Yet, as Skinner emphasizes in *Beyond Freedom and Dignity*, permissiveness is still not the same as positive shaping of learning and creativity, and it also has left us with serious behavioral deficits, delinquency, and feelings of anomie and alienation. He is right to emphasize that it is of the greatest importance to examine how a society might be designed to achieve its ends through positive reinforcements in all our interactions, and to see what it might do to us as individuals and to our collective life. All the experimental and educational results support this claim, that, if positive-reinforcement methods began to be used by parents and teachers (not to speak of law and the courts), and if they were applied to a whole generation, we might see a transformation in our constructive creativity and in the pleasure of life.

COMPLEX BEHAVIORS AND ATTITUDES

A common objection to the application of the Skinnerian methods to man is that "human beings are not pigeons," and that inducing a deprived pigeon in a box to peck a key has little relevance to the learning of complex human behavior. To this, Skinner replies that the reinforcement principle is important in teaching any behavior we can specify. We have seen what complex chains of animal behavior can be taught, even to such relatively free animals as porpoises or chimpanzees in home-labs. For human beings, the reinforcement principle can be used not only for teaching lessons and classroom material to children, but also for teaching good study habits, general problem-solving skills, and such less tangible behaviors as patience, perseverance, self-control, courage, cooperation, and ethical behaviors.

Thus, in "contingency-contracting" classrooms, larger problem solving is taught by "self-contracting," in which the student begins to design and use his own self-reinforcers for improved study habits and exploratory problem-solving steps (Homme et al., 1970). "To teach a student to study is to teach him the techniques of self-management" (Skinner, 1968a, p. 129). Patience and perseverance can be taught by "stretching the ratio," as we have seen. Skinner (1968a) suggests that the perseverance of scientists, or their lack of it, is generated in this way by their early reinforcement contingencies. He describes, fictionally in *Walden Two* and prescriptively in *The Techology of Teaching*, how such virtues and more general ethical behavior might be taught.

The reinforcement method is also a powerful method in self-control, in the reduction of unwanted habits, and in the development of wanted ones. Thousands if not millions of adults have cut out smoking or overeating by using reinforcement methods, which are now taught in many behavioral psychology courses (Stuart and Davis, 1970; Whaley and Malott, 1971). The procedure is the same as that described earlier for eliminating unwanted behavior in children or others—to measure your own behavior and find what R^+s are reinforcing the unwanted habit, then to reduce or eliminate these R^+s, while simultaneously displacing the habit by providing R^+ reinforcements for wanted behavior which is incompatible with it. To change behavior, first change the reinforcers.

This method is very different in its success from such methods as promises or New Year resolutions, which depend on good intentions, or guilt, or self-chastisement and, consequently, have no ongoing reinforcement support and are forgotten in a few days. The R^- method of physical or spiritual flagellation, so familiar in religion, leaves one part of a person fighting the other, so to speak, with self-resentment, escape, guilt, and neurosis, if not psychosis. The R^+ method, by contrast, leaves a person more confident of self-management, with more sense of ease and assurance, and more whole and creative than before. The two are as different as night and day.

We will come back later to Skinner's "two-self approach" to self-control in *Beyond Freedom and Dignity*, and to the problems of self-control and mutual reinforcement for a group.

The effect of changed behavior in changing attitudes is another startling result of the Skinnerian experiments. In the past, most psychologists assumed, like everyone else, that we must somehow acquire new attitudes in order to develop new behavior so that we might then get our new rewards. Skinner has shown that this must be turned around. He says, in essence, that "changed attitudes *follow* or accompany changed behavior. Changed behavior *follows* changed reinforcement contingencies."

Quoting William James, he says that we do not run from the bear because we are afraid, but rather that the fear, set off by the higher adrenalin in our blood and faster heartbeat, is part of our running response. The fear follows or goes with the running behavior. Likewise, in a psychiatric ward that is being managed by the reinforcers of a "Token Economy," when the reinforcement tokens are given to the patients for sweeping and helping to make beds, they speak of the feeling of being appreciated and of the good spirit in the ward. But when the same number of tokens, still exchangeable for the same reinforcements of desserts or privileges, continue to be paid without being contingent on the work, the behavior stops and the feelings of alienation return (Ayllon and Azrin, 1968).

One of the more ironical passages in *Beyond Freedom and Dignity* is the description of the unhappy young man just out of college, whose attitudes are first described in the conventional psychological and popular language, and are then described in terms of the behavior, or lack of it, that is producing them. "He . . . feels insecure . . . (*his behavior is weak and inappropriate*); . . . he feels guilty or ashamed (*he has previously been punished for idleness or failure, which now evokes emotional responses*); . . . he becomes . . . neurotic (*he engages in a variety of ineffective modes of escape*); . . ." and so on.

As Skinner says, this analysis of attitudinal problems in behavioral terms transforms the problems so that, at last, they can be solved. "It helps in two ways: it defines what is to be done and suggests ways of doing it" [pp. 146–147].

NEW EFFECTIVENESS IN TEACHING

Reinforcement methods are now being tested in many areas of social importance, including the management of psychiatric wards (Ayllon and Azrin, 1968), rehabilitation (Cohen, Goldiamond, et al., 1968), industrial management, and urban design. But two areas of application are particularly significant for the larger society: teaching, and behavioral modification in the natural environment.

The role of reinforcers in teaching is especially important. As Skinner emphasizes, teaching is a special situation in which we wish students to learn complex skills or discriminations much faster than they can usually learn them in the natural environment (Skinner, 1968a). Centuries of human achievements are to be mastered in a few years. So we set up training centers, schools, and classrooms for teaching; and we must start off with a compression or simulation of the real-world task, and with such "unnatural reinforcers" as job bonuses, grades, or adult approval, which do not grow naturally out of the task.

To speed up the learning process under these conditions, Skinner invented the "teaching machine" and the more general method of "programmed instruction," which can be used either directly by teachers or in books (Skinner, 1968). Both of these methods transform a lesson into a sequence of small learning steps and immediate reinforcement contingencies planned in advance. This produces much more rapid learning and more retention than the usual methods of lecturing, teaching from a text, or giving repetitious exercises. It completely changes motivation, improving classroom behavior and permitting the management of larger classes (Whaley and Malott, 1971).

Homme et al., in their book *How to Use Contingency Contracting in the Classroom* (1970), give a rather lyrical description of these effects of programmed instruction. They say:

> The parents and teachers now using these rules in their management of child motivation find that children are eager to perform under these conditions. These children do not show the timid or aggressive traits of children performing under duress and coercion. Nor do they exhibit the demanding and "spoiled" characteristics of those who are used to receiving unearned benefits. There is a kind of joy in their activities; they seem to have a feeling of delight in their willing and conscious accomplishment and their well deserved rewards. Observing and participating in this kind of learning is, in turn, the greatest reward teachers or parents can experience.

Anyone who has seen Token Economy classrooms will agree.

Buckley and Walker, in their book *Modifying Classroom Behavior* (1970), explain how these effects are produced. They say: "Programmed instruction is successful because it incorporates (a) immediate feedback, (b) small steps, (c) active responding, and (d) self-pacing."

Of course, after a student has begun to master the problems in the classroom, he needs to be "weaned" away from the classroom re-inforcers to self-reinforcers or the natural reinforcers of the larger world. A way of starting this transfer is by the "self-contracting" mentioned earlier, which helps to teach the student self-management and autonomy in later activities. He finally learns the reward of seeing for himself that, for example, the arithmetic answer checks, or that he can fly the plane by himself.

CREATING NEW REINFORCEMENT PATTERNS IN SOCIAL NETWORKS

Tharp and Wetzel describe other applications of great social significance in their book *Behavior Modification in the Natural Environment* (1969). They worked to solve the behavior problems of many children in a large school system and the surrounding community. They used a sequence of steps, starting with themselves as "outside consultants," first observing and measuring the problem behavior, and then identifying "mediators" in the school or community who could also observe it and who had available some positive reinforcers for any improved behaviors. Mediators might be teachers or adult friends of the child involved. A contract might then be made with the child, so that he would get favorite reinforcers for improved behavior—more TV, or 15 minutes play with his father, or a horseback ride on the weekend. Thus a disruptive child who began to make progressive small steps of improvement in classroom behavior would get immediate notations plus a note to take home two or three times a week so he would get his home reward.

In many cases, under this program, classroom and homework behavior improved, and truancy and stealing stopped. For some three-fourths of the problem children, the disturbing behaviors were turned around in 2 to 6 weeks. (In some of the unsuccessful cases, the parents were moralistic and "did not approve of giving rewards to children for good behavior," or the children were caught in a "double bind" between parents or police and community expectations.)

The Tharp–Wetzel study goes beyond the applications mentioned earlier, in that the new behaviors are not simply being maintained by the outside consultant's reinforcements. Instead, they come to be locked into new reinforcement patterns in the "natural environment" with ongoing new reinforcement transactions between the child, the teachers or mediators, and the pleased parents or truant officers. The consultant can then go away, leaving behind a permanently improved and self-maintaining reinforcement pattern. In the new "family psychiatry," which regards the family as part of a patient's problem, there is a similar attempt to change to a new self-maintaining pattern of relationships in the family group.

But these approaches are quite opposite to the usual individualist attempts to treat mental illness or delinquency either on the analyst's couch or in the detention home or jail. In that approach, a person's behavior and attitudes might change temporarily, but he usually reverts back to his old patterns as soon as he is restored to his original environment, where the same people will renew the reinforcement of his old ways.

AN ONGOING LAW OF MUTUAL BEHAVIOR

All this shows what the reinforcement principle is and how it can be applied. But it is also important to understand what it is not.

It is not a method of manipulation that is simply turned on or off by a wicked dictator or a good fairy. We are all manipulating each other right now, by means of positive or negative reinforcement, and always have been. Skinner regards the principle of operant conditioning as a law of nature, like the law of gravity, by which nature and other people have been pulling and shaping each of us, badly or well, from the moment of birth. It is, therefore, a law that every new design must take into account, if we want more satisfying and less unstable social structures, just as we must take into account the principles of gravity and centers of gravity in designing a table that will not fall down.

Yes, this can be used for wicked ends, like any new understanding of physical principles. But it is also the key to the better implementation of our good ends. And it could be argued that much of the wickedness in society today is due to the types of punitive reinforcements we are now ignorantly using against each other, with the consequences—just as the principle says—of aversion and revenge. We will come back to this question.

The reinforcement principle is also not a one-way principle by which men can control animals, or elites can control slaves, without any recourse. It is true that much of the literature involves asymmetric teaching relations, but the whole point of the reinforcement principle is that our behaviors form a feedback loop, and that either punishments or rewards always bring corresponding counterresponses. A teacher's behavior is, in fact, easily modified and improved—or made worse—by a class that understands reinforcement principles, as has often been demonstrated. In *Beyond Freedom and Dignity*, Skinner stresses that what we are always obeying is a reciprocal rule of control and countercontrol: No animal or human being can shape the behavior of another by response or reinforcement without the other shaping its behavior in return by the response it gives, just as no physical body can pull on another one by gravity without itself being pulled by the other in return.

It might be supposed that this is not very effective countercontrol, but when combined with Skinner's emphasis on positive reinforcement, this could be seen as a modern formulation of the principle of Jesus: Love your enemies, and do good to those who despitefully use you. It is the fastest and surest way of changing or converting the behavior of enemies or masters, far more effective than hostility, which only reinforces their old behavior. In this formulation, all social interactions become chains and networks of mutual transactions that go on and on throughout life as we shape each other. We have always known this in a general way, but now we see the detailed mechanisms of the transactions, and see how they can be improved.

AGAINST INTERPRETATION

The reinforcement method is not a method of electric shocks, brain surgery, implanted electrodes, or manipulation of behavior by drugs.

Such experiments performed by other behaviorists and physiological psychologists sometimes make use of reward-reinforcement and are often mixed up with Skinner's methods by his critics, but they have nothing to do with his principles of behavior shaping or his proposals for methods of improvement in society.

The reinforcement principle does not involve any knowledge of the internal structure or states of the brain, or even of the genetics of the organism. These factors will, of course, limit or guide the responses of different organisms or what they can be taught to do, and Skinner discusses certain underlying evolutionary responses. But reinforcement is a general feedback principle of organism–environment relationships, to which an understanding of these internal mechanisms is largely irrelevant.

This has led to the accusation that Skinner's model is a "black-box" model, in which all the important inside relations are ignored and in which there is no "explanatory theory." Skinner's reply is that his concern is with *behavior*, or with observing accurately what the black box does, and that this is the proper province of psychology, while the other problems can be left to neurophysiology or genetics.

As for an "explanatory theory" of the "internal" type that would satisfy his critics, Skinner's reply is like that of Newton when he was refusing to "explain" gravity; he said, "I do not make hypotheses." Skinner's *Contingencies of Reinforcements: A Theoretical Analysis* gives a Newtonian-operational type of theory, with replies to his critics on these points. What kind of correspondence may finally be found between neurophysiological flow patterns and the behavioral responses of higher organisms is for the future to decide, but it is irrelevant to the application of reinforcement principles in teaching and social interactions. [And the recent findings on the plasticity of internal connections, with single-cell connections and responses themselves being modified by reinforcement principles (Fetz and Finocchio, 1971), suggests that any correspondence may also be plastic.]

Skinner has a more radical critique of the common psychological language of "traits," "drives," and "mental states," which are commonly thought of as "internal" to the "mind" (though in quite a different class from the observable neurophysiology of the brain.) He has always attacked these as "mentalistic" concepts that are left over from medieval "explanatory causes," such as the "dormitive faculty" that was supposed to explain why we sleep. At best, he would say, they are "mediating" terms that are ill-defined and unnecessary in a complete description of behavior.

He says, for example, that to speak of a "state" or "drive" such as "hunger" adds nothing to the behavioral observation that an animal eats or does not eat, or that a boy overeats when he has been reinforced by his mother for doing so. Nor can such a language suggest what to do to change this behavior, as the reinforcement principle does. Even if there are chemical levels in the brain that are correlated with "hunger," this is still fairly irrelevant if the eating behavior is, in fact, changed operationally by a change in reinforcement patterns.

The same is true of "aggression," "industry," "laziness," and "attention," and such terms as "personality," "ideas," "attitudes," "feelings," "thoughts," and "purposes." (He insists that "aggression" is not an inescapable "trait" stored in us by evolution, but a pattern of behaviors that is brought forth by, and can be suppressed by, reinforcement.) All this is reemphasized in the last chapter of *Beyond Freedom and Dignity*, where he renews and clarifies his attack on a number of such terms and usages that he believes are blocking our clear understanding of what man is and how he acts.

This radical attack on the conventional wisdom extends to the physiologists who "regard themselves as looking for the 'physiological correlates' of mental events" [p. 195]. It also extends to psychoanalysts who search for explanations of behavior in terms of "causes" in childhood history, and who try to get their patients to "work through" old hostilities. Skinner would say that any current inappropriate behaviors and the neurotic attitudes that go with them are more easily changed by changing the current reinforcing contingencies than by any attempts to "uncover" and "correct" the original "causes." The successes of behavioral therapy today are certainly showing that this is often true (Stuart, 1970).

Needless to say, professors of these other schools of psychology and psychiatry are fighting back against such a "black-box" and "non-humanistic" ignoring of the "important aspects" of the "mind." But Skinner's critique is in the pragmatic and operational tradition of James, Pearson, Mach, Bridgman, and Carnap. And where these other formulations are often verbal and helpless, the Skinnerian formulation suggests constructive ways to change behavior, ways that have been shown to work experimentally.

Which is operationally more accurate? Which is the more useful psychology?

The ranking of achievements in this field is always a matter of vigorous dispute, but I think we may come to see the importance of Skinner's reinforcement principle and his critique in psychology as being comparable to the theoretical and operational importance of the work of Newton, Bohr, or Fermi in physics, or Darwin in evolution, or Watson and Crick in molecular biology. In fact, considering its already visible effects on education and behavior, and its incipient effects on medicine, the law, and all our social structures, it may be the most important discovery of this century.

"Beyond Freedom and Dignity"

SKINNER'S STYLE

With this understanding of the Skinnerian achievements, applications, and professional controversies, it becomes possible to go on to examine the major new ideas put forward in *Beyond Freedom and Dignity*.

However, it is necessary first to say a word about Skinner's prose style, because I believe this is the key to some of the misunderstandings. With his usual logical consistency, he has applied his radical critique to his language and his method of writing. The result is somewhat like a programmed text, with each sentence intended to reinforce the previous one or to go one step beyond it. This produces a prose that is bland and straightforward, with a measured density of ideas, but reading it is like skating on smooth ice over a very deep pond. You are almost lulled asleep, and then you suddenly find yourself very far from shore on the edge of a hole you had not noticed. This is the result of reading too fast, instead of stopping to digest and underline and bracket the important ideas. In an effective text, as he says, "something happens as each sentence is read" (Skinner, 1968a, p. 163). (I read this book—*The Technology of Teaching*—three times, making notes, because of the intellectual density, before I thought I knew all that was in it. This has happened to me with less than ten books in a lifetime of study.)

Skinner tries to avoid any material that he does not want to be positively reinforcing to the reader, such as the old psychological terms, or the names of his opponents, or even the pronoun "I." The demolition of current and popular psychological ideas is saved until the last chapter, after the reader has been prepared for it. And Skinner introduces his own terms, such as "emit," "reinforce," and "extinguish," in what seems to be a casual way, until you suddenly realize he is reinforcing you with an exact technical usage. When this gets too legalistic in specifying behavior rather than calling names, a translation into the common tongue is often needed. "Contingencies involving positive and negative reinforcements, often of the most extreme sort, are codified." That's roughly, "The Ten Commandments" [p. 116]. "Those who are in a position to exert constructive countercontrol." That's, roughly, "checks and balances" [p. 181]. And so on. It takes practice and perseverance.

But what has led many critics astray is Skinner's irony and wry humor. He can be as sardonic as Veblen or Galbraith. After building up a point, he will contrast it with a dead-pan description of some opponent's naive view, expecting the absurdity of this now to be appreciated. "The problem is to induce people not to be good but to behave well" [p. 67]. Think of a mother's ineffective "Be good!" in quotes. Such bits can be hilarious if read aloud, but the low-emphasis approach has led many casual readers and critics to take these ironical phrases for Skinner's own views.

Thus, in criticizing the mentalistic way of talking about sudden solutions to problems, he says, "The element of surprise makes it easy to suppose that a solution has been triggered by some such prebehavioral event as an idea" (Skinner, 1968a, p. 138). Put the words "prebehavioral event" and "idea" in quotation marks, and the irony is clear, but read casually, it seems to be Skinner's own supposition. Similarly, in *Beyond Freedom and Dignity*, there is a long paragraph describing "reactionary proposals" against people who do not work or are not law-abiding, with the "explanation" that it is "because law enforcement has grown lax; the problem can be solved . . . by increasing the police force, and by passing stronger laws" [p. 119]. It is all exactly opposite to the improved methods he is describing, and must be read tongue-in-cheek.

A little further on, Skinner criticizes the usual "simplification in utopian writing," in which, he says, "the control of the population as a whole must be delegated to specialists—to police, priests, owners, teachers, therapists, and so on." He points out the conflicts this would produce in these imagined utopias, which are one reason why "the word utopian means unworkable" [p. 155]. But the *New York Times* reviewer thought Skinner was recommending this kind of control! And when Skinner objected, in a letter to the editor, saying "I deplore such a culture" (Sennet, 1971; Skinner and Sennet, 1971), the reviewer tried to justify himself by replying "The words . . . are his own"!! And then the reviewer in the *New York Review of Books* (Chomsky, 1971) repeated the identical error five weeks after Skinner's protest.

A final difficulty in reading Skinner is that he insists, as a matter of principle, on using blunt and forbidding lanaguage, such as "reinforcement" and "control" and "shaping behavior," even when recommending what might be called in softer terms, "responsiveness," "influence," "persuasion," "inducement," "political pressure," or "Christian love." Essentially, he says that we are already using adult social control and intention in teaching children, curing patients, or changing social laws and institutions, and we damage our effectiveness when we kid ourselves.

We fear the language of control, but we fear control itself, even when we want it. As Skinner (1968a, pp. 90, 260) put it,

> We fear effective teaching, as we fear all effective means of changing human behavior. Power not only corrupts, it frightens; and absolute power frightens absolutely. . . . Absolute power in education is not a serious issue today because it seems out of reach. However, a technology of teaching will need to be much more powerful if the race with catastrophe is to be won,

and it may then, like any powerful technology, need to be contained. . . .
The issue is important because the government of the future will probably
operate mainly through educational techniques.

He states it more strongly in *Beyond Freedom and Dignity*:

> Good government is as much a matter of the control of human behavior
> as bad, good incentive conditions as much as exploitation, good teaching
> as much as punitive drill. Nothing is to be gained by using a softer word.
> If we are content merely to "influence" people, we shall not get far. . . . To
> refuse to exercise available control because in some sense all control is
> wrong is to withhold possibly important forms of countercontrol. We have
> seen some of the consequences. Punitive measures . . . are instead promoted.
> A preference for methods which make control inconspicuous or allow it to
> be disguised has condemned [opposing leaders] to the use of weak measures.
> This could be a lethal cultural mutation [pp. 180–181].

That conscious and deliberate control is necessary may be true, but
not since the Calvinists have we ventured to say it aloud.

AGAINST "AUTONOMOUS MAN"

Beyond Freedom and Dignity is Skinner's first attempt to develop a full-
scale coherent philosophy. The "freedom" and "dignity" of the title are
ironic and again should be put in quotation marks. But the key word is
"beyond," for he goes past his critics and his debates with conventional
psychology and tries to relate his organism–environmental behavioral
formulations to family and social practices, evolution and death, ethics
and values and cultural survival, and the design of the future. From the
point of view of its scope and its coherent restatement of the relation
between man and society—based, for the first time, on experiment
rather than on introspection or philosophy—it is a masterpiece. It will
have to be taken into account by all future social philosophers, and it
may be the capstone of his life's work.

The "freedom" and "dignity" of the title are not attacked, in this
case, because they are mentalistic "states," but because they have been
key concepts in his opponents' attack on his work and his philosophy.
Skinner sees them as cardboard verbal concepts expressing a fuzzy-
minded and false view of man, a view that is blocking a clear understanding of the relations between man and society, a view that must be
demolished if we are to understand how to make an improved society.

He sees "freedom" as having been a useful watchword against tyranny
and against elites who tried to control others by negative reinforcement
and punishment. To proclaim that men are not inherently slaves or

subjects was a justification of escape or retaliation, and a valuable aid in countercontrol. But, of course, it was also used by the punishers and the moralist elites to justify punishment: if a man was "free," then his acts had no outside causes, and society could apply its controls nowhere but to his own body.

Skinner says this is false, that there is no such "free" or "autonomous man," that the experiments show that all of man's behavior is shaped deterministically by the reinforcements from his environment from the time he is born. Modern social work and criminology come close to this view, and regard most, if not all, of delinquency and crime as being due to genetics, brain damage, sickness, or a poor environment, for which the delinquent was not responsible.

Conversely, Skinner sees "dignity" as society's way of praising "autonomous man" for "uncaused" acts of generosity, self-sacrifice, courage, or defiance under pressure or punishment. But if we had had a search for the roots of this behavior as careful as our search for the roots of crime and delinquency, we might find the environmental shaping to be just as determining in this case.

Skinner concludes that "freedom" and "dignity" are myths that are preventing us from seeing how continually and subtly we are being shaped by our environment. They keep us using gross methods of praise and punishment that are ineffective in preventing each others' delinquencies and malfunctions and do not help us shape the good behaviors that we might achieve.

"FREE WILL" OR DETERMINISM, OR BOTH?

To this, the humanist critic may reply that no experiments on rats, helpless children, or psychotics can prove that his behavior is completely determined, because he feels and *knows* within himself that he has "free will."

This seems a pathetic argument to the scientist, because we know how often men delude themselves with such subjective feelings. Yet I believe that there is more to the argument than has been allowed for in Skinner's presentation, and that a reconciliation on this point would do much to remove the humanist objection to his type of determinism.

My reconciliation argument has two parallel lines of reasoning. The first one is that determinism is limited, for a system as complex as the human brain and the human organism (Platt, 1966). I am taking determinism in the natural scientists' operational sense of linear causality—of being able to predict a sequence of future behaviors completely from a knowledge of the present state and past states of the organisms.

There are several reasons why any such deterministic statement is limited. First, because of statistical randomness, from cosmic rays, somatic mutations, or thermal fluctuations in the nervous system. This, of course, is "noise" and not "free will," but it provides the very variations in behavior on which Skinner's mechanism of shaping, like Darwin's, depends, so it is a necessary limitation on any exact Skinnerian determinism.

Second, even without statistical fluctuations, the "initial state" of a very complex organism, from which prediction starts, is unknowable by any observer of the same complexity. This is true for two reasons: "complexity-indeterminacy" and "privacy-indeterminacy." The physicist believes that the motions of mechanical objects, like rolled dice, are deterministic; but he takes the roll of dice, as they bounce on a thousand unprescribed irregularities of the table, as the symbol of indeterminacy. Yes, an expert swindler may spin a die with considerable control, but he sometimes misses; and, likewise, a human brain of 10^{11} neurons and 10^{14} synapses—many orders of magnitude more complex than the possible rolls of any die—even though it has important regularities of shaping and control, will not always be deterministically predictable.

Privacy-indeterminacy simply means that your eye cannot see my sunbeam and your ear cannot be at this point of resonance, so you cannot know the private and ever-changing inputs of my initial state. The jailer, absolute in deterministic behavioral control, may chain the prisoner to the wall, but he cannot see the cockroach—or the jailer—from the point of view the prisoner has. These complex and private operations determine each of our outcomes and behaviors in ways that no experimenter or controller can entirely measure or predict. If anyone still wishes to say that we are behaving deterministically "in principle," he can; but it is operationally an empty statement if the prediction is, in principle, not possible itself because of incomplete information. And these unpredictable components of behavior could properly be called "self-determining" in the sense that they are reliable brain operations that are not being determined by anyone else.

Third, these private inputs and operations interacting with the environment—with behavior that is being reinforced and leading to new behavior, as Skinner says—can lead to new insight-closure of new organism–environment loops. I see that the moon is in line with my window; and Darwin, on his desert island, sees that all the finches differ from the mainland species. I write a poem; and he makes notes for publication. This is how the individual has always seen new truths, and drawn the whole world after him. Sometimes the delinquent boy can do it, too, or the addict, Malcolm X, in jail. It is not because we have "freedom" from the world—that kind of "freedom" is an artifact of the old self–world, mind–body dichotomy. Insight is environmentally shaped; yet no one else has done it to me or seen it for me. It is an act of creation between me and my environment—and what else should my "free will" or "autonomy" mean?

Recent studies suggest that these acts of insight or closure, or "hierarchical jumps" in complex systems, are not predictable from the separate precursor steps, either from inside or outside the system (Platt, 1970). They are like the evolution of wings, or like Kuhn's "scientific revolutions," which can only be understood afterwards, in the light of the new laws or closures that the hierarchical restructuring has revealed. (They are like "*a priori* ideas," which remain to be discovered, as the aerodynamics of wings and flying remained to be discovered before there were wings that locked the components together into a self-maintaining system.) And yet they can be arrived at in many different ways, as different men can reach the same insight. For an animal that is near flying, bird or bat or reptile, all ways lead to wings. This evolutionary convergence stabilizes our continually discovered relations to the environment, but it is more like teleology than determinism in any traditional sense. It is a form of organism–environment self-determinism that Skinner does not have room for, except in his self-shaped society.

Finally, there are strong interactions between the organism and the environment that could be described as cybernetic. The effort of the organism is enormously amplified by intelligence and designed structures, as in levering up a rock, driving a car, shooting a rifle. Skinner says the organism does not control the environment (as autonomous man) but, rather, the environment controls the organism. Nevertheless, both are true in the feedback loop that has no beginning and no end. These behaviors, with amplified consequences that frequently grow out of private inputs, are the conspicuous trigger actions that men single out as "autonomous" or, in common speech, due to "free will." It does not change their singularity or privacy to know that they were shaped and made more probable by a long chain of organism–environment interactions. As Skinner says, "no theory changes what it is a theory about" [p. 213], and this is true also of a deterministic theory as applied to these conspicuous acts of self-initiative.

The second reconciliation argument is the other face of this reasoning. It is that determinism is, in fact, a necessary basis for the kind of "free will" we have been discussing. For if we mean by "autonomy" and "free will" the privacy of our experiences and the individual insight-closure of the organism-with-environment based on such experiences, and the cybernetic acts based on such insights, then a necessary requirement for such closure and cybernetics is that there be reproducible and predictable relations between the organism and the environment—that is, that the natural reinforcers of the environment act in a deterministic way as they shape the behavior or are tested by it. Otherwise, both the environment and the organism's behavior would be unreliable, and no one would have said that a consistent "self-determination" or "free will" was "responsible" for behavior. Determinism does not belittle man: it enlarges him and makes him dependable, responsive, and creative.

From this same side of the fence, we can also see that insight-closure to new self-maintaining relationships between organism and environment can be regarded as "self-determination." What else would we mean by "*self*-determination"? It is an old idea of the "self" that sees it as bounded by a skin. A truer idea, with cybernetic feedback loops, is that self and environment form an indissoluble complex with no sharp boundary. My voice fills the room; the wave of my hand or the blink of my eye changes all the holograms throughout the space to the distant hills. And if this environment reacts back on me and redetermines my new behaviors, it is self-determination in this larger and truer sense. I—which means I-and-the-environment—have done something and learned something interactively and holistically. Who else?

This self-cybernetics of closure, insight, and manipulation is the cybernetics of interacting man, the only kind of man there is. The humanists and the environmental determinists are simply emphasizing opposite sides of the same interacting subject.

THE EXISTENTIAL BASIS

And yet not entirely. Skinnerian objective determinism, like the determinism of most scientists today, does not and cannot include the total existential and subjective framework within which it has its validity. This primary interaction of ourselves with the world, which precedes all determinism, must also be put in if we are to have a total picture of man, a picture complete enough for us to use in leading and persuading and shaping a better society.

What Skinner omits is essentially that pronoun "I." He writes, "A person may respond . . . ," "A person may act . . . , " "Human beings do all this . . . ," throughout the book, without ever distinguishing between his self-person and the other persons he is describing. He does not distinguish between himself as "I," as observer, behaver, and arguer, and the world of behavior observed. The closest he comes to recognizing this distinction is in discussing his "two-self model" of "self-knowledge" and "self-control," where he says that "the controlling *self* must be distinguished from the controlled self, even when they are both inside the same skin . . ." [p. 206] (a rare use of italics). But he is still speaking of these "selves" as objectively observed in others, and leaving out himself as observer.

It is not that there is a biological difference of "autonomy" or "free will" between the observing man and the observed man. Rather, it is a logical difference—or, more exactly, an ontological difference. In physics or in biology, the observer or experimenter—who "prepares the initial state," who drops the ball, and who draws or does not draw the deterministic conclusion—can never be logically equivalent, in the construction of the experiment or the conclusions, to the experimented-on, even if the experimented-on is another man like himself.

Each of us—as an experimenter on the outside world—starts with some kind of primary totality *within which* are these objects pointed to, and deterministic experiments, and books, and other professors arguing. This is "the canvas upon which the picture is painted," or the "existential-I," as discussed by Mach (1959), Schrödinger (1945), Bridgman (1959), Bohm (1965), and other operationalist philosophers of science. This total framework, this existential-I of being, action, and reaction, precedes anything else that can be said about the world. And it is within this subjective and almost solipsist sphere that each of us listens, and decides whether the determinism is correct, and acts to manipulate the behavior of these other objects or people.

The objective world, the world of isolated and controlled experiments, is the world of physics; the subjective world of knowledge, values, decisions, and acts—the world of the purposes that these experiments are, in fact, designed to serve—is the world of cybernetics, of our own goal-seeking behavior. Determinism or indeterminism lies on *that* side of the boundary, while the usual idea of "free will" lies on *this* side of the boundary. They belong to different universes, and no statement about one has any bearing on the other. Is not this the way the world almost necessarily appears, when seen from the manipulating organism side of an organism–environment feedback loop of the kind Skinner describes?

I think it is his failure to acknowledge this existential basis that each of us starts from that makes Skinner miss the point of the criticisms by Krutch, Maslow, and C. S. Lewis. They claim his determinism "reduces the stature of man," attacks "the 'being' of man," or abolishes man. They say "what is threatened is 'man *qua* man,' . . . or 'man as Thou not It,' or 'man as a person not a thing.' " He sees this as *their* defense of what he has scientifically abolished: "autonomous man—the inner man, the homunculus, the possessing demon . . ." [p. 200].

But it is clear from their language that they are not protesting against the loss of the homunculus from the determinate behavior of "a person" in his experiments, but against the omission of the existential self of our subjective "being," which underlies all experiments. Skinner is not alone in confusing these two categories, because none of his opponents have made the distinction clear either.

When this misunderstanding is clarified, I think it is again possible to bridge the gap between these opposed positions, accepting both the existential basis of all our knowledge and action and the fact of the general determination of behavior by the environment.

[I myself would hold that the world we experience is *simultaneously* (1) *subjective* or existential in its primary reality of a cybernetic, inseparable, self–environment totality; (2) *a priori* in certain self-maintaining loop invariances, or laws of nature, with which we come to achieve closure; (3) *unpredictable*, with complex organisms continually reshaping the future by unforeseeable amplified acts of creation and closure; yet (4) *deterministic* and causal (except for the fundamental indeterminacies of physics) in every study of simple and essentially isolated objective systems. I think that there is no contradiction, as commonly supposed by objective scientists, as well as by humanists, between these characteristics, because they apply to different aspects of reality; and I think, in fact, that they are mutually necessary for a learning, cybernetic organism.]

This larger view makes it possible to see, suddenly, that we exist as organisms manipulating the environment; and that it is our existential business to interact strongly and persuade each other of our own insights into reality and our own desired goals, enlarging the loops of collective behavior-and-consequences—instead of offering unpersuasive explanations, as a pure determinist like Skinner must do, by saying that it is "just our environment and culture that has determined us" to make these persuasions and arguments.

Ethics to Shape a Culture

CONVERSION OF REINFORCERS FOR SELF-CONTROL

After we have gotten the free will and existentialist arguments out of the way, I think we can better appreciate Skinner's effort, in *Beyond Freedom and Dignity*, to put forward a behavioral–evolutionary basis for ethics. It has two components. The first component is a new theory and practice of self-control and group control, by the conversion of long-run large-scale reinforcers into immediate personal reinforcers. The second component is the consideration of the longest-run reinforcer of all, the survival and maintenance of a culture, and how it can be transformed into behavioral rules and practice.

The achievement of self-control by reinforcement mechanisms is surprisingly simple, as we have seen. First, measure the unwanted habit or behavior and identify its immediate reinforcers, R^+, then eliminate or reduce them and displace the unwanted habit by introducing new R^+s for competing wanted behavior. Lifetime habits can often be reversed in 2 to 4 weeks.

But what do we mean by "unwanted," if it is something we actually continually do or try to do? Here Skinner offers the "two-self theory," as we have seen, of the "controlling self" and the "controlled self," as he earlier offered a "self-knower" and a "self that is known" [p. 199]. He says, "The controlling self (the conscience or superego) is of social origin, but the controlled self is more likely to be the product of genetic susceptibilities to reinforcement (the id, or the Old Adam)" [p. 199]. We see that the controlling self is acting somewhat like the "consultant" in the Tharp–Wetzel formulation of behavior modification in communities. It sees the large-scale or long-range values, and applies the new theoretical knowledge to the design of new reinforcers that will shape our more automatic behavior into new patterns that will achieve these values. Or, more briefly, the thing to do is simply to "convert" long-run or large-scale advantages or reinforcements, R_L^+ or R_L^-, into congruent short-run reinforcers, R_S^+ or R_S^-, that will tend to immediately encourage or suppress behavior with long-run positive or negative pay-offs.

In these terms, it could be said that happiness is having short-run reinforcers congruent with medium-run and long-run ones, and wisdom is knowing how to achieve this. And ethical behavior results when short-run personal reinforcers are congruent with long-run group reinforcers. This makes it easy to "be good," or more exactly, to "behave well." The achievement of the latter takes a design for the conversion of mutual advantage into personal advantage. It can be done more easily and effectively by design than by exhortation, as when we make an organizational design to collect garbage, or to feed the poor, or to educate all children—transforming the long-run community payoffs into daily wages, instead of depending on personal neighborliness or charity to do these jobs as we once had to do.

These reinforcement approaches do not create the internal conflicts of the old religious resolves with repeated violations and self-punishment. Rather, by making it easy for our immediate responses to be good, we are able to pursue whatever long-run ends we pursue with wholeness and energy. This means true self-control and autonomy.

This appears to be a real solution to the classical dilemma of St. Paul, which has seemed, for so long, to be an inescapable statement of the human condition. "For the good that I would I do not: but the evil which I would not, that I do" (Romans 7:19). He is speaking of longer-run good and evil, and short-run behaviors. Paul also explained this in terms of what a scientist might call a "two-self theory": "But I see another law in my members, warring against the law of my mind. . . . O wretched man that I am! who shall deliver me from the body of this death? . . . with the mind I myself serve the law of God; but with the flesh the law of sin" (Romans 7:23–25). [Koestler (1968) similarly attributed our troubles today to the higher brain and the lower brain being hopelessly at war with each other, and supposed that to save the human race some *drug* would be needed to harmonize them!)

I believe that this is the first time that the Pauline dilemma, which has plagued all religions and all moralists, has been solved in a practical way; so that again Skinner's method of designing reinforcers for self-control may be the most important contribution to ethical practice in 2000 years.

EVOLUTION, BEHAVIOR, AND SURVIVAL

Groups also need to convert their long-run survival or reinforcers into contingencies bearing immediately on each individual in the short run. This conversion has largely been through the teaching of moral rules. Skinner follows Waddington (1967) in suggesting that the moral codes of a group are subject to survival pressure. Those that have come down to us are a mixture of those that had survival value for the group— such as codes against lying, stealing, and killing within the group— together with others accidentally or superstitiously connected with them, such as certain taboos, and food, dress, and sabbath customs. (Skinner has shown that pigeons also preserve "superstitious" behavior accidentally connected with their first instances of reinforcement.)

Among the codes with group survival value are those that benefit the group at the risk of the individual's life, or after the individual is dead. These include risking life for the group in battle or to save the young or females—as certain animals do—as well as building houses, planting trees, and educating children. Skinner emphasizes that the group must find ways to instill not only these verbal values but this *behavior* by offering present reinforcers of praise and reward for heroes, as well as respect for fathers and mothers and leaders who have built up the family and the community.

He extends this reasoning to the problems of the present survival of our own large-scale culture. The old warring modes and codes that helped the earlier survival of the tribes and nations will destroy us, if they continue in this new world society in which we have all been pushed together. They must be rapidly superseded by a world ethic and pattern of behavior in which men will risk their lives, if necessary, for the world culture, and in which they know they will receive personal praise and reward for such risks.

But what is almost more important is that we must shape the education of our children and the rewards for them so that they will not only
want to preserve the culture that has been achieved—or at least large
parts of it—but so that their *behavior will also be shaped* toward ways
that will preserve it, and that will shape the behavior of their children,
in turn, toward preserving it. "A culture is ultimately no stronger than
its capacity to transmit itself" (Skinner, 1968a, p. 110). Skinner is
obviously influenced by the ethics of his own religious upbringing,
wanting a world in which all men are brothers, but he is scrupulous not
to let this enter his formal scientific reasoning about the survival of a
culture.

The two earlier long-range "goods" that societies have always converted into short-run reinforcers (even though badly) were "the personal
'goods,' which are reinforcing because of the human genetic endowment,
and the 'goods of others,' which are derived from personal reinforcers."
He is saying that to these, "we must now add a third, the good of the
culture" [p. 134]. This is not for culture as culture (because Skinner sees
all cosmic or religious arguments for man's cultures as culturally induced), but only because of its long-run value for people. "If there is
any purpose or design in the evolution of a culture, it has to do with
bringing people under the control of more and more of the consequences
of their behavior."

This strict derivation of ethics from survival and, in fact, from global
survival, is not outside the framework of scientific humanism, but
Skinner has added, I think, two important points. First, that ethics is
ineffective unless it includes actual behavioral and valuing *practices*,
which can only come by conscious and deliberate shaping of the behavioral education of the young, so that they, in turn, will shape *their*
young. And second, that ethics has meaning only within the framework
of its contributions to the longer-run or larger-scale survival of the
larger biological system. This gives us a behavioral foundation for personal ethics that is congruent with our modern ecological consciousness
of the need to preserve the complex global network of life—a congruence
that is absolutely necessary in any viable society of the future.

This conversion-of-reinforcers theory of ethics means that there is
an important confluence between the "good" and the "profitable," just
as in the case of personal wisdom in planning and behavior. The only
power in the world that moves men to large efforts is the gap between
"what is" and "what might be" (Platt, 1971). That is to say, an anticipated improvement or advantage is converted into personal reinforcers
for present action. This is why we work, save, build dams, and invest in
factories and education. All of economics may be found to be only a
narrow application of these behavioral principles.

Correspondingly, all of politics is but a theorem of the profitability and the power of utopias. Utopias are dreams, but it is the hope for improvement in these dreams that makes men tear down governments and remake societies. We invest our votes or our lives in that long-run and ethical payoff for ourselves and our children. Each such step is another collective insight-closure into how we can more satisfyingly survive in our environment, and, in this sense, it is historically inevitable. The forces of history are with us. Seen in this way, there is energy and profit enough for us to solve any social problem, if we anticipate what great payoffs for all of us an improved society could achieve. It is enough to pay off unions into automation, industries into environmental protection, administrations into responsiveness, and perhaps governments into peace. It is better than faith for moving mountains.

BETTER CONTROL, BETTER COUNTERCONTROL

We call this conversion from group or cultural reinforcers to personal reinforcers by the special name of "ethics," rather than "wisdom," because we have not been closely integrated with each other in the past, and it has taken special effort and powerful verbal reinforcers that had to be "drilled in" or "accepted on faith" in order to make our rather clumsy conversion. But Skinner's reinforcement-conversion methods would enable this "group self-control," like "personal self-control," to be easier and more effective, with less punishment and fewer attempts to escape or retaliate than we have with present aversive religious and legal methods of control.

But is it ethical for a group to maintain its own self-control in this way by easy methods rather than clumsy and punishing ones? Is it ethical to make ethics easy? Skinner forces us to face this issue. But certainly, for many distraught parents and teachers and officials today, the answer would be a resounding "Yes!"

Yet this immediately leads to a related question: Who is going to prescribe and impose this more effective ethics on the rest of us? Skinner quotes C. S. Lewis as protesting: ". . . the power of man to make himself what he pleases . . . means . . . the power of some men to make other men what they please" [p. 206].

The answer is, as it has always been, that the controlling elites are teachers, leaders, and officials whose methods and values are accepted or adopted by the whole community. This is a question not of behavioral methods but of social and political structure. How does a teacher communicate new ideas? How does a leader get a following? How does an official get his job, and how is misconduct curbed?

New behavioral methods will force us to rethink these questions, and to redesign the mechanisms and politics of democracy, particularly our traditional adversary methods. These were once designed—in the U.S. Constitution, for example—as checks to protect us against tyranny, but they also engender continuing polarization and hostility throughout our society. Hamilton said that "ambition must be made to counteract ambition," but strengthening it also counteracts goodwill and constructive efforts and attempts to make a more peaceful world order. With new methods, what we have called politics and government might find earlier and more constructive ways of controlling tyranny than by confrontation.

In particular, Skinner has a cogent paragraph on the many tyrannies in our present system resulting from delegation of authority to people who do not know what is happening. His behavioral cure is to redesign the system in order "to bring some important consequences to bear on the behavior of the controller" [p. 171].

I think this is a pioneering concept, to translate the general problem of "controlling the controllers" into a behavioral problem of "counter-control." The symmetry of the reinforcement method, in which all those involved are reinforcing each other for behavioral modification, means that any new methods of control are matched by correspondingly powerful new methods of countercontrol. This is what the better integration of a society means—like the integration of an organism. If the stomach does not get enough blood from the heart, it demands more, and gets it, or we become sick, and the heart may be forced to stop. So leaders or officials managing a society are endangering themselves, as well as everyone else, if the countercontrol demands for equity, rights, or variety are not satisfied and the society tears itself apart. A society, like a man, is educated by events or it does not survive. Both biological and cultural evolution *"make organisms more sensitive to the consequences of their action"* [p. 143]. Our new high-communication society, with enormous powers of mutual destruction, can only survive if it adopts sensitive signaling and feedback and positive reinforcement practices, so as to detect and solve its problems long before they reach the point of malfunction and confrontation. It will have to become more like a cheerful family than like any government today.

DELIBERATELY SHAPING THE FUTURE

Finally, in *Beyond Freedom and Dignity*, these technical and ethical components are put together in a program of designing a culture for the future of man. I think it is a new kind of blueprint of the future. It differs from all past utopias and utopian colonies—except *Walden Two*—in not being derived from the revelations of a prophet or from generally uplifting rules of love and cooperation without much knowledge of good long-run structures and behavioral practices. And it differs from the many books that depict our present disorders and what a better world would be like—hoping all other men will agree with the author's culturally shaped opinions about what is "better"—which commonly end with the pathetic conclusion that "somebody" should create a new politics or a new economics or new attitudes.

Instead, Skinner's book gets down to the theoretical bedrock of the ethical practices logically needed for a satisfying society, and the practical mechanisms of constructing it, with scientifically tested knowledge of human behavioral interactions. His improved behavioral methods are not "unworkable" but are already being practiced daily in hundreds of centers, with improvements in motivation and satisfaction like those described earlier.

What Skinner calls for, at this time of crisis in the world's history when all the old partial and accidentally inherited systems are in disarray, is to accept our cultural or existential responsibility for creating the future and to begin to build according to this blueprint. He sees our refusal to build, because of misgivings about problems of control or about the fact that we might be really effective in shaping our children's ethics and attitudes and behavior, as the surest recipe for disaster. The old behaviors that society has been reinforcing for centuries will destroy us if they continue. "The capacity to be reinforced by food now leads to overeating and illness . . . sexual reinforcement now means overpopulation," and aggressive behaviors "may now interfere with more useful social relations" [p. 176]. The "cultural designer" must "accelerate the development of practices which bring the remote consequences of behavior into play" [p. 143].

To put the psychology of positive reinforcement into practice to change our old behaviors and structures will take manifold efforts of design, and diverse pilot experiments. Yet there is hope, too, of new types of family living, neighborhood relations, town meetings, business management, economic relations, and legal and political structures. New mutual support and a new consciousness. It is, as Skinner says, a new "design of man."

But he insists, like a good evolutionist, that the only long-run survival will be of a society planned for diversity and a constantly experimental approach, to keep from falling into sterile and homogeneous repetitions unable to deal with emerging problems. There may be as many viable life-styles or cultures as there are different kinds of successful organisms. He says that "a standard pattern . . . would be bad design, but if we are looking for variety, we should not fall back upon accident. . . . The only hope is *planned* diversification, in which the importance of variety is recognized" [p. 162].

He also suggests that a society shaped for survival will have to manage leisure, and to make far more effective use of it, in order to avoid being consumed by gambling, destructive behavior, or spectatoritis. "Leisure itself does not necessarily lead to art, literature, or science. Special cultural conditions are needed." Skinner sees it as crucial to create such cultural conditions to shape and "control what a person does when he does not need to do anything" [pp. 179–180]. Probably it will only be our delight in human relations that will finally be able to use up our time, going far beyond the "services" that now make up over half of our national economic activity. New meanings and new behaviors will be needed for work, income, and unemployment. In an affluent society, we might fruitfully shape ourselves into creating new experimental communities, or into spending the days playing with children and teaching them, as in the old, easy, Polynesian societies.

Skinner emphasizes that a new design of society will have to appeal now to most of us. "A new culture must appeal to those who are to move into it, and they are necessarily the products of an older culture." But he recognizes that the long-run design might not be one we have been brought up to enjoy or "to be reinforced for"—with no punishment or threat or compulsive labor and "no need for moral struggle." He says, rather, that "the problem is to design a world which will be liked . . . by those who live in it," a world based on the real "sources of the things people call good" [pp. 163–164].

HELL OR HEAVEN?

Is all this just a benevolent Fascism, as Skinner's critics have commonly asserted? Is it a "blueprint of hell," as an opponent in *Psychology Today* suggested in a remark that has now been quoted in many other reviews?

I think the answer is clearly no. It is true that this is not laissez-faire capitalism, and that it might lead to a very different type of economic system. And it is not a Communist society of the Russian or Chinese type, for these have few large-scale behavior-shaping mechanisms, other than exhortation and censorship, and few effective checks and balances or countercontrols. And it is not a theocratic state, like some pseudo-utopian societies today, with an ecclesiastical hierarchy and punishing moral controls. But it is surely at the opposite pole from the real Fascisms of this century, with their goose-stepping and bloodbaths and need of control by continuous expansion and war.

No, this is a new concept of a society, although it was represented in embryonic form in *Walden Two*. Parts of it have been suggested by other reformers and utopians (or antisuggested, if we include *Brave New World* and the misunderstood passage quoted earlier). Among existing societies, it is perhaps most like a *kibbutz*, with its warm family relations and emphasis on constructive work together for survival. But Skinner's emphasis on diversity and experimentation, and his positive behavioral methods and teaching methods for achieving such goals as group harmony and effectiveness, are quite new.

A society for survival with immediate feedback channels of protest and correction, a society that ends the long reign of punishment and retaliation, a society whose officials are subject to continuous counter-control to insure that they work for the good of everybody, a society that deliberately practices diversity and experimentation with different life styles, a society in which such things are not just wishful dreams but one that actually knows how to accomplish them—from where we stand today, such a society looks to me not like a blueprint of hell but more like a blueprint of heaven. Read the Homme quotation again, and see if this is not a society that most of us would pledge our lives to achieve for our children and grandchildren!

We must look at the realities, and not be like the religious zealots of the past who thought all reforms were from the devil if they were not dressed in their own familiar theological language. It is by their fruits that you shall know whether reforms are good.

OTHER THINGS TO BE DONE

There are many other things to be done in spreading these new patterns or making the needed large-scale transformations based on them. Two will be mentioned here. The first is the further study of mutual reinforcement by adults with each other in families and small groups. Most of the reinforcement studies so far are on such asymmetrical relations as psychologist–pigeon, therapist–patient, or teacher–child. We need studies on the reinforcement contingencies needed to maintain mutual cooperation and mutual respect between lovers, siblings, or friends in groups of various sizes. Adults will have gone beyond baby talk and baby rewards and will need subtle, verbal, high-information discriminating responses. We may need to alternate "shaping" and "being shaped"; and an attitude of openness to being shaped may be the key to maturity and effectiveness in working with others, as the responsiveness psychologists have emphasized. There are reasons for believing that small mutual-support groups to practice and teach behavior-shaping techniques might be natural self-multiplying units for Skinnerian methods, and a rapid and effective mechanism for constructive social change to new ways of behaving, new values, and countercontrol methods where they are most needed today.

Another area in which much more study is needed is that of "non-zero-sum games" and their relation to reinforcement principles and behavior-modification techniques. These "games" include many social conflict–cooperation dilemmas, such as "Prisoner's Dilemma" (Rapoport, 1966), and "The Tragedy of the Commons" (Hardin, 1968). These are our present ways of labeling two-person game situations similar to arms races, where escalating conflict continually reinforces arms makers and government officials on each side; or *n*-person games, like international whaling, where catching the last whales is a temporary national advantage but a collective disaster. Without a superordinate controlling authority, there is now no available mechanism for converting the long-run collective advantages of peace and trade, on the one hand, or of restraint, on the other, into short-run reinforcements for different behavior by the individuals involved. The search for new reinforcement methods and long-run–short-run conversions in such problems, possibly including such new political pressures as the large-scale consciousness of the ecology movement, might be of great practical value in these larger-scale social–structural conflicts.

But there are hundreds of new types of studies that can be made and that will be made in extending behavior-modification methods to other aspects of our social life. The Skinnerian methods are loose in the world and cannot be put back. They offer us the brightest hopes of any methods we now have for rapid restructuring of many of our obsolete and dangerous social institutions, and for building not merely a Skinnerian society, but any new society for the world ahead. Today we stand at the fulcrum of history, between the old societies and ethical values, which developed by accident, and the new culture, which will have to be created by intentional design if we are to survive at all. At this critical moment, we are fortunate to have a revolutionary manifesto like *Beyond Freedom and Dignity* to shake up and clarify our thinking and to lay the foundation of necessary values and practical methods that will be needed, as we finally take up the responsibility of designing and creating a livable and long-run future for man. As Skinner says at the end:

> It is hard to imagine a world in which people live together without quarreling, maintain themselves by producing the food, shelter, and clothing they need, enjoy themselves and contribute to the enjoyment of others in art, music, literature, and games, consume only a reasonable part of the resources of the world . . . and come to know themselves accurately and, therefore manage themselves effectively. Yet all this is possible . . . [p. 214].

It is not a dream. He has helped to make it a reality that is already coming into existence at many centers. These centers are seeds of the first culture that has ever offered people tested and effective ways of shaping each other's behavior so as to reach their full and diverse human potentialities. For the solutions of our deep problems, it is, in the long run, the only hope we have.

3

Behavioral Technology and Institutional Transformation

Dennis C. Pirages

Dennis C. Pirages, a political scientist with a broad background in the behavioral sciences, is currently a research associate in the Department of Biological Sciences at Stanford University. His most recent book, Ark II, *takes up many of the ideas implicit in this article in much greater detail.*

The main theme that Pirages treats in this chapter is the growing imbalance between industrial and social technology. Galloping technology has shaped industrial man's culture, and now this culture seems to offer little guidance for future survival of the species. He points out that there is now a great need for a social transformation in which the old norms, values, and institutions are replaced with others that are more ecologically sound.

In this respect, Pirages sees much that is important in Skinner's message, particularly at what he calls this "critical point in human history." Skinner calls attention to the subtle conditioning that presently exists in our society, he feels, and lays the groundwork for a strategy to turn this conditioning around in starting the needed social transformation.

Industrial society has become technologically overdeveloped while remaining socially underdeveloped. The same society that uses applied science to orbit Mars and put a man on the moon seems incapable of maintaining a stable social order and promoting a more satisfactory life for all citizens. Industrial culture is held captive by a galloping technology that molds values, institutions, and human behavior (Frank, 1966). "Progress" is a one-dimensional progress, no longer defined in terms of human needs but most often in terms of economic growth and other material achievements (Marcuse, 1964).

The publication of B. F. Skinner's manifesto *Beyond Freedom and Dignity* once again calls attention to our failure to develop a technology of behavior sufficient to cope with the results of achievements in the physical sciences. While scientists have been able to split the atom and decipher genetic codes, there have been no equivalent breaththroughs in understanding human behavior or the structure of society in which we live. Technicians produce new types of nausea gas and remarkable weapons for riot control, but little has been done to prevent riots from taking place. It is unfortunate that Skinner has left himself open to so many attacks by overdrawing his case, because the social and political message that is woven through the book highlights some very critical contemporary problems.

Skinner's timely argument focuses attention on the failure to develop a behavioral technology at a very critical point in human history. Never before have so many interrelated problems threatened man with extinction. Galloping technology has created a highly complex and interdependent environment, and man is no longer certain whether he controls this environment or is being controlled by it. The planet is overpopulated, the atmosphere is becoming increasingly polluted, the division of labor is now unbelievably complex, social insulating space is rapidly disappearing, and the level of social discontent seems constantly to rise. Men of good will suggest solutions, but they are told that intuitive ways of solving these problems turn out to be counterintuitive in the end (Forrester, 1971a).

Industrial man has learned too much about his natural environment while knowing too little about himself. He has dominated and "inherited the earth" because of successes in modifying and redesigning his ecological niche. The environment has been shaped to meet man's needs, but man has not yet altered his behavior to meet environmental imperatives. Success in manipulating the physical world has enabled man to avoid facing the unpleasantness of modifying ecologically destructuve behavior.

But the ability to manipulate the physical environment at will is increasingly circumscribed. Even with a "green revolution," food supplies can't keep pace with the increasing numbers of humans. Resources for providing warmth and shelter are in scarce supply. Population growth more than absorbs increased productivity, and consumer goods that have played an important role in insuring social peace over the last century no longer guarantee stability in a society in which the purchasing power remains concentrated in the hands of a very few. It is for these reasons that the social and political aspects of Skinner's message are now so important.

The Social Animal

Homo sapiens differs from other species because it has developed very complex cultures that serve as survival weapons. Man alone is no match for his well-endowed competitors. He cannot run nearly as fast as some animals, his sense of smell is not well developed, and he lacks the sharp tusks and teeth necessary to do battle. But, through evolutionary accident, man has developed a much bigger brain than his competitors. This, in turn, has enabled man to communicate, cooperate, and pass detailed knowledge from generation to generation. Man uses symbols and abstractions to pass on knowledge and to condition behavior, rather than the simple mimesis used by less sophisticated species.

Patterns of behavior passed from generation to generation become institutionalized. Institutions represent parsimonious ways of passing on shared norms, values, and behaviors. Religious institutions have grown up surrounding man's relation to the unknown, political institutions have developed to handle collective decision-making, and social institutions have grown out of patterns of social interaction. Although man is a social animal, cooperation has never been automatic. Countless wars attest to the fact. Over time, however, a core of commonly held values has evolved as a part of the cultures that have aided man's survival. It is these institutionalized values that have made organized social life possible.

But, in spite of man's superior brain size, much of his cultural evolution has been as haphazard as genetic mutation. Values and institutions have rarely been designed or modified to meet anticipated crises.[1] Our present industrial culture has grown as crazily as if man had no powers to rationally plan his future. Man has changed his behavior only in *response* to changing conditions and rarely, if ever, in anticipation of problems.

Skinner alludes to the survival value of a culture and points out that "to the extent that it helps its members to get what they need and avoid what is dangerous it helps them to survive and transmit the culture"

---

[1]The only exceptions to this generalization would seem to be those institutions devoted to war that must be innovative or perish. Much of what is referred to as galloping technology has been related to war research.

[p. 129].[2] For Skinner, a culture represents a set of contingencies (reinforcement mechanisms) by which humans orient their behavior. These
contingencies are embedded in social institutions, values, norms, and
behavior. As cultures evolve, the behavior that has been rewarding in
the past is repeated, and that that has led to the extinction of humans is,
quite naturally, abandoned along with the nonsurvival cultures that
produced it.

Skinner lightly passes over two very fundamental points in his discussion of cultural evolution. The first is that behavioral contingencies
are socially determined and don't exist in a vacuum, and the second is
that contemporary cultures can just as easily hinder species survival
as aid it.

We all engage in certain types of behavior because it is rewarded by
people around us. The child learns values and norms through socializa-
tion processes, although, much to his parents' chagrin, there is no
one-to-one relation between what is taught and what is absorbed. Other
people are the important contingencies in our lives. Humans strive for
approval from those whose opinions are valued. The approval of significant others can be one of the most important reinforcers of social
behavior.[3]

Industrial society consists of an extremely complex web of social
relations, and much social behavior is "mediated" by unseen others.
Although Skinner can easily manipulate the contingencies governing
animal behavior in his laboratory, assessing the structure of reinforcements in a real society is a forbidding task. The study of how contingencies are socially anchored has just barely begun, and the whole question
of organizing attempts to modify human behavior remains in the realm
of science fiction. Although there are, undoubtedly, complex sets of
rules governing human behavior that we may be able to understand at
some future date, there is a world of difference between pigeons pecking
triangles and humans refusing to sell their homes to others of a different
race. It is quite easy to make the pigeons peck the triangle on command,
but it is not so easy to modify the socially anchored behavior of humans.

In traditional societies, the social anchoring of behavior does not
conflict with the role that culture plays in survival. The social structure
is simple, and nearly all members of the culture are exposed to the same
range of critical problems. The structure of reinforcements automatically
aids survival, because those who stray from the commonly accepted
value core find life to be nasty, brutish, and short. Conformity is a virtue

---

[2]Throughout this paper, page numbers in square brackets refer to pages in Skinner's
Beyond Freedom and Dignity (Alfred A. Knopf, 1971).

[3]The social anchoring of behavior and the "exchanges" that take place in everyday
life have been mapped out by Blau (1964).

in traditional society, because the life expectancy of the nonconformist is minimal. Only the living survive and modify behavioral contingencies, and traditional cultures represent ideal survival mechanisms for unchanging environments.[4]

There is now considerable doubt that the culture in which we live has the survival value of its traditional counterpart. The mechanisms by which "survival" behavior is reinforced have apparently broken down. As man has modified his ecological niche, elementary threats to daily existence have diminished. Aside from the very poor, few need worry about finding food or protection from the elements in modern society. Simple survival imperatives make up a diminishing part of the industrial culture. Now that the wolf is no longer at the door, the relation between survival and the sanctioned structure of rewards is no longer close. An entire society now lives in apparent nonconformity with environmental imperatives; but it is clear that we can get away with this behavior for only a limited period of time.

Industrial society is in constant flux. Man is now changing his physical and social environment in ways that he does not completely understand. Behavior that was survival-relevant in the past may have little survival value today. Unless a culture continuously adapts to the environment in which it is embedded, there is little hope that it can long endure: behavior anchored in an agricultural value cannot persist as farmland turns to desert; a hunting and gathering society cannot survive as game becomes scarce; and, most important, a society in which the structure of social rewards is anchored in conspicuous consumption cannot long survive in an environment of increasing scarcity.

The Changing Environment

Throughout most of human history, there has been little need to discuss conscious programs of behavior modification or altering the institutionalized structure of rewards. Those who did not conform to environmental imperatives received summary justice. But remaking the physical environment has given man a cushion that permits more deviance in social behavior. Those who are unwilling to have their lives guided by ecological wisdom can now survive, thanks to the industrial revolution and the spurt of abundance that it has produced. The "deviants" have helped to create a new industrial culture of abundance, a culture that is sowing the seeds of its own destruction.

---

[4]The conformity that characterizes traditional societies has been best explicated by Lerner (1958).

It is one of the ironies of history that the "benefits" that have altered the social contingencies for industrial man and have led him to so readily embrace modern technology now threaten to destroy the human race (see Harman, 1971). Greater abundance has seduced man away from rational evaluation of the ecosystem's potential for continued support of greater numbers of people. New prosperity has led to a global revolution of rising expectations, which places new demands on an already overtaxed supply of nonrenewable resources. Scientific discoveries have produced new drugs to prolong human life and, thus, have contributed to planetary overcrowding. Laissez-faire cultural development has led to the immediate satisfaction of perceived needs, with little attention to aversive long-term consequences.

The emergence of a highly interdependent industrial culture beset by an increasing number of technological "success" problems necessitates more cooperation and planning for unseen contingencies. At the same time that industrial society has become much more heterogeneous, we all have become much more dependent upon others for our continued survival. Sustaining tremendous numbers of people at very high standards of living requires new forms of cooperation not unlike those instilled by simple conformity in traditional societies. Adequate social insulating space no longer exists, and the types of behavior appropriate in modern society are quite different from the "rugged individualism" of an open frontier.

In a very real sense, we all have a veto power over the lives of others that grows every day. Extreme interdependence means that the failure of any part of society to perform as expected results in problems for the whole society. In Great Britain, coal miners clearly demonstrated their importance to the rest of society when, in 1972, they created havoc by walking off their jobs to obtain higher wages. The lack of coal virtually paralyzed the British economy. In the United States, dockworkers demonstrated the same principle. By walking off their jobs, they caused untold inconvenience, including loss of jobs and income, for millions. Strikes became acceptable behavior during the period of intense industrialization, when their effects were localized, but now they remain as a dysfunctional reminder that our institutions are still those of the frontier.

But even on an individual level we all have more impact on our fellow citizens. Dramatic examples occasionally occur in our weapons culture when a deranged individual arms himself and shoots others at random. Such explicit displays of veto power are unusual, and more mundane examples occur every day when careless drivers slaughter innocent people on the freeways. Whether we like it or not, the crowded and complex social environment gives us little choice about becoming our brothers' keeper. Because we are all pressed much closer together in densely populated society, *all* of our actions affect others.

The collective decisions of millions of individuals to consume more have not been without effect on the physical environment. The earth's carrying capacity is not unlimited, and neither are the supplies of non-renewable resources needed to sustain industrial societies. In striving to meet the perceived needs of additional millions, the planet has become increasingly polluted and resource supplies have become dangerously depleted. No amount of technological modification of the environment promises to save mankind.[5] Industrial man must once again begin to conform to environmental imperatives and modify his behavior in accordance with age-old rules. There are limits, clearly, to the extent to which man can transform his ecological niche through imperialistic activities aimed at other species, and we have apparently reached those limits.

Just as galloping technology has unleashed four new horsemen of the apocalypse—Progress, Production, Population, and Pollution—it has begun to develop the rudiments of behavioral expertise to cope with new social problems. Behavior modification and social engineering are at least discussed in polite society, although more often in a negative than in a positive context. In Skinner's terms, we still prefer to remedy mounting problems by "playing from our strong suit" and investing in technological solutions, because they involve little tampering with important taboos against organized modification of institutions and behavior [p. 3]. It is acceptable to perfect birth-control devices but not to frame social policies designed to insure their use. The former requires only technological innovation, but the latter involves interference with social values. Science develops the most expensive pollution-reducing equipment in an effort to keep up with the increasing output of noxious exhausts, but no one dares suggest that society should cut back on its fantastically high rates of consumption. The cult of social laissez faire (freedom and dignity?) encourages development of an increasingly dangerous galloping industrial technology that is extremely important in reducing our freedoms in less apparent ways while condemning efforts to develop and use a technology of behavior.

Institutional Transformation

The contingencies by which human behavior is molded are embedded in social institutions. In order to modify collective behavior, the institutions that shape that behavior must be correspondingly altered. Any pattern of expected behavior that becomes "institutionalized" is, by definition, difficult to change. Men are basically conservative

---

[5]There is an extensive literature on the environmental problems we face. Perhaps the best reference is Ehrlich and Ehrlich (1972).

and resist sudden shifts in behavioral expectations. Organized groups develop vested interests in the maintenance of prescribed behavioral patterns, even though those patterns may become dysfunctional for human survival.

Being social animals, men seek recognition from others in the form of power, privilege, and prestige. Political institutions determine the distribution of power and define the types of behavior that lead to being rewarded with greater supplies. Similarly, economic institutions determine the types of behavior that are rewarded with privilege. Although there is no necessary connection among them, similar types of behavior most often lead to accrual of power, privilege, and prestige. Taken together, the institutionalized rationing of scarce social resources could be called a social "paradigm." In this sense, the term represents the accepted way of parceling out social rewards, a set of commonly understood social wisdoms, and an organized framework for socializing the young and passing on relevant experience. This usage of the term is analogous to that explicated by Kuhn in his study of scientific revolutions (Kuhn, 1962).

The most pressing task for twentieth-century man and his government is transforming the now outmoded industrial paradigm and creating a structure of rewards more in conformity with environmental imperatives. A behavioral "Prometheus Project" is needed, if mankind is to escape the fate of other species that have overshot their niche and suffered the inevitable consequences.[6] Growth in numbers and a revolution of rising expectations have outstripped the planet's ability to provide adequate long-run support, and the gap between perceived needs and realistic possibilities continues to widen. We would expect that, if man is truly different from other species, he will recognize the problem and develop a behavioral technology adequate to prevent the population crash that will certainly result from continued reliance on an outmoded institutional paradigm.

In Skinner's language, the heart of the predicament is that the behavior most rewarded in industrial society militates against man's long-term survival chances. There is great difficulty in making the aversive long-run consequences of present behavior a meaningful contingency. In simpler terms, this means it is very difficult to discourage today's population from bequeathing current problems to unborn generations. Industrial man is told to consume, although the interests of future generations would encourage him to ration. Economies grow

---

[6]A Prometheus Project to exhaust man's creative capacities has been suggested for the physical sciences by Feinberg (1969), but so far no one has suggested such an undertaking in social life, where it is most needed.

when there is a need to stabilize exploitation of natural resources. "Growth" and "progress" are values that are firmly entrenched and until a significant institutional transformation or "paradigm shift" occurs there can be little change in human behavior.

Unfortunately, little is known about the transformation process. Existing institutions have developed slowly over time, and little rational guidance has been employed in their formation. Laissez faire has been the guiding rule. It has taken major visible crises to alter institutions and behavior in the past, and sometimes even catastrophic events have failed to have any impact.

Environmental problems, unfortunately, do not fall into the highly visible category. They seem to have been growing slowly, and their consequences remain remote in time and space for most people. It is difficult to watch a mineral "depleting itself," and no one pays much attention to statistics. Tiny increments in air pollution pass unnoticed, and we adjust to them. Starvation remains a way of life for a sizable portion of the world's population, and poverty is tolerated in the wealthiest country in the world. Yet, little remedial action is taken. There have been no ecological "Pearl Harbors" to alert us to impending dangers, and the consequences of present behavior are glossed over by all but a handful of "prophets of doom."

Even the obvious deterioration of the social environment stirs little apparent critical evaluation. While the centers of our major cities were burning, a few years ago, most went about their business as usual and there was no enduring shift in social priorities. There have been new developments in police science, as new equipment and riot-control techniques have been developed to deal with the symptoms of social discontent, but the causes of social catastrophes are still ignored. As a result, greater quantities of social resources are spent in keeping order through the use of force, while the roots of social problems are ignored.

Crime, violence, and other indicators of social dislocation represent failures of our institutions and not, necessarily, new human weaknesses. Increasing indications of deviant behavior mean that there is a gap between what the structure of rewards offers people and what they have been taught to accept. For example, equality of opportunity is an accepted value in our society, but when a very rigid hierarchy controls the distribution of privilege, conventional paths to wealth may be closed to all but a selected few. Deviant behavior becomes the only way in which oppressed minorities may seek the opportunities supposedly open to all.

In this respect, deviant behavior is but another indication that an institutional transformation is necessary. Expectations are being created that cannot be met. In the long run, the use of aversive controls to maintain order will bankrupt society, as costs begin exceeding benefits.

Terror and coercion are effective only for brief periods of time, and an active or well-ordered society need seldom resort to force.[7] Police protection, for example, cost each of us $36.50 in 1969. In constant dollars, this was double the $18.61 that such protection cost in 1960 (U.S. Bureau of the Census, p. 148; 1971, p. 227). There is no reason that this trend won't continue, in the absence of a large-scale shift to a new social paradigm more in keeping with human needs and environmental possibilities.

It is unfair to contend that all these problems result from evil people. Human nature is certainly no worse in industrial society than it has been in the past, and it seems much more benevolent when we consider past excesses of human violence. If there has been anything encouraging about the environmental crisis, it has been the apparent willingness of people to put in the required effort to solve problems that have become pressing. Most people have attempted to play some role in meeting local problems, whether by operating a neighborhood recycling center or attending city council meetings. Political activism is a sign of concern.

What is most unfortunate is that leadership has been lacking. People will work to solve problems brought to their attention, but contemporary political leaders have done little to emphasize the extent of the crisis we face. Perhaps this is from ignorance, but more likely it is out of concern for their own careers. Growth and consumption behavior is still sanctioned by social support from significant others, even though most knowledgeable people will admit that we can't sustain our society on this level very much longer.

Theoretically speaking, the political, social, and economic institutions in a mass democracy respond to the needs and demands of citizens. In reality, there have always been big gaps between theory and practice. Institutions can and do develop lives of their own and, at best, are responsive to human needs only in the long run. At this point in history, however, institutional lag is a very serious problem. Contemporary institutions inculcate patterns of behavior that have been rewarding to past generations. In times of rapid change and serious crises, however, values that only can change as they are passed from generation to generation rapidly become outmoded. Today's citizen must change his values several times within each lifetime (Lifton, 1968). Just as man cannot physically evolve in anticipation of future environmental conditions—at least not until we better understand genetics—present institutions offer little promise in transforming behavior to help meet future

---

[7]The fact that coercion cannot work forever has been demonstrated repeatedly in communist countries, most recently in the economic collapse in Czechoslovakia. For an analysis of the role of coercion in maintaining stability, see Pirages (1972).

problems. Our old institutions have acted as excellent codifiers of past experience, but anticipatory or planning institutions have been rare in human history.

Although it is a sobering prospect to consider, it is possible that mass democracy cannot transform itself to meet environmental imperatives (see, for example, Ophuls, 1971). The fragile consensus that underlies mass democracy is sustained by economic growth. A society with large inequities in the distribution of wealth can only exist when there is hope among the less fortunate that they, too, may profit from a growing economy and become wealthy. No revolution has ever taken place while the lot of the masses was perceived to be improving, regardless of existing inequities. But environmental problems make it unreasonable to expect large-scale economic growth to continue, and advanced industrial societies have to consider that, at some point, steady-state resource consumption will become imperative (Daly, 1973). There is no exception to the rule that accelerating depletion of finite quantities of resources cannot continue forever, even though we seem to ignore this simple fact.

Who Controls a Transformation?

The real problem in our laissez-faire industrial culture is one of control. We can really no longer pretend that we don't know how to modify human behavior. Private interests working for private gain make full use of the available psychological knowledge. The airwaves are saturated with television commercials designed to instill a desire to consume. Hardly an hour of television time passes without at least one sultry blonde using the oldest conditioning device in the world to sell men's deodorants and after-shave lotions. Sex-sells, subliminal advertising, erroneous logic, deceptive statistics, and outright propaganda are freely used by private interests in their attempts to condition behavior.

It is ironic that our political leaders are so distrusted that the use of such devices by public officials in promoting the common interest is forbidden, although private interests are permitted, with few restrictions, to use them for individual gain. For example, governmental altering of the economic structure to encourage development of nonpolluting industries is still often attacked as unwarranted interference with private enterprise. On an individual level, government financing of television commercials to promote racial integration still meets with intense opposition. The fact is that we have been unwilling to develop and use a behavioral technology in the public interest because we have not yet learned to trust each other. It goes against the grain of hundreds of years of tradition to permit such developments. Because of an inability and unwillingness to come to any agreement on the seriousness of the problem we now face, we ignore the conditioning that takes place every day and restrict government to ruling only by use of the most aversive controlling measures.

Skinner is very correct when he points out that there has never been a society in which freedom and dignity have had real meaning, in the generally accepted sense. Behavior has always been conditioned by others and freedom has never been absolute. What constitutes dignity has always been culturally determined. Most behavior is predictable, given the requisite information, and it would be fair to say that ninety percent of the behavior of ninety percent of the population can now be accurately predicted. The ability to predict, of course, can soon be followed by the ability to control.

If one doubts that freedom and dignity are only relative terms, he need only compare the varying definitions of freedom in the United States, China, and the Soviet Union. In the United States, freedom has meant free enterprise, free economic opportunity, and the right of the individual to defend property for his own use. In the Soviet Union, freedom has meant freedom to serve the people while not criticizing existing institutions. In China, freedom is apparently found in internalizing the words of Chairman Mao. The point is not that one type of freedom is better than another, but simply that in each culture freedom and dignity are defined differently by the institutional paradigm.

To the student of "democratic" institutions, the consequences of these realities and Skinner's observations create a serious dilemma. It is clear that democratic institutions have been very slow in responding to new problems and remolding contingencies. The task for present political leaders is to restructure the social environment so that ecologically sound behavior is rewarded and suicidal behavior discouraged. But this requires a type of bold leadership that has been rare in our history. Present leaders are attuned to the politics of industrial society, the old politics of muddling through. The required bold programs of behavior modification and institutional transformation raise too much opposition among believers in Skinner's "cult of freedom and dignity."

It is uncomfortable, but it is perhaps necessary, to consider that present democratic institutions may not survive in a less affluent future. Times of crisis require resolute action, and democracies have not been noted for encouraging massive transformations. It is not inconceivable that mass democracy and other aspects of our laissez-faire culture will come under sustained attack as the impending crisis becomes clearer. But there is no reason that a democracy *cannot* respond to challenge. The real question is, Will it? There could be no more powerful instrument to promote the needed paradigm shift than a determined, democratically ruled society, but there is a very real question of whence the necessary impetus will come.

Although people in our mass democracy are certainly not malevolent, and although they remain available for any mobilization effort, a silent majority is hardly ready to lead a wholesale transformation of values and institutions. The masses are basically inert, at least until some obvious problem appears in need of solution. In time of war, when there is an obvious enemy against whom we struggle, people can be easily mobilized. It is much more difficult to mobilize people in support of the rights of future generations!

Given the current constraints placed on future growth possibilities by environmental deterioration, democratically elected politicians can hardly be expected to seize the initiative. Given a choice between candidates promising greater economic growth, higher salaries, and general prosperity and "prophets of doom" backing plans for limiting growth and equalizing incomes, there is little doubt as to how people will vote. Voters do not have sympathy with candidates who confront them with ugly truths. Consequently, we can expect little bold leadership from politicians who depend upon mass support.

What is really needed at present is some insulation of public officials from citizen pressures. The immediacy of political campaigns precludes any real efforts at long-term planning. There is no planning branch of government charged with responsibility for the welfare of future generations.[8] Politically, we live for the moment, as if we secretly realize that tomorrow we might well die. Officials are elected by appealing to individual and group interests, and the common interest of the species is neglected.

It would seem that a partial solution to the dilemma is the establishment of an insulated planning branch within the government. In this manner, it would be possible to outline a program of behavior modification and institutional transformation, which seems to be required. This group of "controllers" would be charged with responsibility for designing a structure of social contingencies that would make the aversive long-term consequences of contemporary behavior meaningful at the present time. Perhaps this could be made more palatable by the creation of a new profession that might be called behavioral technology. But first we must accept the fact that survival problems have social solutions that can be solved by scientific inquiry just as readily as other problems have been solved by physicists and chemists.

This should not be taken to mean that we need scrap our democratic

---

[8]A planning branch of government has been proposed in the suggested constitution designed by Rexford Tugwell (1970) at the Center for the Study of Democratic Institutions.

institutions. The "controllers" in the planning branch need not be little philosopher kings. They would be charged with the development of policy alternatives in light of the serious problems we face. The implementation would be up to the elected representatives of the people. As of now, we have no institutions devoted to long-term planning and framing societal alternatives. Such a planning branch or group of behavioral technologists would inject a new and authoritative voice into the political debate. It is hoped that this would be the voice representing the interests of those who will yet live on this planet.

Some Conclusions

The social message in Skinner's book is timely, and it offers an introduction to the major problems confronting twentieth-century man. His work touches a very sensitive nerve in our society. A fairly effective technology of behavior is currently being developed, but we have an inordinate fear of recognizing it and harnessing it for the common good. There still is a great deal of distrust of behavior modification in general, and of the application of these techniques to social problems in particular.

If our culture is to survive, it must be drastically remolded. The data clearly indicate that mankind is headed for a population disaster, and, without effective rational action, the social and physical environments will continue to deteriorate. This occurs in an atmosphere in which the greatest portion of the world's population has been led to expect tremendous increases in standards of living. But social scientists know that worsening conditions in the face of golden promises lead to violent and tragic responses. Man not only responds to institutionalized contingencies, but he can understand them and create new ones. Skinner's behavioral technology offers the hope that man can avert impending disaster by better understanding himself.

We have approached a tremendous watershed in human history that may be equal to all previous "revolutions" combined. The very survival of the species is at stake. B. F. Skinner's warnings and observations stand at the crest of this historic divide. He has made an admirable case for developing a technology of behavior before it is too late. In the end, man will get what he, by his efforts, deserves. If he uses his *material and intellectual resources* to overcome his own challenges to himself, a more golden future awaits him. If he fails to use these resources, the result will certainly be chaos and self-destruction.

4

Controlled Environments
for Social Change

Vitali Rozynko, Kenneth Swift,
Josephine Swift, and Larney J. Boggs

*Vitali Rozynko and his colleagues are associated with the Operant
Conditioning Behavior Modification Project at the Veterans
Administration Hospital, Menlo Park, California. Their project is
partially supported by a grant from the National Institute on Alcohol
Abuse and Alcoholism.*

*Their chapter takes us from the general exposition of operant
conditioning to a practical and applied discussion of its techniques as
they are utilized in an innovative program for the treatment of
emotional and behavioral disorders. In their project, Skinner's methods
are used in treating a group of institutionalized alcoholics. Though this
project has not been in existence sufficiently long to develop longitudinal
statistical proof of the method's efficacy, the authors are confident that
the results will be quite impressive when a full analysis of the data
becomes available in 1973. They also emphasize an aspect of
Skinnerism not touched on elsewhere in this book: the importance of
verbal behavior in operant conditioning. They believe that abusive,
pejorative, or "aversive" words can be as punishing as physical assaults.
Moreover, they believe that for certain general behavioral disorders—
as distinguished, for example, from discrete phobias—verbal behavior
provides the appropriate leverage for making the necessary
modifications. They always refer to those with whom they work (and
to their staff) as students and, in other ways, avoid verbal patterns that*

might condition clients to think of themselves in negative terms.

The authors dedicate this paper to B. F. Skinner and James G. Holland, and would like to share credit with the rest of their colleagues—Garry Flint, Jay Matejcik, Larry Dell'Anno, Christine Danforth, Phyllis Ratigan, Marjorie Fuller, Bruce Bailey, Hazel Tileston, Arvada Pacheco, James Word, John Greenhalgh, Barbara Matejcik, John Sinclair, Jane Rozynko, Peter DeMartini, Stephanie Balter, Clifford E. Hammer, and many others.

B. F. Skinner's statements on autonomous man and his attributes have pervasive ramifications concerning the control of individual and group behavior and, by implication, the kinds of governmental control mechanisms that might be implemented in the future. Not unexpectedly, these statements have been followed by considerable alarm and criticism. The breadth and significance of Skinner's ideas, as well as the genuine concern of his opponents, call for national and international discussion at the highest levels. Our comments are intended to further stimulate such discussion.

Determinism versus Freedom

Skinner's basic statement is that the behavior of all living organisms is ultimately controlled by the environment and the changes in it that occur consequent to their behavior. The behavior of organisms changes as a result of whether or not a given behavior is followed by positive reinforcement (reward) or negative reinforcement (the termination of a "frightening" or an aversive stimulus), punishment, or no discernable consequences. More specifically, the behavior of individuals is a function of (1) their previous history of reinforcement and punishment, (2) the stimulus situation impinging on them at a specific time, and (3) their level of deprivation. The experimental evidence supporting these general statements is unassailable. Thus, Skinner states that human behavior is lawful and determined, and that it can be predicted and controlled. Finally, Skinner observes that present systems of behavioral control are dangerously inadequate and, if not altered, may result in the extinction of our species or, at the very least, the significant degradation of human society. He suggests that we begin to discuss and, ultimately, to devise more effective ways of controlling human behavior.

There is little controversy regarding Skinner's observation that society must begin to behave differently in order to survive. The evidence of social dysfunction at various levels of human interaction is presented to us daily, and ranges from reports of individual acts of murder to the subtle evidence of "duplicity in high places." The necessity for societal change is generally evident and is undeniable. Disagreement exists, however, as to what is to be done, how it can be accomplished, and when.

The central controversy surrounding Skinner's formulation of the problem is his denial of "free will." His critics phrase their objections in a number of ways (for example: the theory ignores the capacity of man to make existential decisions; it is mechanistic; it will create a society in which individual expression is impossible; it will eliminate disagreement and rebellion and stifle necessary social change). This controversy is grounded in discussions concerning free will, which, in many aspects, is a pseudoproblem and only serves to help us avoid the necessary and difficult task of learning better ways of controlling ourselves, in order to insure our survival and our future happiness.

Other objections to Skinner's theoretical structure state that certain behavior exhibited by human beings cannot be accounted for by his theory; that it is overly simple and cannot explain the richness of human experience.

There is no disagreement about the complexity of man's behavior, but one need not posit free will to account for it. W. Grey Walter (1951) has calculated that his elementary electronic organisms, "Machina Speculatrix," which consist of only two elements or circuits, form a system that can generate a new behavior pattern every one-tenth of a second for 280 years. He estimates that the human brain may have approximately one thousand perceptible functional elements, and states that "even if man had only ten, this number of elements could provide enough variety for a lifetime of experience for all the men who ever lived or will be born if mankind survives a thousand million years."

Whether or not all of human behavior can be predicted and controlled on the basis of Skinner's system is an empirical question. There is no question that much of human behavior can be and, moreover, that much of it is already controlled. Skinner contends that human behavior is lawful, predictable, and modifiable, if—and only if—certain specific operations are carried out. If freedom and free will are synonymous with whimsy or are independent from any parameters in the environment—past or present, internal or external—then Skinner's system negates freedom. On the other hand, if freedom means the existence of a multitude of alternatives for behavior, which at any instant may occur lawfully to result in a specific response, then there is no conflict.

The free-will issue stemming from Skinner's formulation of human behavior creates visible controversy only among very select groups of people who are involved in this rather esoteric topic—for example, scientists, philosophers, and theologians. Individuals in the general population do not, as a rule, discuss free will. Nevertheless, as Skinner points out, their attitudes and thinking appear to be based on a free-will model. However, the ramifications of Skinner's position, when applied to government, immediately stimulate the interest of a much broader group. His tenet that society and government should begin "self-consciously" (in response to the data about behavior already available) to control individual and group behavior by systematically modifying the environment stimulates fears of losing individual freedoms. Most objections to designing specific environments are based on the assumption that we have freedom and will lose it if our environments are planned or designed. It is clear that behavior does not occur in a vacuum, but that our present behaviors are controlled by our present environments, just as our behaviors will be controlled by whatever environments we are able to devise in the future. Certainly, we can agree that a proportionately greater number of people who live in ghettos than of those who live in Beverly Hills will commit crimes. Similarly, a proportionately greater number of Beverly Hills residents than of ghetto residents will go to college. In fact, even now, we seem to recognize this state of affairs by our social legislation, which seeks to provide different environments for minority groups in order to modify their behavior.

Alternative Control Methods

We are presently concerned with controlling upheavals and anarchic behavior associated with social change and discontent, but we also share the fear of developing a society that will achieve communal tranquillity at the expense of what we call our individual freedoms. Skinner's proposals stimulate the latter fear and raise the portent of society depicted by Aldous Huxley (1932) and George Orwell (1949).

It is more likely, however, that an Orwellian society may develop from our present system than from extrapolations of Skinner's proposals. People rebel against and resist repressive measures but, at the same time, advocate and support their use on others who behave in ways that are aversive to them. People have learned that punishment is very effective in immediately suppressing ongoing behavior; they have not yet learned that punishment is not very effective in helping initiate new behaviors—behaviors that may be more productive and helpful, both to society and to the individual. In addition, most people see government largely as a coercive force, rather than a potential source of reward for things well done.

During a period of rapid economic and social change, a significant number of the population will suffer, and will be more apt to support repressive governmental measures as a response to their own fears. The last five years have seen much more emphasis placed on law enforcement and strict interpretation of the laws than before, and it is likely that repressive measures will become more prevalent in the near future. The extent to which the present trend toward the use of repressive measures will develop is partly a function of the rate of social change. Because our rapid technological development forces an acceleration of social adjustments, the trend toward repression may be difficult to stem and may result in a technologically sophisticated totalitarian state.

A distinct additional possibility is that, with the rising population, depletion of natural resources, and the increase of pollution, repressive measures may have to be used to guarantee survival of our species. These measures may take the form of forced sterilization, greatly restricted uses of energy, and limits on movement and living location. Some of these measures have a high probability of being put into action suddenly with consequent additional social disruption.

Skinner's proposals not only recommend more sophisticated behavioral control but also advocate a reduction of coercive measures. The literature on operant technology shows that, for the most part, punishment works temporarily and only while the punishing agent is present. Extrapolated to a larger group, the more a society utilizes repressive measures, the more energy has to be devoted to maintaining the control system; consequently, less energy is available for more productive enterprises. The excessive use of punishment sometimes results in behaviors that are more troublesome or damaging than the original behavior—for example, a child who has been subjected to excessive punishment may become apathetic or depressed, or an adult may behave in ways that people call "insane," "criminal," or "dull." Even more energy has to be devoted by society to taking care of the people who respond aversively to aversive methods of control. The use of positive reinforcement as a control mechanism, although not as immediately effective, is more expeditious and less costly in the long run. The energy required to develop such a system is initially high, owing to research and developmental costs, but considerably less in the long run, because it requires less supervision.

Language and Behavior Control

Although the ultimate causes of behavior can be said to lie in the external environment, a vast amount of behavior control is internalized and is a function of learned covert and overt verbal systems (thinking and speaking). Verbal stimuli are rarely considered as stimuli to which the organism responds. However, the verbal systems that we possess and share are directly related to our other social behaviors and determine our concept of the world in which we live. A man does much of what he does as a function of what he thinks (or would say) is real. People vote for candidates, go to the theater, raise their children, or build airplanes and sophisticated electronic apparatus as functions of the overt or covert statements about these things that others direct at them. These statements are learned, sometimes paired with autonomic responses (emotions), and are an effect and consequence of the control exerted by verbal communities—the family, the school, the media, religious groups, and many other subgroups or institutions. People continue to behave the way they do because of the consequences of their behavior in the past; similarly, people continue to talk and think the way they do because of the past consequences of their behavior. As civilization has developed, the prevalence of violent or repressive control of behavior has diminished. However, coercion as a model for controlling behavior has not been replaced. Instead, it is now mediated by our language; and coercion, though expressed in terms less physically damaging to the individual, has significant short-term and long-term deleterious effects. Skinner's advocacy of a reduction of coercive measures, therefore, applies to verbal behavior as well as to nonverbal behavior.

When individuals live in a community that verbally punishes certain behaviors, they learn to behave similarly—that is, they learn to punish others verbally when presented with examples of the socially disapproved behaviors. Similarly, they will make punishing verbal statements to themselves in a like circumstance or when presented with occasions in which the probability of their behaving in a socially disapproved manner is increased. If, on the other hand, individuals live in a society that talks about and reinforces responses that are incompatible with socially unproductive behavior, they are more apt to talk and behave in a way that reinforces productive behavior. The type of control people are subjected to in their environment and in their verbal community is the type of control they apply to themselves and to people around them. The behavioral ramifications and consequences of a society rewarding or maintaining punishment of unacceptable behavior, as opposed to a society reinforcing positive and acceptable behavior, are pervasive and manifest.

What we say is "wrong" with society, or our own behavior or that of some other person, is also a function of the verbal system we have learned in our community, and what we say to others and ourselves will determine where we will look for solutions. In our present society, what we say is a significant part of the problem. Our main control device has been some form of punishment, and much of it is verbal.

Punishment as a means of control is taught in our communities, and it has become an integral part of our ethical system. The backup system for punitive control includes agencies that are sanctioned to generate the sort of aversive stimuli that could terminate life or greatly restrict the environment of, and the behaviors available to, an individual. When solving a problem that is aversive to society or to a person, we have, as a function of our traditional methods and verbal systems, dealt directly with the person or group that we have held responsible instead of with the environment that controls their behavior. We have various penal institutions and mental hospitals designed to punish and somehow change the people who create social problems. All of our systems are, for the most part, trying to stop or restrain "offenders" from emitting behaviors that we have found aversive. They are no more successful in accomplishing their goal than is an individual who chastizes himself for drinking or smoking too much: such a person continues to drink or smoke, sometimes even at a higher rate, but feels guilty and incompetent. Skinner's position is that we are holding accountable the products of the environment instead of the environment that produces these products. Much of what maintains this state of affairs and postpones the application of science to our problems is a function of our verbal systems.

Eventually, social and other environmental crises will force action. Again, these changes, although critical for the survival of our whole group, may nonetheless cause mass upheaval. The negative responses that are likely to be incurred by sudden, necessary changes will also be largely a function of the verbal systems that we all share. Much of this can be precluded by beginning to talk now about long-range plans for our society and about the gradual changes necessary to make our environment a producer of creative, socially successful human beings.

The ultimate causes of our covert and overt verbal behavior lie in the environment. If societal agencies begin to consider events in terms of their consequences, and if they also begin to regard punishment, verbal or otherwise, as a temporary and injurious expedient, individuals within the society will also modify the way they talk to, and behave toward, themselves and others.

This extrapolation of operant principles to thinking, or covert verbal behavior, smacks of "thought control." The term is anathema to just about everyone. However, the objections to "thought control" are also a function of our verbal systems. Objections to "thought control" imply that we are free to think whatever we want. Apparently, we think or talk to ourselves in ways that we have been taught or reinforced to think or talk; our thinking is controlled now by our present verbal communities and society just as it will be by whatever society we devise in the future.

Controlling the Controllers

Even if readers agree with the statements made above, they may resist more efficient "self-conscious" behavioral control by government. The question of most concern is this: If we construct more efficient behavioral control systems, who will run these systems and who will determine what is best for the population? Who will control the controllers?

We seem to be in relative agreement that the present system of controlling the controllers is not satisfactory. The pages of the *Center Magazine* testify to the dissatisfaction with governmental policy concerning international relations and treatment of minority and special-interest groups. The need to devise alternative methods of controlling the controllers was expressed in a speech given by John Gardner in December, 1969. Gardner stated that many of our present institutions are unable to respond quickly to the needs of the population that they serve. He called for the construction of mechanisms that would make possible the evolution of institutions concurrent with the changing needs of society. He referred to the presence of riots, demonstrations, and other signs of social dysfunction as an index of the deterioration of the efficacy of our social institutions. Presumably, Gardner's initiation of Common Cause was a preliminary step directed toward the solution of this problem.

The initial step in the process of devising more effective techniques in controlling controllers is the identification of the controllers themselves, their areas of operation, their behavior, and the reinforcers that control their behavior. Controllers are not only public agencies but also private corporations whose investments and operations alter the physical and social environment of our society. Identifying significant organizations, their behaviors, and their reinforcers creates conditions under which their behavior becomes subject to control. Appropriate application of reinforcers to organizational behavior in turn can direct their responses into more productive areas. For example, if government makes monies or other reinforcers available in one area of endeavor but not in others, organizations will respond by shifting their efforts to the area of greatest payoff.

This statement implies controlled economies—controlled, but with an empirical bias, in that sufficient feedback mechanisms and technology should be involved to insure rapid adjustment to changing situations. It also has to involve sophisticated analytic capacity for simulation studies that would reduce the possibility of error. Jay W. Forrester (1971b) describes a computer-mediated social-simulation system that is capable of analyzing the interactions of various environmental variables over time and producing predictions about the proximal and long-term effects of social manipulations. Forrester points out that intuitive solutions to social problems often have long-term effects quite opposite to those desired. The example he cites is that the provision of low-cost housing alone in an impacted area will, in the long run, greatly exacerbate the original problem of overcrowding and the excess of unskilled labor in that area.

Objections to a controlled economy can be answered by the fact that the economy and consequent environmental changes are already controlled, as evidenced by present governmental attempts to control inflation, salaries, and prices. The only additional factor would be the utilization of a much more sophisticated technology, which is already within our capabilities.

Another objection to a behaviorally controlled society is based on the assumption that individual initiative and creative nonconformity will be stifled if such a society comes to pass. Behaviors that we call creative sometimes result in novel solutions to problems. Because problem-solving activities appear to be closely related to survival, contingencies could be arranged that would promote such activities among individuals and groups, channelled in directions likely to produce salutary environmental change with a minimum of social disruption.

Planned societies can be sterile, stifling, and coercive, but they can also be creative, free, and open. It seems reasonable to assume that we are more likely to evolve into a society that we like if we plan for it and construct environmental contingencies to increase the probability that creative and productive behavior occurs, than if we proceed without plans and without sufficient awareness of what variables control our behavior.

The question "Who shall control the controllers? can be rephrased *What* will control the controllers? The answer to the latter question is that different forms of feedback data will control the controllers, who will themselves be under a set of specific environmental contingencies designed to increase the probabilities of appropriate responses to the data.

Some Contingencies Controlling Organizational Behavior

In political life, it is difficult to identify the actor, much less his behavior and the consequences of that behavior. In fact, part of the function of bureaucracy is to diffuse accountability, in order to avoid criticism and blunt resistance to administrative acts. However, the same system that protects and reinforces the administrator also makes the system less responsive to modification if the effects of policy are not salutary. The tendency of humans to avoid criticism and, consequently, to conceal their behavior or to diffuse accountability often has tragic, sometimes monumental, consequences. The consequence of concealment or restriction of information to a select group is that the behavior of that group is almost entirely controlled by its intragroup verbal behavior. Such organizations as General Motors, the American Bar Association, the American Medical Association, and the State Department are cases in point. The policy and behavior of these organizations appear to be but little affected by communication from outside groups. Problems and difficulties arise when the behavior of one group impinges on, or restricts the behavior or the reinforcers of, people outside these groups. Because "outsiders" have neither the opportunity nor the power to modify an organization's behavior, that behavior will continue until a crisis occurs, with consequent social disruption. Richard Barnet (1971) makes a similar point regarding the State Department. He states that the great majority of State Department policy makers come from a few large cities with professional offices within ten blocks of each other; that they meet together, give each other awards, and, in effect, reinforce each other's verbal behavior. With little feedback from other communities, it is no wonder that these circumscribed verbal communities often find themselves in conflict with other groups and, in some cases, with the conceptions of reality held by the majority of the population. The present situation in Vietnam is a case in point; the operation of the CIA during the Bay of Pigs disaster was a similar case. In these two situations, relatively small groups of policy makers—reinforced by, and under the control of, their specialized verbal communities—acted in ways detrimental to the population at large.

The solution to the problems of secrecy and diffusion of accountability is a society in which behaviors are identified, actors specifically named, the consequences of actions documented and revealed, and contingencies established to define behavioral alternatives. In order for this concept to be implemented, considerable study needs to be given to innovative systems of checks and balances, to new and more responsive feedback systems, and to more comprehensive systems of monitoring agencies or organizations engaged in significant behaviors, the consequences of which may affect both our own and other populations. Rexford G. Tugwell's (1970) proposal for a new Constitution is one example of an alternative system with checks and balances more attuned to the state of present-day technology. Experiments in this area will, of necessity, continue indefinitely to insure that governmental systems can stay astride of accelerating technological development and social change.

But new systems of checks and balances, although necessary, are not sufficient. Monitoring systems and systems of checks and balances are dependent upon the willingness of organizations to cooperate. As long as agencies are subject to severe criticism and the threat of being replaced because of failure, their cooperation will be difficult to obtain. The problem then becomes how to insure that individuals and organizations will cooperate with whatever monitoring systems may be installed.

Cooperation can be broken down into specific behavioral subsets— for example, accurately recording events or transmitting an account of each event to the monitoring agency. Once critical behaviors have been identified, contingency management can increase the probability that selected behaviors will occur. However, if the transmission of accurate information is likely to result in severe public criticism or in the elimination of the reporting agency, the specific contingencies established will not produce the desired behavior. In such a case, the dominant contingency will be related to survival, and the information reported will be invalid, unreliable, or biased.

Some techniques already have been developed to reduce the tendency of organizations to indefinitely perpetuate themselves. Task forces with limited scope and tenure are often established; but even the information reported by task forces is partly a function of the consequences expected to ensue after the release of the final report.

There has been considerable criticism of the present welfare system to the effect that the present mode of distributing funds appears to encourage and reward nonproductivity. Similar criticisms can be leveled at governmental and other organizations at all levels. Administrators frequently are rewarded with additional staff, salary, and influence as the problem with which they are dealing grows larger; they are punished by reduction of their budgets as the problem situation declines. Under this system, it becomes rather clear that problem-solving activities are not encouraged, while the maintenance of nonproductive behaviors is rewarded.

If a problem is solved and an organization completes its mission, the usual result is that a significant number of individuals quickly lose their jobs or, at the very least, a significant source of satisfaction. It is not unusual, with the present set of contingencies, that the introduction of novel techniques and problem-solving efforts is resisted. Society has not developed techniques of smoothly substituting alternative goals, once the original goal has been reached. Numbers of people find themselves with outdated skills when their jobs are eliminated by automation. They do not have a sufficient number of alternative skills to maintain themselves, and, consequently, they experience depression and apathy. The environment has simply not provided them with readily accessible alternative sources of reinforcement.

Criticism of institutions partially stems from the same set of verbal statements (concepts) that deter the agency itself from cooperating with evaluation or monitoring efforts—namely, that the organization is fully developed and capable of solving the problem, and is remiss if it fails. Organizational attempts to solve problems are rarely conceived of as a process that proceeds by successive approximations guided by appropriate feedback measures. Because error is not tolerated, the organization resists evaluation and deprives itself of opportunities to correct its methods and to adjust to changing environmental conditions.

In summary, if an organization cooperates with evaluative or monitoring systems, and utilizes novel or experimental techniques, it exposes itself to criticism and possible extinction. Moreover, if it survives by escaping criticism and solves the problem to which it has addressed itself, it is eliminated, and many of the individuals within it have to face major dislocations in their lives. On the other hand, if an organization utilizes established noncontroversial methods, and if it conceals—either by commission or by omission—its failures or limitations, it is less likely to be criticized and, hence, more likely to survive. It will also be less likely to solve the problem.

Under the present contingencies, it is highly likely that the majority of organizations will fit the second description, because immediate survival is the strongest reinforcer we have available. The survival of nonproductive organizations, however, is incompatible with the survival of society as a whole. Unless the contingencies controlling the behavior of organizations are altered, the likelihood of our society surviving will be markedly reduced.

Dividing Up Society's Reinforcers

Organizations, including productive ones, have difficulty in accomplishing their missions—even if they are not criticized, and even if they have ample funding. Tasks assigned to organizations, particularly governmental agencies, often include dealing with several groups having conflicting interests or reinforcers. In operant terms, one group's positive reinforcers are another's negative reinforcers—that is, one group's obtaining satisfaction necessarily excludes the possibility of the other group's obtaining satisfaction.

In certain environments, survival requires conflict, and the stronger group survives at the expense of the weaker. The environments in which conflict is necessary may be characterized as scarcity environments, in which certain essential commodities, such as food and water, are sufficient only for a limited number of people. However, in this country, as contrasted with the rest of the world, conflict over basic necessities is unnecessary because an ample supply of these basic necessities exists. Nevertheless, conflict exists between different ethnic, racial, and professional groups, and between sexes. The conflicts between groups are based on disagreements as to how society's reinforcers—that is, material goods, status, and prestige—are to be divided. These disagreements are buttressed, maintained, and expressed by attitudes, and they are manifested by the verbal behavior of society and of the groups in conflict.

The professional-group conflict with which we are most familiar is that between psychologists and psychiatrists. This conflict, over the years, has included a variety of issues, two of which are (1) who should have society's legal sanction to give psychotherapy, and (2) who should head mental-health programs. Obtaining official sanction to give psychotherapy or to head mental-health programs is associated with the receipt of positive reinforcers—namely, high salaries, prestige, and greater control over one's environment. Because members of both professions do not lack basic necessities, the conflict is entirely based on the distribution of "surplus," or social, reinforcers.

Surplus reinforcers become reinforcers as a function of the verbal behavior of societies. Our present society's verbal behavior reinforces the acquisition of money and power and honors those who have achieved high positions; yet society provides extremely limited opportunities for achieving the social reinforcers that it establishes. In other words, our present social system has created an environment of artificial scarcity. Humans respond to socially conditioned reinforcers in a manner similar to the way they respond to primary reinforcers. Thus, an artificial-scarcity environment, like an environment lacking a sufficient amount food or water, increases the probability of intergroup and interindividual conflict.

In ethnic or interracial conflicts, the basic disagreement appears to be similar—namely, how to divide up the available reinforcers. Racial strife appears to be greatest between groups of people close to each other in economic or social status. Severe social strife is apparent between blacks and groups of eastern-European origin. Both groups occupy adjoining steps on the socioeconomic ladder, but the eastern-European group sees the blacks as competitors for jobs, money, and housing. In a scarcity society, groups must do battle for the few reinforcers available or face conditions that society itself establishes as degrading.

This situations calls for a different distribution of the reinforcers, as well as changes in our verbal behavior. If society's verbal behavior places value on wealth and status, it reinforces behavior aimed at *acquiring* wealth and status. In a scarcity society in which all or most groups are reinforced by wealth or status, conflict is inevitable. Not only will the lower economic status groups demand a greater portion of wordly goods, but, simultaneously, the higher socioeconomic groups will fight to retain what they have.

Such organizations as the Office of Economic Opportunity find themselves continually caught between groups, each group striving to obtain its "share" of the available reinforcers. The verbal behavior of the conflicting groups supports the claim of each group and reinforces antagonism. Psychiatrists and psychologists often talk about each other as unqualified, needing supervision, and uneducated in either human relations or medicine. Ethnic conflict is characterized by similar deprecations, such as lazy, "uptight," prejudiced, or uncultured. It is interesting to observe that many of the terms used by each of the groups in reference to the other are often considered descriptive when their intent is clearly pejorative.

Wealth distribution cannot occur, without severe social disruption, in the absence of a concomitant change in values and attitudes; in other words, changes in verbal behavior. Verbal behavior creates our reality, establishes our reinforcers, and, to a great extent, controls our nonverbal behavior. In beginning the process of social change so necessary for the survival of our society, we have to address ourselves first to the problem of how to change both our overt and covert verbal behavior, and in what direction.

Prescriptions for Change

Skinner maintains that it is necessary, for our society's survival, to recognize the role of the environment in controlling our behavior. We currently stress the importance of being free and being able to make our own decisions. When we talk and think in this manner, however, our attention is diverted from a consideration of the relevant factors in our environment that control our behavior. It is Skinner's thesis that, if, instead of talking about freedom, we directed our attention to the contingencies in the environment controlling our behavior, we would be more likely to be able to change it. It is also Skinner's contention that changing our environment would, in turn, change our own behavior in ways that would reduce the probability of the occurrence of a variety of social and intergroup problems.

The ramifications of talking about behavior as determined and controlled by the presence or absence of reinforcement and punishment are manifold. Predictions about the consequences of behavior will have to be different, because the effects of reinforcement and punishment as determined by scientific experiment differ from prevailing thought and practice. Attention will then be directed to a consideration of the kinds of reinforcers society establishes, as opposed to the kinds and varieties of reinforcers that are available and, consequently, to the kinds of environmental changes necessary to attenuate artificial-scarcity situations. Attention will also be directed to a consideration of the kinds of control that society must exert in order to be able to achieve full productivity. This would include a specification of the patterns of incentives and contingencies that must be available to encourage problem solving and creative endeavor, as well as to reduce the number of social casualties produced by the social system. The consideration of different feedback, control, and monitoring data systems will also be a necessary consequence, because the initial stimuli for social change will be those data that measure the consequence of institutional and group behavior. Such changes cannot be achieved immediately, of course, but they will occur step by step in successive approximations, as prescribed by the data.

Specific examples of societal change due to changes in verbal behavior may include the following:

1) In a typical interpersonal situation, unruly children may be punished or scolded less frequently, because the consequence of punishment is usually only more unruliness and guilt. Instead, attention might be directed to the environment in which a child lives—for example, to opportunities for play in a separate room, to availability of friends or playthings, and to the parents' own verbal and nonverbal behavior that maintains or reinforces unruly behavior. Changes that might result from this way of talking or thinking about the situation range from spatial rearrangement of the home to changes in the parents' patterns of reinforcing their child.

2) In a social problem, such as alcoholism, social action might take the form of providing for the establishment and the reinforcement of social activities incompatible with heavy drinking, as well as opportunities for training in social skills and relaxation. Parenthetically, thinking in terms of behavior consequences would also reduce the number of moralistic lectures an alcoholic might receive.

3) In prisons in which homosexuality is considered to be a problem, the environment might be changed to make conjugal visits and visits by girl friends possible. An even better alternative might be to provide situations in which inmates would be able to learn to interact with women in a more rewarding way and in which sexual intercourse might

become available only after certain interpersonal skills have been learned. The long-term effects of this kind of treatment could include a reduction in the number of sexually oriented crimes, as well as a reduction in drinking. (Many people drink heavily in order to interact socially.)

Prisons also house violent people. Violence is a behavior that terminates stimuli aversive to the actor only to result in severe long-term consequences. Learning procedures can be instituted by which inmates can learn to identify the aversive stimulation to which they respond violently and can acquire alternative ways of interacting. As long as prisons are necessary, appropriate enforced contingencies placed both on staff and on inmates would also reduce the amount of punishment dealt out in prison, such as solitary confinement, restriction, or physical assault.

4) In the operation of government, monitoring systems would become more reliable and accurate, were criticism sharply reduced and appropriate incentives installed, and the organization would become more problem-oriented, successful, and creative. It would also give the organization a greater repertoire and a greater sophistication in dealing with the problems assigned to it, inasmuch as any problem assigned includes the control or modification of behavior.

The alteration of verbal behavior concerned with the distribution of wealth (different allocation of reinforcers) is unlikely to occur immediately because the media are controlled by groups who have a large investment in the status quo and will naturally protect their interests. However, the alteration of verbal behavior concerned with social casualties—for example, criminals, the mentally ill, alcoholics, and problem children—is more likely. The initiation of different ways of talking and thinking about behavior is likely to have a cumulatively "self-reinforcing" and exponential effect. People are controlled by reinforcement: if the novel behaviors are reinforced, if the unruly child becomes more pleasant, if criminals begin to reinforce society, then the behaviors that are responsible for such positive effects will be reinforced and, therefore, will increase in frequency.

Any behavior, including verbal behavior, undergoes a process technically called stimulus-and-response generalization. If, on the one hand, the stimulus situation remains unchanged, the same response is still likely to be emitted. If, on the other hand, the stimulus situation is somewhat changed, the response also changes slightly. As long as the response emitted is reinforced, this "drift" will continue. If thinking and acting in terms of behavioral principles are effective in a variety of situations, it is highly probable that this practice would spread to different areas of human interaction. If we find that we are effective with our children, with prison inmates, or with alcoholics, we will gradually learn to respond in a like manner in other problem situations. In this way, major societal change may be implemented, at first gradually, and then with increasing momentum, but with much less accompanying social disruption, because verbal behavior will have kept pace with, or will have preceded, social necessity.

Problems Facing Operant Practitioners

Society will not be suddenly "converted" to an "operant philosophy," but total acceptance of operant statements is not a prerequisite for utilizing operant techniques. Instead, operant technology will be partially accepted, and such terms as "successive approximations" and "shaping" are operant ways of talking about partial acceptance. A newcomer to the operant reality can be taught only in a step-by-step fashion, through a series of partial acceptances. This problem is, of course, not peculiar to the operant neophyte. All newcomers—be they babies, students, immigrants, apprentices, recruits, or religious proselytes—appear to go through the same process. The operant statement about such phenomena is not that the newcomer "decides" to accept the new behaviors, but rather that each "partial acceptance" (new response or series of responses) is reinforced. The problem of a limited repertoire (partial acceptance) is also not peculiar to the student of operants. A baby who can only crawl is limited in its travels, and apprentices are limited by their level of competence. Generally, we do not speak of this as partial acceptance but, rather, as partial learning. However, the person who partially "accepts" the operant reality is therefore also limited to that extent in the kinds of phenomena that he can deal with successfully.

The phenomenon of partial acceptance has always been with us and is perhaps most clearly documented in the history of science. Scientific knowledge accretes at a steady pace as a function of countless observations and experiments. Although the lay person may be aware of the contributions of Newton and Einstein, the physicist is also aware of the hundreds of scientists on whose work Newton's and Einstein's theories are based. Moreover, the physicist is aware of the many successive approximations (partial acceptances) that took place in the interval between the lifetimes of the two men.

In relation to the rest of the population, a scientist can be said to be someone who partially accepts abnormal ways of talking about the universe. The problems that the scientist encounters when he makes abnormal statements about the universe depend upon the state of the normal world. Giordano Bruno's partial acceptance of some abnormal statements about the relation of the earth to the sun (heliocentrism) caused him to be burned at the stake. B. F. Skinner's abnormal statement (behavior is determined by environment) has occasioned numerous verbal attacks by the normal (other than operant) verbal community. The foregoing are typical examples, and they occur predictability. It appears, therefore, that the biggest problem of those interested in applying operant principles today is that of surviving in a normal environment.

At this time (1972), operant research is respectable in academic settings with animals other than humans. By contrast, the operantly oriented person experiences many more difficult problems when he is immersed in an environment designed to modify human behaviors *normally*—that is, a traditional institution for the mentally ill, or traditional educational and penal institutions. These environments may also offer the best opportunities for the operant practitioner, inasmuch as many of them are little more than custodial way-stations and are relatively ineffective in meeting the problems that society assigns them. However, to survive and expand systematically in such settings, it is necessary to perform an "interpretive functional analysis" of who is reinforcing whom, with what, and to what effect throughout the entire organization. The informal interpretive functional analysis (IFA) is used in lieu of the more formal and accurate functional analysis, which requires an order of cooperation and control of the environment not likely to be given to an operant interloper, grant in hand or not. The IFA generates an informal operant "description," as contrasted with a normal "description," of the environment—that is, "the person called a therapist and the person called a patient appear to be mutually reinforcing each other's behavior" rather than "the therapist was helping the patient work through his problems." Things are seldom what they appear to be, and the IFA increases the accuracy of one's predictions and, hence, increases the probability of surviving and eventually modifying the so-called patient. In most institutions, the IFA will point up the fact that many of the so-called problem behaviors have either been acquired through, or are being maintained by, the *normal behaviors* (reinforcing undesirable behaviors or punishing desirable behaviors) of the staff of the institution in question. Partly as a function of being understaffed and partly as a function of the normal orientation, passive behaviors are generally reinforced and independent behaviors (behaviors useful outside an institution) are generally punished.

The next task is identifying the staff members who, in fact, would be reinforced by a change, not simply those who say they would like a change. Change generally requires more work; for many of the staff, this will be aversive and, therefore, avoided, thus insuring failure of the project. It is critical, then, to identify the reinforcers (both positive and negative) of the staff members with whom one wishes to work. Helping a staff member terminate an unpleasant or aversive situation is probably more important initially than any other form of behavioral control. It is only later that positive reinforcement becomes important. Staff, like other humans that survive, terminate aversive stimuli or negative reinforcers first, be they conditioned or unconditioned. Then, and only then, can they be positively reinforced. Attempts to positively reinforce the staff for new behaviors can, hence, be wasteful and can lead to erroneous conclusions that the staff are uncooperative, lazy, sadistic, not interested in their "charges," and so on.

Assisting a staff member terminate aversive stimuli is often difficult because much of what is aversive to the staff member is determined by what is aversive to higher-level staff members. In a normal institutional setting, even a temporary increase in disturbing patient or inmate behaviors results in aversive consequences for the line staff. In such cases, responsible staff are often "counseled," investigated, or reprimanded. In order to avoid such aversive consequences, line staff act to immediately suppress disturbing behaviors. The consequences controlling the behavior of higher-level staff are similar—namely, criticism from the "Central Office" or from the community.

The greatest difficulty, but also the first requirement in initiating an operant program in an institution, is to obtain at least partial release of control over the line staff from higher staff echelons. Some higher-level staff members are able to release control because of expectations that the project, if successful, will enhance their own positions, status, or professional reputations. In any case, the effectiveness of alternatives to aversive control and punishment must be demonstrated piecemeal and, initially, in noncritical areas.

Controlling and modifying behavior via reinforcement is abnormal behavior for institutional staff because the administration of punishment for disapproved acts in the prevalent mode of operation. In order to change the line staff's behavior toward patients or inmates, the verbal behavior of the staff has to be altered first. Some alternative statements to be reinforced include the following: (1) If I punish or criticize behavior I don't like, it will suppress that behavior only temporarily, but will not change or modify it in the long run. (2) I can weaken behavior I don't like by ignoring it and not responding to it. (3) I can also weaken behavior I don't like by reinforcing incompatible behavior that I like. (4) Changing the behavior of another person takes a long time and results are at first slow in coming. (5) Recording behaviors that I like will help me in detecting initial behavior changes that, in turn, will help maintain my own behavior. (6) If the other person does not change, my own behavior is part of the problem.

The ability of line staff to make the statements listed above and to behave in a manner consistent with those statements will increase the likelihood of staff–client interactions becoming productive of desirable behavior changes in both parties.

The changes in verbal behavior recommended for line staff can only be effective if aversive control from higher-echelon staff is significantly attenuated. If aversive control from above is not attenuated, the most likely result will be that the newly learned verbal behavior will occur only in the classroom or in the company of the instructor, but not in interactions with the patient or inmate.

Operant theory directs the attention of the behavior modifier to the environment of the subject. Line staff constitute a significant portion of the client's environment, and changes in the staff's behavior away from punishment and toward reinforcement of desirable social behaviors will change that environment significantly.

When the environment changes, the behaviors of persons within the environment modify very quickly, because behaviors previously reinforced are no longer maintained and new behaviors take their places. Altering the environment of at least part of the institution, therefore, becomes the first objective of the operant practitioner. It is a complicated, difficult, but very rewarding task.

Some Current Research Findings and Issues

This paper may appear speculative and utopian to many. There is, however, nothing speculative about the efficacy of behavioral techniques in the analysis and modification of a wide range of human behavior.

Over the last quarter of a century, operant conditioning and behavior therapy have been utilized in a variety of settings. A partial list would include mental hospitals, prisons, schools for wayward youths, public and experimental schools, institutions for the mentally retarded, outpatient mental-health clinics, and experimental research laboratories, as well as the home. Operant conditioning has also been used with success on a broad spectrum of populations, including normal and autistic children; delinquent adolescents; individuals labeled alcoholic, psychotic, neurotic, and senile; couples engaged in marital conflict; and prison inmates. Specific behaviors modified by operant techniques include smoking, overeating, the drinking of alcoholic beverages, angry or aversive behavior between marital partners, the frequency of vocalizing certain words or phrases, vocally expressed hallucinations, confusion and apathy among geriatric patients, self-destructive behavior, and uncontrolled toileting behavior in children. In addition, responses usually considered as not under "conscious" control—for example, blood pressure, heart rate, and muscle tension—have also been modified and, in some cases, placed under "voluntary" control.

Operant research grew slowly at first, but more recently it has grown at a vastly increased rate. The growth rate of operant research is partially reflected by the proliferation of professional journals devoted to publishing the results of such work. In 1958, the *Journal of the Experimental Analysis of Behavior* was established. *Behavior Research and Therapy* started in 1962, *The Journal of Applied Behavior Analysis* in 1968, *Behavior Therapy* and *Behavior Therapy and Experimental Psychiatry* in 1970, and the *Journal of Behavioral Technology* in 1971.

THE USE OF POSITIVE REINFORCEMENT

Behavior change can be accomplished by varying any of several factors that control and maintain behavior. New responses can be inserted in an individual's repertoire or existing ones can be eliminated or weakened by the adjustment of contingencies. One such adjustment can take the form of providing positive reinforcement after a specific response or chain of responses has been emitted. In an early experiment, Fuller (1949) was able to teach a vegetative human organism (a bedridden idiot) to raise his arm "in order to obtain milk." Fuller followed any incipient arm-raising response with the introduction of milk into the subject's mouth. By gradually raising the requirements for reinforcement, the experimenter was able to shape the subject's arm-raising response to the point where the subject held his arm vertically and responded three times per minute, a rate that approximated the maximum, inasmuch as it took some time for the milk to be proffered and ingested. A much more complicated response chain was conditioned by Pumroy and Pumroy (1965). These experimenters taught their children (1) to ask to go to the toilet, and (2) to urinate in the toilet. The positive reinforcer used was a candy mint given to the children immediately after urination was completed. The application of the positive reinforcer (the candy mint) in this case resulted in a number of behavior chains being "fixed" in a particular sequence.

Positive reinforcement has also been used to control verbal behavior. Greenspoon (1955) was able to increase the rate of using plural nouns in his subjects by verbally reinforcing them at any time they vocalized a plural noun. The positive reinforcer utilized by Greenspoon was the vocalization "mmm-hmmm." Other researchers, Staats et al. (1962) and Kapostins (1963), have used different reinforcers (trinkets and money) to maintain verbal behavior in their subjects. Similarly, Ayllon and Michaels (1959) were able to increase the amount of socially acceptable conversation in a psychotic person by only paying attention to her when she spoke "sensibly." Further, Pumroy and Pumroy and Ayllon and Michaels were able to eliminate competing responses—namely, urinating in places other than the toilet and speaking in a psychotic manner, respectively. Positive reinforcement can, under certain circumstances, eliminate or reduce the rate of certain behaviors by increasing the rate of incompatible behaviors.

Several supplementary methods have been used to accelerate learning complex behavior. For example, instructions may be given, or the desired response may be modeled by a person already familiar with the task. The subject is then asked to perform or to imitate the desired procedure; if he is successful, he is reinforced. Ayllon and Azrin (1968) give examples of "response exposure" procedures, in which the subject first is asked to observe someone else performing work and then is given the opportunity to carry out the task himself. If the desired behavior is very complex or is usually avoided by the subject, behavior rehearsal may be used in which the participants practice certain difficult interactions. The successful accomplishment of the selected task is then positively reinforced by social approval or other reinforcers.

THE USE OF AVERSIVE STIMULATION

Another adjustment possible in contingency management is to present an aversive stimulus immediately after a particular response has been emitted. Depending upon other associated conditions, the result can be the reduction or the elimination of the response. The result may also be any of a variety of responses leading to the elimination of the aversive stimulus—escape or avoidance training.

Punishment was technically defined by Azrin and Holz (1966) as "a reduction of the future probability of a specific response as a result of the immediate delivery of a stimulus after that response." In their literature review on the effects of punishment, these authors have shown that punishment is probably the most effective of all the available techniques in eliminating a response. Perhaps the most outstanding example of the effectiveness of punishment was reported by Lovaas (1965). In a series of studies on the problem of suppressing self-destructive behavior in autistic children, Lovaas was able to demonstrate the rapid and complete elimination of this behavior in a number of children. The aversive stimulus was electric shock applied to the body of the child immediately after the self-destructive response was emitted. Lovaas also contrasted the results of punishment to the effects of an extinction procedure on one child. In this case, the self-destructive behavior decreased significantly after eight 90-minute sessions. During this time, the child was released from restraints and allowed to hit himself without interference or any reinforcement. During these eight sessions, the child hit himself more than 10,000 times. This experiment was possible only because this particular child was a "careful" hitter. With other patients, the result might have been severe injury or death.

Azrin and Holtz (1966) listed 14 conditions under which punishment is effective; but these conditions are quite restrictive and are difficult to obtain outside the laboratory. They also pointed out that the principal disadvantages of utilizing punishment in human interaction are that the punished individual is driven away from the punisher, thereby destroying the social relationship, and that counteraggression (or aggression toward nearby individuals) is also likely to occur. Another factor not mentioned by the authors is that, by utilizing punishment, the punisher is reinforced for punishing and is, therefore, more likely to engage in similar behavior in the future. Azrin and Holz indicate that the disadvantages of punishment are particularly critical "since survival of the human organism appears to be so completely dependent upon the maintenance of harmonious social relations."

Aversive stimuli can be used to cause the acquisition or elimination of certain behaviors, if conditions are constructed so that escape or avoidance of aversive stimulation is contingent upon a selected response being emitted. The aversive stimuli to which people respond may be unlearned (such as electric shock, cold, or loud noise) or learned (such as frowns, derogatory statements, or critical comments). Learned aversive stimuli are acquired by pairing previously neutral stimuli with aversive stimuli. A child, for example, may learn that a frown on the part of a parent is followed by spanking; thus, in the future, a parental frown may stimulate the child to emit a response that terminates the frown. The terminating response—for example, a verbal statement like "I'm sorry"—may be an avoidance response with respect to the physical or unconditioned aversive stimulus (spanking) but an escape route with respect to the conditioned or learned aversive stimulus (the frown). The escape response, whether it is escape from a conditioned or an unconditioned aversive stimulus, is reinforced by the termination of that stimulus. If, after saying "I'm sorry," the frown disappears and, at the same time, physical punishment is avoided, this vocalization will be reinforced. Consequently, saying "I'm sorry" in the presence of a frown will be more likely in the future.

Lovaas et al. (1965) describe a striking series of escape and avoidance experiments on autistic children. The children who were subjects in this experiment had never in their lives been able to follow instructions or to respond positively to social approaches. They spent most of their time in self-destructive and self-stimulatory activity (rocking, making unintelligible sounds, and so forth). After their self-destructive behavior was suppressed through punishment, the children were taught to come to adults when called. Electric shock was administered to a subject's feet, but it was terminated immediately when the child began to move toward an adult who was calling him. After the escape behavior (coming to the beckoning adult) was well established, the contingencies were altered. In the second step of the training procedure, shock was administered only if the child failed to respond to the call of the adult. The approach behavior became extremely stable after three sessions of 50 trials per session. The behavior of coming to an adult when called was maintained by the children for nine months without the necessity of further training.

In another significant experiment, Erickson and Kuethe (1956) utilized avoidance-training procedures to demonstrate the "learning of forgetting." Their subjects were asked to give verbal associations to a list of words provided them by the experimenters. The subjects' associations to a certain number of the presented words were punished (the subjects were administered an electric shock immediately after the verbalized association). In further trials, the verbalized associations changed. (Changed associations were not shocked.) The experimenters had apparently discovered the contingencies under which at least one form of "Freudian repression" occurs. Some of the subjects became aware of the experimental purpose and could verbalize it, but others did not. In both cases, however, the behavioral response—that is, the tendency to give other associations instead of the original ones, was similar.

A very important characteristic of avoidance responses is that they are extremely resistant to change. Lovaas's results, in which responses learned in several days of training remained constant over a period of nine months, demonstrate this characteristic. One of the factors that makes avoidance responses so difficult to unlearn is that the organism rarely has the opportunity to learn that the situation under which the avoidance response has been acquired has changed. If a rat has been trained to avoid a shock by pressing a lever, and the training has been thorough, it will press that lever very consistently. If the experimenter alters the contingencies so that the shock is no longer administered if if the lever is not pressed, the well-trained rat will only rarely be subject to the novel contingency. Only when the shock fails to be administered when the rat fails to press the lever can the rat learn that the contingency has been changed.

Many avoidance responses that are not beneficial to the individual in the long run are learned in human interaction. Such behavior may include: (1) the inability to engage comfortably in social interaction (that is, shyness, indirectness, inadequate approach behaviors); (2) non-productive aggression or counteraggression (aggression is a common response to aversive stimuli); (3) sexual impotency and frigidity; and (4) alcoholism and drug abuse. The avoidance behaviors may eliminate or attenuate the immediate aversive stimulus, but they have severe long-term effects on the quality of the individual's life.

The Conditioning of Involuntary Behavior

The concepts of anxiety and depression have occupied a central position in many traditional theories of psychopathology. The operant model, however, regards emotions, for the most part, as learned autonomic responses that may appear concurrently with operant behavior, not as causative agents. When unconditioned aversive stimuli (shock, loud noises, and so forth) are presented to an organism, an activation syndrome is evoked. Although autonomic arousal patterns are highly individual (Lacey et al., 1953) the modal response includes such events as increased heart rate, pupil dilation, and higher blood-sugar level. As learning proceeds, neutral stimuli that are paired with the unconditioned aversive stimulus become aversive themselves. Eventually, a condition is reached in which these formerly neutral stimuli (now called conditioned aversive stimuli) also elicit an activation syndrome. It is this type of learning process that causes individuals to respond emotionally to certain verbal expressions.

A number of experiments have demonstrated the control of autonomic or involuntary responses via operant conditioning. Miller and DiCara (1967) were able to raise or lower the heart rates of rats by stimulating the pleasure centers in their brains immediately after a momentary slowing or speeding of their heart beats. With human subjects, Engel and Hansen (1966) and Engel and Chism (1967) were able to show slowing of heart beat and heart speeding as functions of positive reinforcement, respectively. Crider et al. (1966) reported having operantly conditioned a human galvanic skin response and Sasmor (1966) was able to operantly condition very small-scale muscle contractions. These experiments suggest that "emotions" are also learned, and that they persist as a function of the reinforcement following the appearance of autonomic responses.

The recent introduction of sophisticated instrumentation capable of amplifying normally unreportable responses (biofeedback techniques) makes possible the learning of "voluntary" control over a number of autonomic and involuntary behaviors. Kamiya (1969) trained his subjects to control their cerebral alpha rhythm, and Budzynski et al. (1969) reported success in training their subjects to reduce chronic muscle tension. Other experimenters reported similar successes in training their subjects to exert "voluntary" control over a number of other autonomic responses, including galvanic skin response (Stern, 1970), heart rate (Brener and Hothersall, 1966), and blood pressure (Brener and Kleinman, 1970). The techniques now being developed in this area hold considerable promise for the eventual control of emotional and psychosomatic problems.

Other Clinical Procedures in Behavior Modification

The task of the behavioral technologist is to create conditions under which undesirable emotional and avoidance responses can be unlearned and replaced with more productive behaviors. A number of methods stemming from the behavioral theory have been developed. Some of these methods are experimental, but they demonstrate the variety of procedures that have been derived.

DETECTING DISCOMFORT OR TENSION

Techniques for detecting discomfort or tension (identifying aversive stimuli) include relaxation training patterned after Jacobsen (1938) and the autogenic training techniques developed by Schultz and Luthe (1959). The subject, trained in relaxation, is thus more able to discern sudden increases in tension as a function of the presentation of aversive stimulation.

SYSTEMATIC DESENSITIZATION

The technique of systematic desensitization, originally developed by Wolpe for the treatment of phobias (Wolpe, 1958; Wolpe and Lazarus, 1967), requires the client, while in a relaxed condition, to imagine a series of aversive, anxiety-producing scenes. The aim is to maintain the relaxed state while visualizing such scenes. In this method, the aversive scenes are previously identified and graded on the extent to which they produce tension or anxiety. The client practices visualizing the least tension-producing scenes first, and progresses to the more potent stimuli as he masters the earlier ones. Kraft (1967) has also used a variant of this technique to reduce social discomfort (Social Anxiety

Hierarchy). The goal of systematic desensitization is reached when the aversive stimulus or image is no longer avoided and does not produce autonomic arousal or tension.

THE IMPLOSIVE OR FLOODING TECHNIQUE

The implosive or flooding technique, introduced by Hogan (1968), consists of identifying and elaborating a scene that is extremely frightening to the client. The client is asked to imagine this scene, and the therapist supplements the client's efforts by means of statements designed to vivify and further elaborate it. The therapist, thereby, tries to block any avoidance responses and to insure that the client keeps attending to the selected episode until tension and anxiety subside.

ASSERTIVE TRAINING

A variety of techniques has been developed in the area of assertive training, including the rehearsal of social situations difficult for the client to manage successfully, such as asking for a job, saying "no" to a salesman, or asking for directions or assistance from a policeman. Other examples include learning to positively reinforce (Rozynko et al., 1972) and learning to respond "emotionally"—for example, with anger, sadness, or fear (Serber et al., 1969). Assertive training provides the client with behavior repertoires alternative to existing unsatisfactory ones.

Establishing Alternative Ways of Talking or Thinking

In any treatment, the therapist trains the client how to talk about his problems. Each school of therapy has its own language. The kind of statement that a behavior therapist is most likely to teach his client is that the troubles the client has, as well as his anxieties, are learned habits over which he has no control, and that intellectual effort and intelligence have no relation to his problem. Consequently, no person, the client included, can be blamed for his condition. In addition to such general verbal training, certain specific affirmations are introduced as more productive alternatives to existing verbal habits. Garfield et al. (1969) reported the use of this method in conjunction with systematic desensitization. A client who was successfully treated for impotence was taught to stop worrying (talking to himself) about his sex partner's orgasm and to say instead "I will think of enjoying myself."

Meichenbaum (1971) evolved a technique of "self-instruction." This

technique consists of (1) modeling the performance of a task with vocalized self-instructions; (2) the performance of the task by the subject
initially with self-instructions said aloud; then (3) performance of the
task with self-instructions whispered; and, finally, (4) the performance
of the task with self-instructions stated silently. The improvement of
performance by subjects utilizing self-instructional techniques in addition to modeling and behavior rehearsal was superior to the improvement observed in subjects utilizing modeling and behavior rehearsal
alone. This technique was first used successfully with impulsive children,
and later with schizophrenic patients, test-anxious subjects, and phobic
clients. Meichenbaum suggested that a variety of techniques of altering
behavior—that is, imitation, behavioral rehearsal, and systematic de-
densitization—may be more likely to generalize to other situations if
concomitant alternative affirmations are also conditioned.

Society and Behavior Change

Behavior technology is becoming more effective, and the research and
treatment literatures testify to a growing range of discrete behaviors that
now can be successfully modified. The most powerful agent of behavioral
change, however, is society itself. The fate of any new behaviors that
may be established in the laboratory or in a treatment situation ultimately depends on whether the contingencies in the environment at
large will support them. Bucher and Lovaas (1968) recognized that their
formerly self-destructive children would quickly return to self-destruc-
tiveness if they were returned to the environment that originally produced the behavior. It has also been long recognized that former prison
inmates and drug addicts are much more likely to return to their self-
destructive, antisocial habits if they return to association with their
former companions. On the other hand, Baer and Wolf (1970) demonstrated the power of the social environment to shape behavior in its
positive aspects. The two experimenters trained a withdrawn child in
basic social skills. Once the child's social-skill level enabled him to enter
his peer group, training was discontinued. From that point, the peer
group was able not only to maintain the child's basic social skills but
also to reinforce the development of more sophisticated social behaviors.
    The behavior technologist takes into consideration the effect of
society's contingencies on whatever novel behavior he wishes to install.
Certain behaviors are very likely to be supported. Withdrawn or socially uncomfortable individuals, for example, will probably be reinforced at a higher rate if they become more comfortable and learn to
hold social conversations. On the other hand, when a person learns to

be more assertive with his employer or his wife, the expected immediate response is punishment or criticism. The benefits of assertiveness may only become apparent after some delay. Therefore, new behaviors will have to be relatively resistant to extinction to make it possible for the delayed reinforcement to become effective.

Meichenbaum (1971) has suggested that the conditioning of alternative instructional sets in conjunction with other types of retraining may result in greater generalization. It is possible that conditioning of alternative verbal systems may also make newly acquired behavior more resistant to change. Behavior change in one family member necessitates change in other members; if novel behaviors can be sustained for a period of time, reciprocal reinforcing change in the behavior of wives, husbands, and children will be more likely.

If society at large reinforces incompatible verbal systems, however, even conditioned changes in an individual's verbal behavior are not likely to persist. Certain societal problems, such as alcoholism and violence, are at least partially the product of society's verbal behavior, which encourages and reinforces drinking and displays and models violent human interaction in the public media.

Some behavioral contingencies in society at large must change in order to lessen the extent of social dysfunction. Although changing societal contingencies may seem to be a very complex task, some group behaviors have been altered by relatively small changes in the environment. Disorderly classroom behavior has been easily controlled by Madsen et al. (1968) and Osborne (1970), and littering behavior in movie houses has been controlled through the use of positive reinforcement (Burgess, 1971).

The alteration of contingencies governing verbal behavior is constantly proceeding in the mass media via commercial advertisement. It may be possible to utilize this resource also to alter the verbal contingencies of our society for our long-term benefit. Much experimentation remains to be done, but behavioral technology may be ready to begin such experimentation in the near future.

Conclusion

Consideration of behavioral technology at all levels of society is critical. Behavior control has always been with us, but now, for the first time, we are aware of the variables that make it work. If we respond to behavioral control with our outdated verbal systems, we will regard it as a calamity, when actually it should provide us with great optimism. For the first time in the history of man, we have acquired conceptual and technological tools that make it possible for us to control ourselves and others to the mutual benefit of society.

In the epilogue to his book *Verbal Behavior*, Skinner states:

> I have been trying to get the reader to behave verbally as I behave. What teacher, writer or friend does not? And like all teachers, writers and friends, I shall cherish whatever I subsequently discover of any "influence" I may have had.

We also will cherish whatever we subsequently discover of any "influence" we may have had.

5

Operant Behaviorism:
Fad, Fact-ory, and Fantasy?

Karl H. Pribram

*Karl H. Pribram, an associate of the Center for the Study of
Democratic Institutions, is professor of psychiatry and psychology at
Stanford University Medical School. Technically a brain surgeon, he
has spent much of his professional career investigating brain
physiology from the standpoint of electrophysiology: how the brain
is "wired."*

*Recently, Pribram summed up the results of his own investigations,
as well as of the findings of others, in an extraordinarily
comprehensive treatise,* Languages of the Brain. *He is one of the very
few scientists to have subjected the general theories of behaviorism,
as well as the special theory of operant conditioning, to a rigorous
scientific analysis of how they comport with what is known about brain
functioning. In the following chapter, he summarizes the results of this
research, adding his own evaluation of the more general doctrines
contained in* Beyond Freedom and Dignity.

Fad?

In 1959, George Miller, Eugene Galanter, and I came to a conclusion
that surprised us. We were completing a book—*Plans and the Structure
of Behavior*—and, when we took a look at what we had done, we de-
clared ourselves (Miller et al., 1960, p. 211) to be *subjective* behaviorists:

As our debate progressed and our conception of Plans became clearer, a conviction grew on us that we were developing a point of view toward large parts of psychology. We then began to wonder how we might best characterize our position so as to contrast it with others more traditional and more familiar. The question puzzled us. We did not feel that we were behaviorists, at least not in the sense J. B. Watson defined the term, yet we were much more concerned—in that debate and in these pages, at least—with what people did than with what they knew. Our emphasis was upon processes lying immediately behind action, but not with action itself. On the other hand, we did not consider ourselves introspective psychologists, at least not in the sense Wilhelm Wundt defined the term, yet we were willing to pay attention to what people told us about their ideas and their Plans. How does one characterize a position that seems to be such a mixture of elements usually considered incompatible? Deep in the middle of this dilemma it suddenly occurred to us that we were subjective behaviorists. When we stopped laughing we began to wonder seriously if that was not exactly the position we had argued ourselves into. At least the name suggested the shocking inconsistency of our position.

In my case, this declaration followed a decade of work in operant conditioning—work that resulted both in the first demonstration that operant techniques were applicable to primates (Skinner, 1958) and in a spate of studies on the experimental analysis of behavior and modes of behavior modification disturbed by selective brain lesions.

Why then the shift? Simply that the concepts and techniques of operant conditioning were too restrictive to solve the problems that were under investigation. I signalled my departure (Pribram, 1962, pp. 119–120) as follows:

As a rule, the extreme behaviorist has become overly suspicious if the psychological concepts derived from behavioral observation too closely resemble those derived introspectively (the "mental"). The position accepted here is that behaviorally derived concepts *are* to be compared with those derived introspectively. Two extremes must be avoided, however. When the behaviorally derived concepts, because of a lack of empirical evidence, are indistinguishable from those derived from introspection, confusion results; when the two classes of concepts are so distinct that no relation between them is recognizable, the behaviorally derived concept is apt to be trivial.

Specifically, I had found that the procedure of frontal leukotomy (or lobotomy), so widely applied during the fifties, disrupted the sequential organization of behavior. Study of the effect of such lesions on behavior controlled by various schedules of reinforcement gave insufficient insight into the mechanisms of disruption; the advent of digital computers, not operant techniques, provided the key to the problem.

Psychology as a whole apparently went through a similar experience, as indicated by the following quotation from G. H. Bower (1970, p. 18):

> A modest revolution is afoot today within the field of human learning, and the rebels are marching under the banner of "cognitive organization." The clarion call to battle was sounded by Miller, Galanter and Pribram (1960) in their book, *Plans and the Structure of Behavior*. The immediate precursors to the ideas in this book were the work by Newell, Shaw and Simon (1958) on computer simulation of human thinking, and the work by Chomsky (1957) on syntactic structures in languages. Although there is little altogether new under this psychological sun, the newer organization man does have a different perspective and slant of attack on memory problems than do his S–R associationistic progenitors. The result has been a changing emphasis in what research gets done by the rebels and how they talk about it. The nature of this changed emphasis will be illustrated by reviewing my recent research on some very potent organization factors in human memory.

The result *has* been this swing toward "cognitive" psychology—cognition, knowing, became the first "subjective" topic to yield to the experimentalists' attack.

The lessons we learned in the late fifties are applicable today, despite the undeniable and well-deserved success that operant behaviorism is enjoying. This occasion thus provides me with a vehicle for undertaking an exciting journey in criticism on which I have long wanted to embark. My trip is made in two stages. One surveys the larger issues of psychological enquiry and the stance of operant behaviorism within those issues. The other addresses the specific relationship of operant behaviorism to physiology and to measurement. Let me begin the voyage with these specifics, in part to get them out of the way of the more interesting vista.

Fact-ory?

In view of the fact that my own investigative endeavor centers on brain–behavior studies, what I have to say about the relation between psychology and physiology may come as a surprise. In general, I *agree* with Skinner's main propositions: behavioral science can function (although at a limited level) independently of physiology; physiologizing *is* often deleterious to clear thinking; the neurological and behavioral languages describe universes of events that ought to be kept separate. My position, however, is that there is a considerable overlap of these universes and that, in order to do justice to the overlap, both neurological (physiological) and behavioral data are demanded. My prejudice is that one misses a good deal of the fun and richness of the field by ignoring the brain–behavior interface. For an operant behaviorist, perceptual constancy poses little in the way of a problem. For one concerned with the variations of the retinal image and the reconstructions that have to be made from them in order to perceive at all, there is a world of investigating to do—and operant techniques can help in the doing, as shown by Tom Bower's classic studies on infants (T. G. R. Bower, 1966). But, *chacun a son goût.*

The parochialism of the operant behaviorist is what is dismaying to encounter. Why, for instance, are references given, with few exceptions, exclusively from the operant literature? When neurological results, cognitive-psychological results, or the results obtained by other disciplines are discussed, they are almost never referenced. Is the work on the fixed-interval schedule really so overridingly precise, holy, and important that, when hypothalamic hyperphagia is at issue, the details of procedure, analysis, and interpretation need not be evidenced?

But so much for physiology. The operant behaviorists' views of the role of measurement are often confused: although they may have an excellent grasp of what measurement means in their own discipline, they seem not to understand what other disciplines are about when they measure. Certainly, measures of response rate are useful, but why not loosen the usual operant shackles sufficiently to allow measurement of choice and latency, in addition to measurement of the canonized rate? I have had an automated discrimination apparatus for discrete trial analysis (DADTA) working for more than ten years (Pribram et al., 1963; Pribram, 1969). It is a computer-controlled device that measures response choices, latencies, and—if so desired—rates. Each response is recorded at the time it is performed, and a summary is collated at the end of each run by the computer. If one wishes to perform statistical manipulations on the data, one can; if there are obvious conclusions to be drawn without the need for statistics (such as the development, or lack thereof, of position habits), one draws them and goes on. Further, latency is not to be discarded as completely useless, provided one has the wit to use it. Lindsley, for instance, has made this measure pay off in his studies of attention (Lindsley, 1961); and my colleagues and I have found latency an effective gauge of distraction (Douglas and Pribram, 1967). I grant the operant behaviorists their fad for interresponse times (I use such histograms in studying neural-unit activity) but ask, in return, that they occasionally look around the world of behavioral science and see what effective use is made of other response measures— yea, even, occasionally, of statistics and of models. For instance, response-operator-characteristic curves (ROC) have been extremely useful adjuncts in psychophysical studies and, more recently, in studies of verbal learning.

ROC analysis might prove equally fruitful when applied to physiological work, as investigators in my laboratory have done) Spevack and Pribram, in press), and to operant learning. Finally, whether one uses one or several subjects depends on how many variables one is juggling, not only on how good one's control over these variables is. If one is interested, as I am, in the relation between brain and behavior variables, one usually needs more subjects than one, just to be reasonably sure of the generality of the results. Mechanization and statistics are two types of technique by which control can be enhanced—they are neither inimical, exclusive of one another, nor infallible.

I want now to venture to the larger issue of psychological inquiry. Operant behaviorism plays two roles in psychological research, and these two roles so often become confused in the minds of the practitioners that the charge of cultism can fairly be levelled against them. Inasmuch as operant conditioning encompasses a set of techniques, operant conditioners serve as behavioral engineers. In this capacity, they have served well. There is still a tinge of restrictiveness here—but it is hardly noticeable when I consider an incident that occurred not so long ago when, during a meeting that was to lay the foundations for the *Journal of the Experimental Analysis of Behavior*, someone suggested that perhaps it might be fruitful for operant behaviorism and ethology to join forces: this suggestion elicited a stony silence, some polite chit-chat, and the break-up of the meeting for the time being.

Despite their current excellence as behavioral engineers, I foresee some dangers for operant behaviorists even in that role. Already the equipment they use so fluently is completely out-of-date. Unless they catch up with computer technology, with its flexibility enhanced by facile hierarchical programming, better and more varied input–output equipment, and the like, operant behaviorists are likely to become obsolete, good technicians of an outmoded technology. And by catching up I mean more than using a Linc-8 to analyze interresponse times. With the precipitous drops in the price of general-purpose computers, there is little excuse for failing to seize the opportunity to use fully these powerful and flexible instruments.

But operant behaviorism purports to be more than a technology. It is also addressed to a set of problems. Yet one must look long and hard before discovering just what that set of problems is; and when one does, the confusion is woefully compounded. One must continuously work one's way through a blinding array of often brilliant applications of a technology. Animal psychophysics is the stellar example where the application of this technology to human behavior has been used even in studying *subjective* (!) processes (see, for instance, Boakes and Halliday, 1970). But what is the core of interest, the conduct with which operant behaviorism is concerned?

The answer is, of course, the problem of reinforcement. The usual operant behaviorists' pride is the cleanliness of the operational definition of reinforcement in terms of its effect on preceding responses. But I must say that a high point of my journey in criticism came in reviewing an article on the Skinnerian analysis of behavior. The authors (Boakes and Halliday, 1970), openly and without shame, displayed their scrubbed and sterilized conception with the comment, "Learning is a process about which Skinnerians have said little"!

I pointed out to them that they here do a grave disservice to Skinner (as so many Freudians have done to Freud, and so on). Only a month earlier, I had heard a superb talk by Skinner (1968b) on the occasion of an IBRO meeting on the brain and human behavior sponsored by UNESCO. Skinner discussed his *theory* (his term). He stated that it is *not* an S–R theory. It is, in fact, an R theory and, therefore, much more defensible—inasmuch as stimulus and response mutually imply each other, unless one is talking exclusively about correlations among "distal" (that is, environmental) events operated upon by the organism. [See Estes (1959) for a detailed discussion of this issue.] He also portrayed his *model* (his term) of reinforcement: he described this as an attempt to so *arrange the contingencies of environmental events that reinforcement can and will occur*. Note that, by this approach, reinforcement becomes a process internal to the organism, a process that can legitimately be studied by neurological methods.

I was, of course, delighted to hear this, because my own interest lies in the neurological process produced by behavioral reinforcement. I have elsewhere tried to make the proposal that behavioral reinforcement is an organizing process that takes place when sequences (that is, temporal patterns) of behavioral outcomes fit into the neurological context (memory) created by prior such sequences. This view of reinforcement as consequence is dismissed by many operant conditioners—but just why it is has never become clear to me. Perhaps it is the reference to a central organizing process that is so distasteful to them. But now they must deal with Skinner himself on this issue, so I wonder whether he or they would object to my treatment of the problem when I suggest that, neurologically, reinforcement may well proceed by a brain mechanism not unlike the one that produces embryological differentiation, the mechanism of induction (Pribram, 1971).

The point is that neuropsychology (by contrast to what some operant conditioners say about operant behaviorism) has a great deal to say about the mechanisms of learning—both in data and in fascinating possibilities that need exploring. Yet, neuropsychology—or physiological psychology in general—would hardly be able to make its contributions if it paid no heed to those contributions, both technical and intellectual, that operant behaviorism has to offer. Perhaps operant behaviorism would have more to say about psychological problems—which are, of course, of a piece, and do not care for our arbitrary distinctions—were its practitioners to attend wholeheartedly to the explorations of their nonoperant colleagues.

The experimental analysis of behavior within the framework of operant behaviorism has a great deal to offer to students immersed in psychological inquiry. As of the moment, with few exceptions (for example, the work of Premack, 1965), the contributions are coming from those who only *use* operant behaviorism and stand solidly outside it. This is, to my mind, due largely to the abysmal provincialism and cultivated bigotry of so many who remain within the operant confines. I do *not* advocate any abandonment of operant behaviorism as a scientific enterprise in its own right. Rather, I want to see it strengthen its core by admitting the contributions that other disciplines within psychology are making and by usefully incorporating and improving them whenever they are relevant. The problem to which operant behaviorism is addressed is reinforcement. Reinforcement (by whatever name it is called: outcome, consequence, law of effect, feedback, stamping in, and so forth) is a central problem in psychology. Thus, the demand for a sophisticated operant behaviorism pervades psychology. But the converse also holds, or should hold: psychology must pervade operant behaviorism, if either is to remain viable.

Fantasy?

I had hoped that such revisions would come following Skinner's UNESCO presentation, which I mentioned above. Therefore, I followed closely the operant literature and Skinner's own productions. With the publication of *Beyond Freedom and Dignity*, this renewed interest came to a head, and I felt again moved to take up my pen.

My first reaction was anger. There is much good in the book, but I felt that its mistaken polemics would achieve just the opposite of what was intended. A second reading confirmed my initial impression, but it left me sad rather than angry.

Beyond Freedom and Dignity has two messages interwoven. The first is that a behavioral technology has been developed that can go a long way toward curing the ills that beset men. The second concerns the mind–body issue and centers on the conception of man's autonomy.

Skinner makes a good case for this behavioral technology. For those not acquainted with his achievements, the book could be enlightening. Skinner has applied to the social good his insights into the control of behavioral operants—"Behavior which operates upon the environment to produce consequences . . ." [p. 18][1]—obtained in the laboratory. He has been effective in sparking "behavior therapy" for obsessional and compulsive disorders that are resistant to other therapies. He has been instrumental in providing "programmed texts" to the educational community. Both have been achieved by making immediately clear to the behaving individual what the outcome of his behavior entails. Behavior has consequences. These consequences are shaped by the environment in which they occur. Proper arrangements of these contingencies produce the desired "reinforcement." The task for the behaviorist is clearcut: arrange the environmental contingencies of reinforcement and so control behavior. All else is irrelevant.

Much as I admire Skinner's contributions to our knowledge of the environmental contingencies that lead to reinforcement, I was again disappointed by his limited view of the problem. After all, other forms of behavior modification exist. As I pointed out to him almost twenty years ago, our legal system is a reasonably good deterrent of unwanted behavior. What was needed, and what his techniques could provide, were better methods for rewarding *wanted* behavior. Our educational and psychotherapeutic communities, which are dedicated to this task, have developed remarkably during this period. Changes in grading systems, computer-assisted instruction, transactional and Gestalt therapies, and encounter groups are only some of the social inventions that have occurred since midcentury—inventions that speak to Skinner's goal of a better behavioral technology for man. It might even be added that behavior therapy is merely a modification of Reich's discovery that psychoanalysis must proceed by "analyzing" away defenses—the most superficial defenses first, the deeper ones when they become accessible. Verbal "analysis" has been bolstered by more generally effective techniques of behavior modification—a major contribution, but not necessarily the innovation that its practitioners claim. A careful scientific analysis of the occasions for effective use of all these new tools would serve us better than the one-sided claim.

Much of the power of *Beyond Freedom and Dignity* comes not from Skinner's behavioral contributions, however, but from his clearcut stance on the mind–body issue. Skinner is against freedom and against dignity and against feelings and against values. He is against anything that smacks of mind, because mind is soft and ghostly and gets in the way of clear thinking about the control of behavior. In short, philosophically speaking, Skinner is a straightforward, naive realist—no ifs, ands, or buts. We are to go beyond dualism by becoming realists. But, of course,

[1]Throughout this paper, page numbers in square brackets refer to pages in Skinner's *Beyond Freedom and Dignity* (Alfred A. Knopf, 1971).

the Cartesian trap has been sprung: Skinner can only sell his views by referring continuously (almost to the point of boredom) to the mental—to feelings, freedom, dignity, values. In his very denial, he acknowledges the dualist problem. But in his naivete, there is simplicity and strength, and this can beguile the unwary.

I myself have gradually, through my research on brain and behavior, come to a realist position (Pribram, 1970, 1971). My realism is constructional and biological (rather than physicalistic) and suggests that mental language, brain language, cultural language, and behavioral language are multiple embodiments of basic biobehavioral structures, much as biologically related persons are embodiments of the same DNA potentialities. (This view differs from a multiple-*aspect* monism—that of Feigl, for example—but is, in part, derived from it.) So it is not Skinner's realism to which I object but his deliberate cop-out in favor of the easier "naive" position—especially when he makes what is then unfair use of mentalism, in his book and chapter titles, to promote his viewpoint:

> The dimensions of the world of mind and the transition from one world to another do raise embarrassing problems, *but it is usually possible to ignore them, and this may be good strategy,* for the important objection to mentalism is of a very different sort. *The world of the mind steals the show* . . . [p. 12, italics added].

According to William James (1931), G. K. Chesterton once remarked that

> for a landlady considering a lodger it is important to know his income, but still more important to know his philosophy. We think that for a general about to fight any enemy it is important to know the enemy's numbers, but still more important to know the enemy's philosophy. We think the question is not whether the theory of the cosmos affects matters, but whether in the long run anything else affects them.

James, Skinner's forebear at Harvard, states simply: "I agree with Mr. Chesterton on this matter."

I want, therefore, to try your patience by showing, in the following examples, that Skinner's retreat to naivete is, in fact, wrong and, therefore, harmful:

1) Skinner claims that physics and biology no longer concern themselves with "indwelling agents . . . references to purpose are still to be found in both physics and biology, but good practice has no place for them" [p. 8]. Can you imagine what planning the moon landing would have been like if we carried out Skinner's "good practice" and never

referred to gravity? Was it really sinister, as Skinner would have us feel, to describe the weightlessness of men on the moon relative to the fact that the "pull" that the moon exerts is weaker than that exerted by the earth? And where has Skinner been during development of cybernetics, which has given rise to the second industrial revolution? The very word *control*, of which he is so fond, has been scientifically shown to be related to "purpose," to teleology. Computers *are* machines that can show purpose, in a very technical sense. It is this revolution in *scientific* thinking that, twelve years ago, led George Miller, Eugene Galanter, and me (1960), into reevaluating what behavioral science is all about. And, of course, biology, in its adherence to evolutionary conceptions, is "purposive," and has been since Darwin. It is pre-Darwinian biology that simply classified (the biology of Linnaeus, for example). It is the science of genetics that has, since Mendel, developed teleonomics (Waddington's *very* scientific conception) as an explanatory tool with which we have revamped agricultural practice. I, too, was taught by Ralph Gerard in my elementary biology course *not* to think teleologi-cally—but both Gerard and I have abandoned old views when they were superseded. Skinner accuses Koestler [pp. 165–166], and rightly so, of being "approximately seventy years out of date" in misrepresenting behaviorism. Skinner is equally out of date in misrepresenting the physi-cal (especially the information-processing) and biological sciences. Per-haps that is why Skinner and Koestler found responsive chords in each other—we are privileged to watch and enjoy an encounter between such antediluvian titans.

2) Skinner tries to make point after point against mentalism. Let us look in on him for a moment:

> A third example, a "cognitive" activity, is *attention*. A person responds only to a small part of the stimuli impinging upon him. The traditional view is that he himself determines which stimuli are to be effective by "paying attention" to them. Some kind of inner gatekeeper is said to allow some stimuli to enter and to keep all others out. A sudden or strong stimulus may break through and "attract" attention, but the person himself seems otherwise to be in control. An analysis of the environmental circumstances reverses the relation. The kinds of stimuli which break through by "attract-ing attention" do so because they have been associated in the evolutionary history of the species or the personal history of the individual with impor-tant—e.g., dangerous—things. Less forceful stimuli attract attention only to the extent that they have figured in contingencies of reinforcement. We can arrange contingencies which ensure that an organism—even such a "simple" organism as a pigeon—will attend to one object and not to another, or to one property of an object such as its color, and not to another,

such as its shape. The inner gatekeeper is replaced by the contingencies to which the organism has been exposed and which select the stimuli to which it reacts [pp. 186–187].

But on another occasion, Skinner (1969, p. 283) remarked:

In a more advanced account of a behaving organism "historical" variables will be replaced by "causal." When we can observe the momentary state of an organism . . . [and] when we can generate or change a state directly, we shall be able to use it to control behavior.

In a recently completed series of experiments, my colleagues and I did what Skinner proposes. And we did find a brain system that appears to perform the function of a "causal inner gatekeeper." The experiment showed that the brainwaves of a monkey reinforced for responding to the *color* of a multidimensional pair of cues are different from those recorded when *pattern* is responded to. Further, these differences in brainwaves occur some 50 milliseconds before any overt behavior is manifested. So we describe our findings in terms of selective attention. What is wrong with this? In the opening paragraph of an article on energy and information, Tribus and McIrvine (1971) stated: "Science does not hesitate to give precise definitions to everyday words such as 'work,' 'power,' and 'information,' and in the process to transform proverbial truths into scientific truths."

3) I am interested in what goes on inside the organism, but that does not preclude my interest in how what is inside got there. Why cannot Skinner be equally tolerant? He insists that "the feral child has no language, not because his isolation has interfered with some growth process, but because he has not been exposed to a verbal community" [p. 141; see also the relevant footnote].

We now know (see Pribram, 1971, chapter 2) that brain growth is dependent on appropriate stimulation. Skinner should have left out some negatives: the feral child has no language because his isolation has interfered with the growth of his brain, which depends on his being exposed to a verbal community—much as a child fails to read when, during the first two years of life, he suffers, due to a congenital cataract or severe squint, from a lack of patterned visual input, which has been shown to be necessary to the development of the human visual system.

In summary, proper concern for what goes on inside the human organism—especially the brain—leads to conclusions opposite to those drawn by Skinner in *Beyond Freedom and Dignity*. The brain, in fact, is modified by experience; without such modifiability, the brain would be incompetent to process the environmental consequences of behavior. The brain, in fact, is sensitive to chemical influences that determine dispositions to behave, and these dispositions affect the environment just as environment affects dispositions (Bandura, 1971; Sidman, 1966). Designs of cultures, therefore, cannot, in and of themselves, completely specify behavior. Inherited individual differences in reactivity will assert themselves, unless the cultural design is so impoverished as to allow no alternatives. And, to do him justice, this is not what Skinner advocates. Complexity in design begets options in behavior, and with them comes the possibility—in fact, the necessity—of choice and autonomy. The very feelings of freedom (and, I might add, the feeling of responsibility that freedom entails) that Skinner wants to deny are part and parcel of the consequences of a sophisticated behavioral technology, as is evidenced by the title of his book and its chapter headings.

For Skinner has got it all backward. What behavioral *science* is all about is to use observation of behavior to explain and understand such feelings as freedom and love; such perceptions as green and red and circle and square, and memories of such things as faces and phrases. Whether feelings and images and thoughts are causal in the behavioral chain is a deep question that I am not yet prepared to answer—but certainly, once such feelings and percepts and thoughts are communicated, they can become causal in the social scene. That, however, is not really the point. Science is knowledge; engineering is the application of that knowledge to human purpose. Skinner's interest is that of the engineer, and we are much in need of good engineering in our culture. But it is one thing to advocate good engineering and another to try to make it encompass all of science and human enterprise. The journey ends. I am sad.

6

Great Expectations

Arnold Toynbee

Arnold Toynbee is a distinguished British historian whose major work,
A Study of History, *has attracted a wide readership in this and many
other countries.*

*With this chapter, we leave the expository material on operant
conditioning and move to more philosophical and speculative
treatments of the general implications of contemporary behaviorism,
with particular reference to the leading themes of* Beyond Freedom
and Dignity. *Toynbee's is a dispassionate review of Skinner's thesis.
He concludes, "I part company with the behaviorists over their belief
that behavior is determined wholly and exclusively by heredity and
environment." In working toward this conclusion, he details aspects of
behaviorism with which he agrees and others that he takes exception to.
As an example of the latter, Toynbee writes, "I do not think that
either heredity or environment, or these two forces together, fully
account for the behavior of Hosea, Zarathustra, Jeremiah, the Buddha,
Socrates, Jesus, Muhammad, and Saint Francis of Assisi."*

Manifestly, we ought to give the most serious consideration to a doctrine
whose exponents see in it a means of saving mankind from imminent
catastrophe and a means of guarding ourselves against being treated by
each other with cruel injustice. These are large claims; they hold out

great expectations; and they deserve to be examined impartially, insofar as impartiality is attainable by human minds when they are engaged on thinking about human affairs.

A great deal of the behaviorists' thesis is, today, undisputed common ground between them and other students of human affairs who are not convinced by the behaviorist doctrine in its entirety. Few serious observers and thinkers now deny that our genetic endowment and our social setting determine our behavior to a greater extent than we find it agreeable to admit.

It is now believed that a human being's set of genes contains genetic information that is as old as life itself on this planet. A gene that may determine decisively a human being's capacity and govern his behavior may be derived from some palaeolithic human ancestor or, perhaps, even from a prehuman forebear. It is also true that, now that biologists are discovering so much more about the nature, structure, and transmission of genes, they are beginning to contemplate the possibility that some day—perhaps before very long—they may become able to bring the selection and transmission of genes under human control. It would then be within human power to decide what each new human being's genetic endowment is to be. This suggestion sounds, already, far less fantastic than it did when it was propounded as a *jeu d'esprit* by Aldous Huxley in *Brave New World*.

However, the control and manipulation of genes is still only an uncertain possibility, and Skinner, therefore, does not give more than a passing consideration to it in this book. The book is concerned mainly with the control and manipulation of the social setting, and this is reasonable; for it is an indisputable fact that we are social animals, and it is probable that our ancestors were already social animals long before they had evolved into human beings. Perhaps all social animals— for example, wolves, beavers, and termites, as well as human beings— are governed to some extent by their social setting as well as by their genetic heritage. But it is recognized that the relative effect of the social setting on behavior is so much greater in humans than it is in any other social species of living creature that this amounts to one of the distinctive characteristics of man. The effect on a human being of his social setting begins at birth and continues throughout life. It is what we call "education," in the broadest usage of the word. It is disputable whether education accounts for everything in human behavior that is not accounted for by our genetic heritage; but it is acknowledged by everyone that the effect on us of education—at least in the broad meaning of the word —is enormous.

Human beings are conscious social animals. Consciousness is not the same thing as freedom, but we may make the mistake of identifying these two different things with each other. Our awareness of how we are behaving may lead us to believe that we are determining our own behavior. This may or may not be at least partly true, but even its partial truth must not be taken for granted. This needs to be proved—or at least we are under the onus of demonstrating that self-determination is an indispensable explanation of some facts about human behavior for which no alternative explanation can be found.

The fallacy of equating consciousness with freedom is exposed tellingly by Voltaire in a passage that Skinner quotes. "When I can do what I want to do, there is my liberty for me; but I can't help wanting what I do want." Voltaire's point is that our consciousness of our desires does not reveal their source. Since Voltaire's time, the psychologists have tracked down much of our volition from the conscious surface of the psyche to its subconscious depths, but they have not demonstrated that our behavior originates there, either. Is part of it caused by an inherited "collective subconscious"? Is another part of it caused by the pressure of a human being's social setting during his lifetime? Without attempting to give positive answers to these questions, we can agree that a large part of our behavior does not originate in, and is not determined by, ourselves, and that the thesis that our behavior is determined entirely by ourselves is confuted by incontestable facts.

No one would disagree with Skinner if he had limited his counterthesis to asserting that a human being is only partially free. We might perhaps all go so far as to agree that a major part of a human being's conduct is not self-determined. The disputable point in Skinner's thesis is his denial that the human being himself may be even a partial, if only a minor, determinant of his own behavior.

Skinner makes effective play with the "pathetic fallacy." Human beings are conscious that they have impulses, desires, motives, and plans. Our prescientific ancestors explained the behavior of nonhuman living beings and of inanimate objects and phenomena by attributing to these the psychic behavior of which we are conscious in ourselves. The implication was that both human beings and other constituents of the universe are self-determining. We have now come to recognize that the behavior of inanimate objects and phenomena—and of nonhuman living beings, too, to a large extent—is determined by forces that have not originated in these entities. In other words, the causes of their behavior are impersonal. Skinner adroitly turns the tables on human nature. Now that the "pathetic fallacy" has been recognized to be untenable in respect of nonhuman nature, must we not conclude that it is also untenable in respect of human nature? The supposedly humanlike power of self-determination must, Skinner suggests, be illusory when attributed to human beings, now that we have conceded that it is illusory when attributed to the rest of nature. This point of Skinner's is as telling as his citation of Voltaire's dictum.

Skinner points out that much of the imagery of human language, and perhaps most of its vocabulary and syntax, has been shaped by the assumption that, in a human being, freedom to will, and to plan for the achievement of what he wills, is a reality, not the illusion that Skinner believes it to be. Skinner, therefore, holds that, in order to give a meaningful explanation of human behavior, we must translate the traditional prescientific way of describing it that is still prevalent into forms of words that avoid attributing freedom to human behavior. Given Skinner's own assumptions, this procedure of translation is reasonable and is, indeed, necessary. Yet I am made uneasy by Skinner's behaviorist scientific language, as I am by the Christian Scientists' comparable language. Both the Christian Scientists and the behaviorists are driven, so it seems to me, into linguistic contortions by their theses of nonreality (of freedom, for the behaviorists, and of disease, for the Christian Scientists). These contortions that are required in order to avoid making the admissions that are made in traditional language lead me to suspect that the traditional language may, after all, come nearer to expressing the truth than the artificial language that, so it is claimed, is required for stating the truth scientifically.

I know of a case in which a Christian Scientist—confined to his bed by what would be called, in non–Christian Scientist parlance, a feverish cold—sent a message to a committee, in which he was due to take the chair, that he "preferred to stay in bed." The discourteous words dictated to him by his creed seemed to his non–Christian Scientist colleagues to be further from the truth than the words that they would have used had they been laid up; but, knowing that their colleague was a Christian Scientist, they did not take offense at the apparently discourteous message; they realized that he was inhibited by his beliefs from explaining his nonattendance at their committee in any other language.

Some of Skinner's language gives me just this uneasy feeling of unreality.[1] For instance, he writes, in more than one passage, that a

---

[1] It is unfortunate that, in *Beyond Freedom and Dignity*, Skinner has not given explanations, in everyday language, of his technical terms. I take it that the book is intended to be read by nonbehaviorists. Yet the meaning of the technical terms is taken for granted without being explained, as if this were an esoteric work addressed solely to readers who are already well-instructed behaviorists. In the language that Skinner uses in order to avoid attributing any power of initiative or freedom of choice to human beings, the words "contingencies," "reinforcers," and "reinforcement" are evidently key terms. They are also apparently being used in a technical sense, and the uninitiated reader has to guess at their technical meaning, at the risk, if he guesses wrong, of failing to do justice to Skinner's argument. I guess that, in this book, "contingencies" means "sets of circumstances in a human being's social environment that, in the author's view, determine a human being's behavior." I also guess that "reinforcers" is a substitute for "rewards" or "incentives"—words that a behaviorist is inhibited from using because they imply that a person's reaction to his environment is at least partly spontaneous. I hope these guesses of mine are not too wide of the mark.

culture "induces" a human being to make efforts to change this culture. In this formula, Skinner has surely been driven into the "pathetic fallacy" by the exigencies of his thesis. Skinner points out that a culture is not the aggregate of human bodies that is delineated in the famous frontispiece to Hobbes's *Leviathan*. Skinner holds, surely correctly, that a culture is not a crowd of human beings, but is a network of relations between human beings. Now we all agree that a network of relations cannot "induce" anyone to do anything; so how can a behaviorist, of all people, write that a culture "induces"? If it is a fallacy to say that a human being "induces," then, *a fortiori*, it must be a fallacy to say that a network of relations between human beings "induces." Yet, in avoiding the attribution of "inducement" to human beings, Skinner has been driven into attributing "inducement" to a network of relations between people.

It seems to me that, in translating from traditional language into behaviorist language, Skinner has here failed to avoid using a form of words that is inadmissible according to his own behaviorist thesis. This makes me doubt the validity of the thesis—not as a partial explanation of human behavior, but as a complete explanation of it, to the exclusion of all others.

If a human being's genetic endowment and his social setting, between them, determine the whole of his behavior, how is it possible for a human being to have a policy? Yet Skinner does attribute policies to human beings. "When an individual engages in intentional design of a cultural practice, we must turn to the culture which induces him to do so and supplies the art or science he uses" [p. 210].[2] "He is indeed controlled by his environment, but we must remember that it is an environment largely of his own making. The evolution of a culture is a gigantic exercise in self-control" [p. 215]. "What we need is a technology of human behavior" [p. 5]. "To refuse to control is to leave control not to the person himself, but to other parts of the social and non-social environments" [p. 5]. These passages in the book assume that some, at any rate, among the participants in a human society design cultural practices, create cultural environments, control the behavior of other human beings, and do these things by operating a technology of human behavior. These assumptions are surely incompatible with Skinner's fundamental thesis, which is that freedom is a delusion; that human beings have no power of taking the initiative; that their behavior is determined wholly by their genetic endowment and by their social setting; and that whatever part of their behavior is not caused by one of these two forces is caused by the other.

---

[2]Throughout this paper, page numbers in square brackets refer to pages in Skinner's *Beyond Freedom and Dignity* (Alfred A. Knopf, 1971).

We can all agree with Skinner that these two forces, between them, do determine human behavior to some extent—indeed, to a large extent —but this does not commit us to agreeing with him that these are the exclusive determinants of human behavior. Skinner does not present us with any demonstration that these two account for the whole of human behavior, and it is improbable that they do. Taken by themselves, they leave human behavior partially unexplained. In order to explain parts of it, Skinner himself has been constrained, in the passages quoted above and in others of the same tenor, to attribute part of a human being's behavior to the person's own initiative. It is quite credible that a person's behavior, besides being partly determined by his genetic endowment and by his social setting, is also partly determined by the person himself.

Self-determination or self-control [the term used by Skinner in the passage quoted, on p. 117, from p. 215 of his book] is another name for life. Every living being is a part of the universe that has tried to separate itself from the rest of the universe in order to erect itself into a counteruniverse. The individual member of any species of living beings is striving to keep itself alive by exploiting the rest of the universe for this purpose. The species that the individual represents is striving to perpetuate itself by reproducing individuals on an unchanging pattern.

Of course, this self-determination is never more than partial and temporary, in any case. The species changes, in spite of its attempt to remain true to type. It has originally evolved out of some other species, and it will eventually evolve into another; or, alternatively, its line will become extinct. Any individual member of a species is still more ephemeral than the species itself. The individual is procreated and it is foredoomed to die. Life on this planet is, of course, younger than the planet. The planet may survive for aeons after it has once again become uninhabitable for any form of life. Moreover, the earth is a very recent body; it is younger than its own sun, and it is vastly younger than the whole of the cosmos, in which the earth is a physically insignificant speck of dust. The self-determination possessed and exercised by living beings on the earth is thus manifestly imperfect or even minimal, but it is not, on this account, necessarily illusory or unreal. On the evidence at our disposal, self-determination has as good a claim as heredity or as environment to be reckoned as one of the causes of human behavior.

An account of human behavior that explains it solely by heredity and environment, to the exclusion of self-determination and any other possible cause, might be plausible were we to cut short our retrospect of human history at a date, say, about 2700 years short of the year 1972 A.D. These last 2700 years are a minute fraction of the total span of human history, and, in surveying the millions of years before the eighth century

B.C., we could explain most things in that major period of human history as being products of the environment, with the nonhuman part of the environment preponderant at the start and the social and technological environment gradually gaining in importance.

The history of the environment's determination of man's behavior is reflected in the history of religion. Religion may be defined as man's attempt to keep in touch with, and to live in harmony with, some presence, or presences, in the universe that are more important than man himself. So long as man was at the mercy of his nonhuman environment, he conceived of these presences, and worshipped them, in the form of nonhuman natural phenomena. After man had at last begun to get the upper hand over nonhuman nature through the development of his social organization and his technology, he went over to the worship of his own collective human power. Athena, who had been orginally the deification of the olive tree, was subsequently conscripted to serve as the deification of the power of the state of Athens, while Poseidon, the deification of seas and earthquakes, came to serve as the deification of the state of Corinth.

The worship of human power is, no doubt, the real religion of most of mankind still today, but the nominal religions to which most of mankind now pays lip service tell another story. In the course of some twelve centuries, beginning with the age of the prophets of Israel and Judah and ending in the generation of the Prophet Muhammad, a number of "great souls" (mahatmas) proclaimed that a society's established beliefs and practices do not have an absolute claim on the allegiance of the participants in that society. They appealed to some spiritual presence or spiritual objective that has a paramount claim on a human being's loyalty. All these "great souls" broke, in some degree, with the society in which they had been born and brought up. Some of them were consequently persecuted and even put to death. They suffered as martyrs— that is, as witnesses to their conviction that they were following a spiritual call that took precedence over their society's claims and demands upon them.

I do not think that either heredity or environment, or these two forces together, fully account for the behavior of Hosea, Zarathustra, Jeremiah, the Buddha, Socrates, Jesus, Muhammad, and Saint Francis of Assisi. I believe that these "great souls" did have the freedom to take spiritual action that has no traceable source. I also believe that there is a spark of this creative spiritual power in every human being.

These "great souls" have influenced the behavior of millions of human beings ever since they communicated their messages. They have influenced posterity, but they have not "conditioned" us, in the sense of depriving us of the possibility of refraining from following their

directives. Man has learned the art of "conditioning" inanimate matter—
for example, the air in a room, or metal extracted from ore dug out of a
mine. But living creatures cannot be "conditioned" more than partially.
Try to "condition" a goat, mule, camel, or horse; you will find that
the exercise is counterproductive. They can be coaxed, but they will
resist being coerced. And there is a goatlike, camellike, mulelike vein
in human nature that makes "a technology of human behavior" or
"a science of social engineering" a forlorn hope. It is true that human
beings can be partially dehumanized by being subjected to military drill,
but the hypnotic effect of drill is precarious. In a soldier, human nature
is inhibited but not eradicated. Under provocation, it may reassert itself.

At the beginning of *Beyond Freedom and Dignity*, Skinner points out
that we are living today under the threat that mankind may liquidate
itself at short notice. When time is short, people look for short cuts,
and the application of a technology of human behavior would be a
providential short cut to the salvaging of mankind, if the methods of
technology, which have worked such wonders on inanimate nature,
could really be applied effectively to human nature, as Skinner holds
that they could be. As I see it, this belief of Skinner's is vitiated by an
inner contradiction. A technology of human behavior would be practicable only if it were true that behavior is wholly determined by heredity
and environment and if it were also true that techniques could be devised
for manipulating a human being's genetic endowment and his social
setting. But, if human freedom is truly an illusion, no human being
would be free to plan and carry out the requisite biological and social
"engineering." The blind cannot lead the blind, and a camel cannot lead
a string of camels. Experience has proved that a donkey is needed to
do that.

I therefore believe that the behaviorists' objective is unattainable.
Human behavior seems to me to be determined partially, but only
partially, by forces outside the human being himself. I part company
with the behaviorists over their belief that behavior is wholly and exclusively determined by heredity and environment.

7

Behaviorism's Enlightened Despotism

Chaim Perelman

Chaim Perelman, professor of philosophy at the Université de Bruxelles, is author of Justice *and* The New Rhetoric, *as well as of numerous earlier works.*

Continuing the philosophical evaluation of Beyond Freedom and Dignity, *Perelman finds Skinner's arguments unconvincing. He objects particularly to Skinner's thesis that man's environment, not man himself, is responsible for his actions. Perelman suggests that, in a Skinnerian utopia, responsibility would be held by those who could transform the environment to condition their fellow men, and finds the prospect of a "behavioral scientist's enlightened despotism" frightening.*

In *Beyond Freedom and Dignity*, Skinner presses his behaviorist views to their extreme consequences. His answers to the philosophical problems that his views raise are not philosophically convincing. In order to show this, I propose to analyze more closely some crucial points concerning his conception of value judgments.

Let us look at this text: "To make a value judgment by calling something good or bad is to classify it in terms of its reinforcing effects" [p. 105].[1] Or,

---

[1]Throughout this paper, page numbers in square brackets refer to pages in Skinner's *Beyond Freedom and Dignity* (Alfred A. Knopf, 1971).

When we say that a value judgment is a matter not of fact but of how someone feels about a fact, we are simply distinguishing between a thing and its
reinforcing effect. Things themselves are studied by physics and biology,
usually without reference to their value, but the reinforcing effects of
things are the province of behavioral science, which, to the extent that it is
concerned with operant reinforcement, is a science of values.

Things are good (positively reinforcing) or bad (negatively reinforcing)
presumably because of the contingencies of survival under which the species
evolved [p. 104].

Behavioral science is thus the science of efficacious values (operant
reinforcement), philosophy being reduced to the study of inefficacious
conditioning. Only by divesting philosophy of the fiction of man's
autonomy will we be able to build an efficient science of values, to pass
"from the inaccessible to the manipulable" [p. 201]. Thus, instead of
reasoning about freedom and dignity, about justice and fairness, we
should turn "to good husbandry in the use of reinforcers" [p. 125].

Consequently, if, in conformity with Skinner's ideas, we wish to know
whether he has written a good book, we must not ask whether his
argumentation is close and coherent, whether he is not making a confusion about the notion of value itself by reducing it to psychological
states, whether he is not himself introducing value judgments of a
nature other than that of those he has defined; rather we must ask who
has been reinforced by reading the book. The answer is clear: the
behavioral scientist—he who, relying on efficacy only, becomes the
great manipulator of mankind by neglecting "weak methods of control,"
which do not depend on individuals but on other conditions [p. 99].

The author will not be surprised if those of us who are not behaviorists are not convinced by the argumentation in his book, for he was
only presenting us "weak methods of control." If he wanted to be sure
of convincing us, he ought to have conditioned us so as to make us
feel the same sense of power that his book is supposed to give behaviorists [see the "wonderful possibilities" he mentions on p. 214].

Every military leader who has to fight an urban guerilla or a resistance
movement cannot avoid facing the problem of torture. Must he use the
most efficacious means, including torture, in order to get information?
The idea of human dignity may somehow keep him from using the most
cruel means, but why hesitate if they are indeed the most efficient means?
Why should a doctor be restrained by medical deontology and hesitate
to send men that are sane but opposed to the régime into lunatic asylums?
If he does hesitate, the men in power may well use some "bad reinforcers" on him, and he will think that he is fighting chimeras. The idea
of responsibility seems to be a metaphysical construction that has no
counterpart in reality, when everything is a matter of more or less

efficacious conditioning. According to Skinner, man is not responsible for his actions: "A scientific analysis shifts both the responsibility and the achievement to the environment" [p. 25]. It is difficult to grasp what this means, if not that—"the contingencies of action" being alone efficacious—a change of behavior can only be obtained by working not on the person but on the factors that condition his reactions. However, when it comes to "responsibility" and "achievement," the responsible agent will not be the environment, but those that have the power to transform it, while the behavioral scientist indicates in which direction it ought to be changed. In the behaviorist's outlook, the latter replaces the philosopher as auxiliary to the men in power. However, as a matter of fact, he will only be a tool for them. The ends of action will be determined not by him but by those having authority to manipulate him by all sorts of "reinforcements" in order to reward or to punish him. Indeed, the point is to know who will manipulate whom and to what end [p. 25].

We may wonder who will still bother about "good reasons" [p. 137]. The main thing is not to present what is true or right but what is expected to reinforce the sense of well-being of those whom one addresses. Skinner defines a better world as one "that would be liked by those who live in it because it has been designed with an eye to what is, or can be, most reinforcing" [p. 164].

But men yearn for immortality, and the ideas of an everlasting salvation or everlasting punishment in Hell have always seemed highly "reinforcing" for the bulk of mankind. So why not favor all efficacious myths, whether they be religious myths, the myth of the superiority of a race, or that of the dictature of the working class? Should we object to those myths because they are not in conformity with truth, as Skinner seems to suggest when he mentions an "explanatory fiction" [p. 201]? He has, no doubt, been badly conditioned himself, for the value of truth consists solely in the way in which it serves as a "positive reinforcement." If the myth is well-designed for our aims, the belief in it must be spread by conditioning men to accept it as true. The only criterion of a value being the way men "feel about it," they must be conditioned accordingly. If Skinner does not agree, it must be because he has been conditioned by a decadent society that rejects traditional values for the sake of an ideal of scientific truth. He should be taught his lesson by being sent to one of those camps where they use brainwashing techniques, such as Plato proposed in the *Laws* more than twenty-three centuries ago.

It may be that Skinner is right and that all ideas of liberty, dignity, truth, and justice are the result of centuries of conditioning with the aim of leading men away from the animal tradition that was originally theirs. But then traditional education has, before him, done no more than adopt those methods that appeared most efficient for the survival of mankind. Such methods may not be objected to in the name of truth but only on account of their inefficacy. Should we say that efficacy is the only consideration that matters when it comes to action? If so, why stop at behavioral techniques of reinforcement? Why not use still stronger manipulations, such as those presented by Aldous Huxley in *Brave New World*?

Actually, Skinner undertakes to show us that the methods he advocates could lead mankind towards "wonderful possibilities." Why not towards "frightening possibilities?" In the course of history, all types of conditioning have been used by the men in power in order to get their subjects to submit. Why should it be otherwise in this case?

Skinner is guilty of supposing erroneously that values express what men feel, not what they should feel when they are faced with certain situations. Values are normative. However, though we all agree that truth, justice, and happiness are values, we do not, by any means, agree about the way in which they are to be interpreted in particular situations. When disagreement crops up in this respect, are there reasons why Skinner should resist suppressing it by conditioning the opponents, by giving them drugs, or by submitting them to a lobotomy so as to render them less aggressive? We know plenty of means to get rid of our opponents, but the advancement of civilization consists in a desire to convince them by arguments instead of by some kind of conditioning; this has been the age-old ambition of philosophy. I do not think the methods he advocates can solve the fundamental problem concerning which methods to use when men disagree about what ends to aim at in real situations. Does he suggest that we replace the various political systems, monarchies, oligarchies, or democracies by the behavioral scientist's enlightened despotism?

8

Some Aversive Responses to a Would-be Reinforcer

Max Black

Max Black is Sage Professor of Philosophy and Humane Letters and a senior member of the Program on Science, Technology, and Society at Cornell University. Black is the author of Models and Metaphors, The Labyrinth of Language, *and* Margins of Precision. *He is a past president of the American Philosophical Association.*

Here is a philosopher's attack on Skinner's theories. Black finds Skinner incoherent and dismisses Beyond Freedom and Dignity *as a "melange of amateurish metaphysics, self-advertising 'technology,' and illiberal social policy [which] adds up to a document that is a disservice to scientists, technologists, and to all who are seriously trying to improve the human condition."*

The spectacle of a convinced determinist *urging* his readers to save the human race is bound to be somewhat comic. But Skinner is very much in earnest in his latest book, and no traces of the irony and self-deprecation that occasionally enlivened *Walden Two* are here allowed to mollify the urgency of a call to behavioristic salvation. For "we have the physical, biological and behavioral technologies 'to save ourselves'; the problem is *how to get people to use them*" [p. 158, emphasis added].[1]

---

[1]Throughout this paper, page numbers in square brackets refer to pages in Skinner's *Beyond Freedom and Dignity* (Alfred A. Knopf, 1971).

That a requisite "technology of behavior" [p. 5] is already at our disposal may be doubted. I shall discuss later whether Skinner can say, consistently with his own principles, that we should work to achieve such a technology.

Skinner's call to action, if that is what it is, is marred by endemic ambiguity, repeatedly manifested in his uses of the key terms of his vocabulary of exhortation. Thus, survival, according to him, demands "control" of the "environment"; but equivocation upon both of these terms makes it doubtful whether radical changes are in question.

Consider the following characteristic remarks: "A scientific analysis of behavior dispossesses autonomous man and turns the *control* he has been said to exert over to the environment" [p. 205, emphasis added]. (Here, it should be explained that "autonomous man" refers simply to the "myth" of men's responsibility for their actions. We notice that "control" is to be assigned, characteristically, to a supposedly impersonal environment.) "To refuse to *control* is to leave *control* not to the person himself, but to other parts of the social and non-social environment" [p. 84, emphasis added]. "When we seem to turn *control* over to a person himself, we simply shift from one mode of *control* to another" [p. 97, emphasis added]. "Attacking *controlling* practices is, of course, a form of *countercontrol*" [p. 181, emphasis added]. "Good government is as much a matter of the *control* of human behavior as bad, good incentive conditions as much as exploitation, good teaching as much as punitive drill" [p. 180, emphasis added]. And so on.

It seems, then, that "control" is ubiquitous in social relations, and any attempt to change oneself or others, whether by conditioning, persuasion, or argument, is sure to count as "control." In this loose and obfuscating usage, "control" means no more than "have some effect upon," and the admonition to facilitate human survival by "control of the environment" becomes vacuous and somewhat fatuous, inasmuch as it urges us to do anything we please, with the assurance that we shall thereby be controlling our environment. Of course, this is emphatically not Skinner's intention, as we shall see.

A similar shift from a natural and restricted sense to a vacuously inflated one will already have been noticed in connection with the term "environment." One might reasonably gloss it as "*physical* environment," because this is the sense that Skinner needs, but he repeatedly renders his call for human conditioning persuasive by stretching the word to cover *persons*. Thus, "setting an example" counts as changing the environment, and counts also, therefore, as controlling those influenced by the example [p. 92]. In this expansive sense, changing others and ourselves, by whatever means, will count as changing the "environment."

Because "control" and "environment" are used in these reckless ways, it is not surprising—although, to be sure, it is unintentionally amusing— to find Skinner speaking of the "control" exercised by a laboratory animal on his handler. "His apparatus exerts a conspicuous control on the pigeon, but we must not overlook *the control exerted by the pigeon.* The behavior of the pigeon has determined the design of the apparatus and the procedures in which it is used" [p. 169, emphasis added]. It reminds one of the old joke about one pigeon boasting to another of how it had conditioned Skinner to provide food whenever it pecked a button.

Skinner might seem to have anticipated such objections by admitting that "the text will often seem inconsistent" [p. 23]. But he misses the point when he goes on to say that "English, like all languages, is full of prescientific terms which usually suffice for purposes of casual discourse." His own preferred technical terms, being theory-laden only in a very weak sense, are scarcely more than common expressions in fancy dress (so that a "response," for instance, is nothing but a bit of behavior under a physical description), and he *needs* the ordinary senses of "control," "reinforcement," and the like for his message to sound plausible. As for his promise that "acceptable translations [of 'mentalistic expressions'] are not out of reach" [p. 24], we shall see later that that is merely a bluff.

The increased and more effective control advocated by Skinner is not merely the taking of whatever measures may improve society: he really intends the special and controversial modes of control known as "classical conditioning" and "operant conditioning," and especially the latter. He is able to equate whatever needs to be done with conditioning because he holds that *only* conditioning will be effective.

Operant conditioning consists, basically, of the application to animal subjects of carefully planned schedules of positive or negative "reinforcements," by which the subjects' favored responses are "shaped and maintained" [p. 169], or "strengthened," by being rendered more likely to occur. To such procedures, the term "control," in its dictionary sense of "exercise restraint or direction over," does apply without dilution or extension of meaning. A Skinnerian psychologist, engaged in conditioning a pigeon or a man, is quite literally shaping, restricting, directing— in short, controlling—his subject's responses.

We must remember that, on Skinnerian principles, what the subject thinks about the routines imposed upon him is causally irrelevant. (Sometimes, however, Skinner seems willing to admit the efficacy of the subject's "interpretation" of the situation, with the usual promissory gesture in the direction of an eventual translation in behavioristic terms.) Skinner regards serious reference to such allegedly "mentalistic" factors as motive, intention, and the like as being, at best, Aesopian and, strictly speaking, inadmissible in a truly scientific account. So, it is reprehensible in the end even to talk about "mental" features, and unwarranted to assign causal efficacy to any of them. The pigeon, we may presume, cannot reflect upon his conditioning, and if a man under conditioning knows what is being done to him, that makes no difference to the administered reinforcements.

Given the postulated irrelevance of the subject's awareness of his training, and hence also the irrelevance of his knowledge and consent, a better label for the procedure would be "*involuntary* control," or its more familiar variant, "manipulation." Skinner's true doctrine, barely veiled by his habitual equivocation, calls for the wholesale manipulation of human beings, willy-nilly, for their own good, or, rather, for the survival of the species.

Skinner will retort that men are controlled anyhow, whether by propaganda, the threat of force, education, indoctrination, or love. Well, all these things affect us, to be sure, but that hardly amounts to control, in the sense of manipulation. Common sense would hold that men are sometimes manipulated and sometimes not. The differences, turning as they do upon the knowledge and consent of those involved, are crucial. To ignore them is to leave "control" without any clear sense.

In its familiar and proper use, "control" implies a controller or controllers. Skinner's right to control pigeons is sanctioned by our society's tolerance for scientific research. But who is to choose the Grand Manipulators of all of us? And what is to be their authority to manipulate us without our knowledge? This question Skinner repeatedly dodges, by using his favorite device of speaking of control by the "environment," as if the envisaged display of "reinforcers" were not to be designed and employed by hidden managers. It is a safe, if somewhat pessimistic, rule of thumb that unintended consequences of technological innovations are likely to turn out badly. Skinner himself says that "what is needed is more 'intentional' control, not less, and this is an important engineering problem" [p. 177]. He might have added that it is also an important political and moral problem. For if a manipulator stands behind each "engineered" environment, his moral and political restraints are of keen interest to his "subjects."

Skinner has a short way with the question of control over the social controllers. He tells us that "such a technology [the extension of deliberate human conditioning] is ethically neutral" [p. 150]. Here lurks the old fallacy that the introduction of "technology," even when its human consequences can be reasonably foreseen, is, from the moral standpoint, neither good or bad. We need some assurance that wholesale conditioning will not have results as deplorable as the introduction of some stupefying drug. Skinner says that "the great problem is to arrange effective countercontrol and hence to bring some important consequences to bear on the behavior of the controller" [p. 171], but he seems to regard this as a mere technical hitch: he is conveniently vague about who is to exert the requisite "countercontrol" ("restraint," in plain English). For the rest, we get the ritual obeisance to democracy: "In a democracy the controller is found among the controlled, although he behaves in different ways in the two roles" [p. 172]. Indeed he does, as the case of Joe McCarthy may remind us. The promoter of the Great Lie is not deceived (or, if he is, so much the worse) and the controller of the Great Social Conditioning Experiment is likely to have enough sense to stay out of the Skinner box. In evaluating what are, properly understood, political proposals, we need specific descriptions of the envisaged political and social institutions and the restraints under which they will operate. Faced with Skinner's skeleton design, we can only be reasonably sure that manipulation will be more congenial to an authoritarian than to an imperfectly democratic form of society—if only because dictatorships, as we know, pride themselves upon "efficiency." Mussolini boasted of making the trains run on time; a Skinnerian dictator may be expected to have all of us running on time.

As for the allegedly "scientific" basis for these far-reaching recommendations, a lay observer can perhaps do no more than register an impression of implausibly sweeping generalizations from a narrow empirical base. Suppose Skinner and his associates to have been conspicuously successful in training pigeons and other experimental animals —does it reasonably follow that similar methods will be equally effective with human beings? The scope of conditioning may well be wider than common sense suspects, but that is something yet to be established— and, if necessary, guarded against.

Suspicions of unwarranted generalization are roused by finding Skinner using the technical term "reinforcer" (roughly speaking, any event that increases the likelihood of occurrence of some associated item of antecedent behavior) in ways unsanctioned by his own self-denying methodology. One finds him freely using "reinforcement" for social approval (or, strictly speaking, the noises and gestures by which such approval is expressed), money, friendship, the joy of achievement, love—indeed, anything that we should ordinarily regard as a reward. If "institutions may derive effective reinforcers from events which will occur only after a person's death" [p. 135] (a neat trick, from the standpoint of operant conditioning) we are certainly a long way from the pigeon in its controlled apparatus. Similar doubts arise when Skinner claims that "the accidental appearance of a reinforcer strengthens any behavior in progress and brings it under the control of current stimuli" [p. 176]. That what Skinner calls "superstition" is quite so universal in its incidence may well be doubted. And is there really enough evidence to show that "how people feel about facts is a by-product" [p. 113]? Does Skinner know this? Does he have reasonable grounds for believing it? I very much doubt it. The extent to which feelings (and intentions, motives, ideals, and so on) are, in fact, casually effective in particular situations is a question for detailed empirical investigation. Common sense tells us that feelings sometimes make a difference, sometimes not. (The anger felt by a father whose child has been killed by a reckless motorist may move him to commit murder.) Pending the presentation of relevant evidence to the contrary, uninstructed common sense may reasonably continue to tell us that what men feel and believe *does* often make a substantial difference, and is not a mere "by-product."

When scientists, professionally committed to cautious and well-hedged hypotheses, indulge in universal generalizations that denigrate entire categories of entities as fictions, one may well suspect some metaphysical bias. That Skinner has such a bias against "mentalism" is abundantly clear from his writings. Consider such a revealing remark as: "The world of the mind steals the show. Behavior is not recognized as a subject in its own right" [p. 12]. Can the original sin of "mentalism" be that it sets bounds to the inferences drawn from empirical associations between what have been called "colorless movements"? At any rate, extensive debates in the past between behaviorists and their philosophical opponents have made it very clear that science cannot, on the basis of the historical record of scientific achievement, be identified with the mere correlation of observables: the introduction of suitable theoretical terms, ultimately but only indirectly linked with observation, deserves to be regarded as of the essence of scientific method. Skinner's inveterate propensity to identify his favored methodology with "scientific analysis" is simply unacceptable. There is also, by now, an impressive body of testimony to the severe difficulties that must be overcome by anybody committed to behavioristic translations of the commonplaces of ordinary life, for which such terms as "intention," "goal," "attitude," and "feeling" still seem indispensable.

The last point is amusingly illustrated by Skinner's exercises in translating some "mentalistic" assertions. The assertion that "there is nothing he [a college student] wants to do or enjoys doing well, he has no sense of leading a purposeful life, no sense of accomplishment" is to be translated, according to Skinner, as "he is rarely reinforced for doing anything" [p. 147]. (The man in question might console himself by the reflection that reinforcement of some sort is always in progress, as we have seen.) "He feels guilty or ashamed" becomes "he has previously been punished for idleness or failure, which now evokes emotional responses" [p. 147]; and "he experiences an identity crisis" is paraphrased as "he does not recognize the person he once called 'I'" [p. 147]. One wonders what this unfortunate man (like the old woman in the nursery rhyme who complained "This is none of I") now calls the person he once called "I." Does he perhaps refer to himself as "He"— or even as "*K*"? Skinner disarmingly says that the "paraphrases are too brief to be precise" [p. 147]. Well, some of them don't even have the charm of brevity. There are weighty reasons for thinking that no such paraphrases, long or short, will be satisfactory, and that the vocabulary of ordinary life and literature has a genuine point.

Given Skinner's theoretical commitment to behaviorese—or at least to ordinary language that is to be ultimately translated into the new jargon—it is perhaps unsurprising to find him belittling what he pejoratively calls "the literature of freedom and dignity" (that is to say, any discourse that imputes responsibility and choice). It is, however, disconcerting to find him displaying such open and steady animus against what, under a more persuasive description, is merely the common language of ordinary life, literature, and history. (After all, the members of *Walden Two* were great readers.) How are we to explain such remarks as "[There is a] threat posed by the literature of freedom and dignity" [p. 177]? Perhaps the answer is to be found in the following remark:

> What we may call the literature of dignity is concerned with preserving due credit. It may oppose advances in technology, including a technology of behavior, because they destroy chances to be admired and a basic analysis because it offers an alternative explanation of behavior for which the individual himself has previously been given the credit [pp. 58–59].

So the prime mistake made by humanists is to attach blame and praise ("credit") to persons. We might say, on Skinnerian principles, that the fault is not in ourselves, dear Brutus, but in our reinforcers. That we are on the right track is shown by another remark: "A scientific analysis shifts the credit as well as the blame to the environment, and traditional practices can then no longer be justified" [p. 21]. Or, again: "It is in the nature of an experimental analysis of human behavior that it should strip away the functions previously assigned to autonomous man and transfer them one by one to the controlling environment" [p. 198]. Here is that ostensibly impersonal "environment" again, presented now as a bearer of praise and blame. Skinner might more consistently have placed praise and blame on the index. (I seem to recollect that nobody praises, blames, or even gives thanks in *Walden Two*.) Once the myth of personal responsibility has been rejected as superstitition, not even the controllers can count as responsible. For this is what is really at stake in Skinner's polemic against the humanistic standpoint. It is disingenuous, on his part, to depict the "literature of dignity and freedom" as a device for flattering its readers, for he knows as well as all of us how often the teachings of history and literature have been derogatory and pessimistic. The blunder of humanism, according to him, is to hold men to account for their deeds. It would be interesting to hear a good, or even a persuasive, argument that absolved Skinner from responsibility for the book under discussion.

Skinner claims that purging the "myth" of responsibility (my description, not his) will be a step forward.

> What is being abolished is autonomous man—the inner man, the homunculus, the possessing demon, the man defended by the literature of freedom and dignity. His abolition is long overdue. . . . Science does not de-humanize man, it de-homunculizes him, and it must do so if it is to prevent the abolition of the human species [p. 200].

Here, at least, is one place in which Skinner agrees that ideas (the myth of responsibility) make a difference. Would it be "a step forward" [p. 215] to be in a "behavioral environment" arranged by skillful hidden manipulators, in which the very language of responsible action had been expunged by effective conditioning? Would this be a sanitary removal of some obfuscating myth? We might justifiably regard the end product as a dehumanization, in which men were no longer accorded the dignity of being treated as persons. A world of well-controlled bodies emitting physical movements in response to secret reinforcements, might perhaps seem hardly worth preserving. It may, after all, be better to be dead than bred—like cattle.

Throughout these comments, I have been regarding Skinner as a reformer who offers admonitions having the form, "You (we) *should* do such and such." That he does wish to "control" us in this way seems plain enough. Given the inconsistency of his language, it is hard to determine whether he really wants us to do much or little. But let us suppose that he does wish his readers to approve of certain actions, and to work toward them—perhaps by instituting managers trained in Skinnerian conditioning techniques and licensed to condition all of us to the hilt. Call the advocated actions *A*. Then how, from the perspective of a radical behaviorism, are we to understand the admonition "You should do *A*"? For it is not, on the face of it, a statement of fact of the sort that Skinner admits.

Skinner provides us with the materials for an answer when he says that we might translate a "value judgment" of the form "You should (you ought to) tell the truth" into "If you are reinforced by the approval of your fellow men, you will be reinforced when you tell the truth" [p. 112]. Because the reference to truth-telling is only illustrative, we may take it that, in urging us to do *A*, Skinner would be content to have us understand him as saying "If you are reinforced by the approval of your fellow men, you will be reinforced when you do *A*." Taken as a conditional statement, this last statement may well be false. Even the parallel behavioristic surrogate for the injunction to tell the truth is false, if it refers to the reinforcement of *all* "fellow men," because lying is approved by thieves, schoolboys, advertisers, and politicians, among others. The commandment should presumably be relativized to run: "If you are reinforced by those who approve of truth-telling, you will be reinforced when you tell the truth."

To which one wants to reply, "Of course!" The translation proposed is saved from tautology only by the weak presupposition that the man addressed will, in fact, be in the presence of those who approve of truth-telling. Grant that, and the truth of the conditional follows at once. In that form, it can be cheerfully affirmed, by habitual truth-tellers and liars alike. Ananias (Acts 5:1–10) might readily have agreed that, *if* he was reinforced by the approval of the approvers of veractiy, he would try, like other liars, to appear as a truth-teller in the presence of veracity-approvers. But Ananias might have been *negatively* reinforced by the approval of veracity-approvers, preferring the approval of his wife Sapphira. Given the falsity of the antecedent in the doctored command, it then gets no grip upon him—which is perhaps why Peter needed to intervene with so drastic a negative reinforcement. In this example, Skinner seeks to reduce the motive force of the "should," in a way that is clearly unsuccessful, to a hypothetical prediction about the effects of other persons' approval.

We are entitled to make parallel responses to Skinner's own recommendations, on his own interpretation of what he is saying. "If you are reinforced by the approval of those who approve my recommendations, you will follow them." I think I am not deceiving myself in claiming not to be "reinforced" by Skinner's recommendations or by the approval of those who agree with him, but rather the reverse. So, I can agree with his hypothetical prediction—and do nothing at all.

It would be wrong to suppose that this argument *ad hominem* disproves the possibility of some more sophisticated behavioristic reduction of "should" statements. But the most plausible candidates for naturalistic interpretations of such statements invoke the concept of attitude, which is beyond Skinner's behavioristic ken. Enough has been shown, I think, to demonstrate the incoherence of Skinner's position.

Such incoherence can be found throughout the book. Skinner's arbitrary identification of science with the procedures of operant conditioning, his unsupported and dogmatic rejection of the notion of human responsibility and, hence, of human agency, his extravagant testimonials to a "behavioral technology," which is, I am confident, still no more than a future threat—all this *mélange* of amateurish metaphysics, self-advertising "technology," and illiberal social policy adds up to a document that is a disservice to scientists, technologists, and to all who are seriously trying to improve the human condition.

If the book has here received more attention than it deserves on its merits, the excuse may be that it has received wide circulation. In this, there is little cause for alarm: few of those who buy the book will read it, fewer still will understand, and even fewer will change their actions in consequence. If some who favor manipulation are "reinforced" by Skinner's approval, that need not disturb us much, either, because those who wish to manipulate and dominate can always find some "justification" or other when they think it politic, even while they decry the very notion of justification as an absurdity.

9

Can Any Behavior
Be Conditioned?

Robert Rosen

*Robert Rosen, a visiting fellow at the Center for the Study of
Democratic Institutions, is a theoretical biologist at Michigan State
University and author of* Optimality Principles in Biology *and*
Dynamical Systems Theory in Biology.

    *Rosen's chapter introduces a group of analyses by scholars whose
work is in systems analysis. They apply the assumptions and
procedures of their disciplines to evaluate operant conditioning and
behaviorism from the standpoint of producing a coherent model of
human behavior. Rosen examines the question of whether the behavior
of any system can be conditioned so that it will respond to stimulus in a
predictable way. He concludes that a technology "based on
conditioning alone is most unlikely to accomplish the good results that
Skinner expects of it; [and] that these results can only be accomplished
by an appropriate combination of . . . technologies."*

The thrust of Skinner's *Beyond Freedom and Dignity* is, as I understand
it, to offer an intelligent lay readership a glimpse of the kind of "behavioral technology" that, he argues, must be developed and implemented if the serious problems facing us as a society are to be solved.
Such a behavioral technology, like any other technology, must rest upon

an underlying science (in this case, "behavioral science") that specifies the scope and limitations of the technology. Skinner and his school have been attempting to develop a set of foundations for such a behavioral science over the past several decades.

Any behavioral science—and, more particularly, any behavioral technology—is bound to raise a host of important questions of social, political, philosophical, and scientific nature. This is particularly true of Skinner's work, for he clearly articulates a number of serious incompatibilities between the ideas he advocates and some of the prevailing and deeply held convictions of important elements of our society. Most of these, important as they are, will not be considered in this essay, but will be left to others more competent to deal with them in their full generality. Instead, I will concentrate on some of the purely scientific implications underlying Professor Skinner's approach to behavioral problems. In particular, I shall be concerned with analyzing the basic concept that underlies Professor Skinner's work: the concept of *behavior*.

The word "behavior," like so many other important words in the biological and social sciences, defies exact definition; it cannot be defined formally, but only ostensively. However, unlike most other important ostensively defined concepts, such as "living," "regulation," and "fitness," it is difficult to give examples of things that are *not* behavior in some sufficiently broad sense. As with the word "system" to which it is conceptually closely related (because, speaking roughly, behavior is what systems do), it is a word of exceptionally broad semantic field, and, as such, it is more than usually difficult to speak about it in useful scientific terms. Most of the analysis that follows is aimed at narrowing the kinds of system properties we want to call "behavior" down to the point where it is possible to say sound and meaningful things about them.

To do this, it is necessary to specify a definite set of processes, occurring in a well-defined class of systems (large enough to be of interest), and identify these processes with the *behaviors* of the systems in the class. In this way, "behavior" becomes a meaningful concept, *relative to that class* of systems, and its properties can be investigated in detail and with rigor. (It is, of course, always possible to argue that the word "behavior" should be applied to system processes other than those we have chosen, but this is a matter of detail; the strategy of approach remains the same.) Indeed, this is the strategy that was employed in the creation of a quantitative and powerful physical science out of its ostensively defined precursors, and is today being employed to do the same for biology.

It may be helpful to give a specific example of the way in which this kind of approach works, in an area close to that considered by Skinner. This example concerns our attempts to formalize and understand the basis of biological memory (where "memory" itself is, of course, another important ostensively defined concept). In its broadest terms, we may say that a system exhibits memory if its past experience can modify its future behavior. As such, we can identify the ostensively defined concept of "memory" concretely in many different classes of systems. For instance, any physical system that exhibits hysteresis can meaningfully be said to possess a memory; by making the identification of the ostensive term "memory" with the precisely defined term "hysteresis," we can inquire into the detailed mechanisms of memory within the class, and actually use the knowledge thus obtained to devise valuable technologies (most computer "memories" involve hysteresis in an essential way). Or, in the class of neural nets, we can consider any network with a regenerative loop as intuitively possessing a "memory," and identify the ostensive term "memory" with the properties of such loops. The mechanisms by which these two kinds of "memory" work are entirely different in the two classes (and in the many other similar classes that could be proposed), but, in each of them, the term has a precise meaning from which precise conclusions can be drawn; the problem of "biological memory," then, reduces to a technical question of showing that the biological systems of interest fall into one or another of the classes we have defined, in such a way that the biological behaviors we intuitively call "memory" can be identified with the corresponding precisely defined concept in the classs. Of course, a certain amount of care must be taken in such studies; we cannot, for example, learn about the *mechanisms* of hysteresis by studying loops in neural nets, and, indeed, much nonsense has been generated by extrapolations to other properties of classes of systems merely because a word such as "memory" can be attached to certain of their particular properties.

All this is important because it is tempting to generalize about ostensively defined terms—to say, for example, that "memory is an adaptive response," or that "memories inevitably decay." It is clear that assertions like these may sometimes be true and sometimes false—that is, there are classes of systems for which, under the identifications made between the ostensively defined terms of interest and the specific properties of the systems in the class, the assertion becomes true, and there are other classes of systems for which the assertion is false.

Returning now to the Skinnerian treatment of "behavior," and in particular to the generation of technologies for the control of behavior, we find a parallel situation to that just outlined for "memory." Indeed, the entire thrust of the proposed technologies of behavior arises from a generalization implicit in *Beyond Freedom and Dignity*—namely, that *any behavior can be conditioned*. (Actually, this generalization is rather stronger than necessary, as will be discussed below; however, it certainly implies anything that Skinner would want for his technologies, and, in any event, the same kinds of arguments as I shall employ would also be valid for any weaker assertion). It should now be clear, however, that a generalization of this kind must take the form of an existence argument within well-defined classes of systems, which may hold for some classes and fail for others. In the next two sections, we shall consider examples of both types; the final section will be devoted to the possible implications of this state of affairs for behavioral technologies in general, considered from a general system-theoretic perspective.

"Behaviors" That Cannot Be Conditioned

MODEL I

Let us begin by defining a family of elementary units. These units will be capable of receiving *inputs* ("stimuli") from the environment, and will be capable at any instant of time of producing one of two alternate *outputs* ("responses"), which will be called *on* and *off*. Such a unit might be diagrammed as follows:

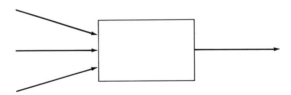

The input lines themselves may be of two types, either *excitatory* or *inhibitory*. If an excitatory line is on at a given instant of time (that is, if it is actually carrying an input), it is assigned a weight of 1; if an inhibitory line is on at a given instant, it is assigned a weight of −1; if either kind of line is off at a given instant, it is assigned a weight of zero. An elementary unit produces an on response at time $t + 1$ if, and only if, the sum of the weights of the input lines at time t is greater than zero; otherwise, the unit is off at time $t + 1$.

These elementary units can be assembled into a variety of networks by attaching the input lines of some of the units to the output lines of other units. A behavior of such a network is the response pattern of a

particular family of the units in the network at a given instant. A simple
network is shown in the following diagram:

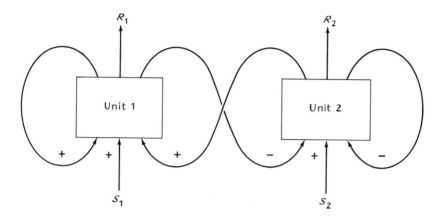

The $+$ denotes an excitatory line; the $-$, an inhibitory line. Let us
consider the *behaviors* of this network when the line R' is *on*: Can we
condition this behavior, in the sense of finding sequences of input stimuli
S_1, S_2 that will always produce the behavior in question? It may be
easily seen from the diagram that, although the on response of R_2 is
possible, it will extinguish itself immediately through the inhibitory loop.

This network may be made more realistic through the use of continuously variable responses R_1, R_2, instead of the all-or-none units we
have employed. In this case, the same network will find it harder and
harder to express the behavior R_2; the more it is stimulated to do so,
the faster the behavior R_2 will disappear. It is, therefore, a network that
cannot be conditioned to exhibit this behavior through any manipulation
of environmental stimuli.

The network in question is not simply an artificially contrived system
designed not to be conditionable. It is, in fact, a network that was
originally developed as an example of a system that *"learns"* the behavior R_1. If we call the basic units in these networks *neurons*, or *neuro-
elements*, we have, in neural terms, an example of how simple kinds of
"learning behavior" can arise. It is also interesting to observe that
exactly the same network (with the units called *operons*) was independently proposed as an example of how one of two alternate modes
of genetic expression could be exhibited without any loss of genetic
information. It thus appears to be a common type of system organization
in biological systems, manifesting itself at many different levels of
biological organization.

To give these examples some neuristic content, let us suppose that the response R_1 corresponds to a kind of behavior we would call "agressive," and the response R_2 corresponds to a kind of behavior we would call "pacific" or "nonaggressive." Under these circumstances, we would never be able to condition the pacific response, nor could we cause the aggressive response to fail to be expressed, by any schedule of reinforcement. Under all circumstances, the pacific response will more or less gradually become extinguished (a result more or less in accord with what has been learned by observing aging mammals).

MODEL II

Skinner has drawn interesting parallels between the selection of behavior by a conditioning environment and the selection of biological properties (through natural selection) by environments favoring particular types of adaptation. In this class of evolving systems, "behavior" takes the form of adaptive responses of biological structure or function, or both, to the particular environmental circumstances. However, there are many clearly evolutionary behaviors that cannot arise through the translation of simple reinforcement ideas to the context of evolving systems. A particularly interesting one is that of a species of insect possessing two generations a year—a winter generation and a summer generation. These generations alternate; the winter generation consists of the offspring of the summer generation, and vice versa. Their modes of life are naturally quite different, and each generation is adapted to the appropriate climate. However, it is clear that such an adaptation of alternate generations could not arise through ordinary Darwinian selection mechanisms: if the adaptation, say, to warm summer were hereditarily transmitted to the offspring of the summer generation, it would render them totally unfit for winter existence; indeed, the better the adaptation to the climate in which a particular generation finds itself, the faster the species would become extinct. Thus, the classical Darwinian behavior must be selected *against* in this case (note, for formal similarity, the self-extinguishing loop in the previous example). Examples of this kind could be multiplied at great length.

Thus, we have at our disposal at least two classes of systems that are biologically significant and realistic, systems in which a reasonable identification of system "behavior" in the class leads us to kinds of behavior that cannot be conditioned. Indeed, in evolutionary biology, it is frequently the rule that, once a certain kind of "behavior" has been selected for (that is, once the evolving organism has become *specialized* to survive in a particular set of environmental circumstances) it can no longer adapt to other environments, and a chage of environments becomes lethal and leads to *extinction*. In behavioral terms, this means that certain kinds of behaviors, once conditioned, lead to an *irreversible loss* of other kinds of behaviors, even though these other behaviors might be essential to survival in a different set of circumstances. This possibility, if it is manifested in the kinds of systems with which Skinner wishes to deal, would raise important limitations for any behavioral technology we might wish to construct within the class; and, inasmuch as this seems to be a general property of biological evolution, we might expect it to be true of human behavior as well, because this, too, has evolved.

Returning to the example of aggressive versus pacific responses in the present evolutionary context, it is possible to envision a class of processes in which the selection of aggressive behavior causes irreversible loss of the capacity to exhibit pacific behavior, and vice versa. Note that this class of evolutionary models differs significantly in interpretation from the class considered in the first model. The first model dealt essentially with a *developmental* process, considering the changes occurring in a single individual in the course of real time. The second model, as an *evolutionary* model, deals rather with changes occurring in populations of organisms in an evolutionary context. Despite the many formal similarities between evolutionary and developmental processes (expressed by the famous phrase "ontogeny recapitulates phylogeny"), the exact relations between the two kinds of processes are far from clear. The point is simply that the same kind of extinction of behavior, with corresponding loss of conditioning ability, arises in both contexts.

MODEL III

In the previous section, we gave examples of classes of systems for which it was false to say that any behavior could be conditioned. It is equally instructive to seek classes of systems for which this important generalization actually is true. I can think of only one such class; because this class is also of interest for many other reasons, it may be worthwhile to briefly describe it.

An *algorithm* is a recipe or set of rules for accomplishing a particular task. Many mathematical procedures are algorithmic in character, such as the ones we all use for obtaining the square root of a number or the quotient of two numbers. Many other common procedures are also algorithmic, such as constructing a building from a blueprint, or playing many kinds of games. Typically, an algorithm provides a rote or canonical way for solving all the problems in a particular well-defined class of problems. A class of problems for which an algorithm can be constructed that solves them all is called *effectively solvable*, and any process that can be put into algorithmic form is called *effective*.

The English mathematician A. M. Turing was interested in whether certain simply statable problems in number theory were effectively solvable or not. To investigate this question, he invented a class of formal machines that now bear his name, the so-called Turing machines. He based his constructions on abstractions from the way in which human beings perform numerical computations (and, of course, other mental processes as well). For this reason, his machines have found a central place in the literature of "artificial intelligence" and "self-organization."

A Turing machine consists of a device (the *reading head*) that can be in one of a finite number of *internal states* at any instant of time. Serving as the environment of the machine is a tape (which, in theory, could be infinitely long) divided into squares. On this tape there can be initially printed any string of symbols (such a string is called a *word*) taken from a finite set that constitutes the machine's *input alphabet*. The machine scans one square of the tape at a time, and can take a variety of actions, depending on the symbol it is scanning at a given instant and its own internal state at that instant: (1) the machine can erase the original symbol and print another symbol on the scanned square; (2) the machine can *move the tape* any number of squares to the left or right; or (3) the machine can change its own internal state. The rules governing these operations constitute the *program* of the machine. The fact that the machine can move its tape to the left or right means, in effect, that it has access to what it has already done, and can use this information to decide what to do next.

It turns out that the Turing machines can carry out any effective process and, conversely, any effective process can be carried out by an appropriately programmed Turing machine. The Turing machines are thus, in a sense, the most general kinds of machines that can be built. Two important theorems about Turing machines will have a bearing on our subsequent discussion:

1) There exist (simple) classes of problems that are not effectively solvable—that is, for which no Turing machine can be programmed to solve every problem in the class. Thus, there are (many) things that Turing machines cannot do. This result is closely related to Kurt Gödel's celebrated theorem about completeness and consistency of an axiom system.

2) To each Turing machine, T, we can uniquely assign a numerical index; we can denote by T_n the machine associated with the number n. We can describe the operation of T_n by specifying, for any initial word

w written on the tape, what the corresponding output word is—that is, what is written on the tape when the machine has stopped. This output word can be denoted by $T_n(w)$. Turing's most important theorem is the following: There exists a Turing machine U such that, if the input tape to U has written on it the word *wn* (that is, if the machine U scans first the index *n* and then the word *w*) we will have $U(wn) = T_n(w)$, for all indices *n* and all words *w*. Such a machine U is called a *universal Turing machine*; if we give a Universal machine a description (the index *n*) of any particular Turing machine, then U will imitate the computations of the particular machine.

Now there are many different aspects of the Turing machine's dynamical organization that can reasonably be called the "behavior" of the machine. We can, for instance, call the "behavior" of the machine the total correspondence between whole input words and their corresponding output words; or we can call the "behavior" of the machine the specific action it takes when it scans a particular input symbol; or we can look, instead of at the output words, at the corresponding sequence of internal states. Perhaps the most natural selection is to identify the alphabet symbols with our *stimuli*, and the corresponding action of the machine as the *response* to a given stimulus. The problem of conditioning then becomes: Is there an input sequence to a particular Turing machine such that, subsequent to the scanning of that sequence, the machine will always respond to a stimulus with a preassigned response?

The answer to this question is clearly "no" for arbitrary Turing machines, but it is "yes" for universal Turing machines; for there is certainly a specific Turing machine that always gives the desired response upon seeing the proper stimulus. This machine has an index *n*; by showing the universal machine this index and then the stimulus, the proper behavior will always be forthcoming. Thus, the universal Turing machines are an example of a set of systems in which Professor Skinner's hypothesis is true.

Before we turn to a consideration of the implications of these various examples, it is interesting to note that this very same class of Turing machines provides a counterexample to the assertion that any behavior can be conditioned, if we define "behavior" to mean a correspondence between input words and output words. This follows from the existence of unsolvable problems, which is the first of Turing's theorems stated above. Thus, even within a given class of systems, the identification of the ostensive word "behavior" with a particular kind of system activity is crucial in ascertaining the validity of propositions concerning it within the class.

Implications for Behavioral Technology

We have seen, from the examples given above, that it is far from obviously true that "any behavior can be conditioned." If this proposition fails, it follows, then, that there are inherent limitations imposed, at the outset, on any "behavioral technology." For instance, some kinds of "pacific behavior" we might want to condition may, in fact, fall outside the class of conditionable behavior. It may be that these limitations are not serious, in the sense that any kind of behavior that we might find to be useful is also conditionable; but this proposition is even more difficult to deal with than the one that we have been examining.

Even if we stay within a class of systems and system behaviors for which it is true that any behavior can be conditioned, does it follow that a useful "behavioral technology" can be constructed? We shall now inquire into this question, and we shall see that the answer is "not necessarily." Much depends on the kinds of problems that we will require the technology to solve. To illustrate this, we shall consider several kinds of plausible behavioral problems within the class of systems described in the preceding section, for which we know that any behavior is conditionable.

1) Can we *effectively* design a sequence of inputs that will cause a universal Turing machine to exhibit a particular behavior? We have not yet answered this question affirmatively; all we have shown is that there *exists* an internal state of the universal machine such that, when the machine is started in that state, the machine will exhibit its characteristic imitative activity. In a real behavioral situation, however, we have no assurance that the given machine will be in the appropriate initial state. Thus, we must preface any input word to the universal machine with another word that will bring it from whatever internal state it happens to be in to the correct initial state. (This is the form of a standard problem in control theory: to bring a system from an arbitrary initial state to a desired end state at the end of a definite time.) This, in turn, raises further problems: (a) can we effectively tell which internal state our machine is in initially; and (b) does there, in fact, exist a sequence of inputs that will take our machine from any arbitrary initial state to the one appropriate to exhibit the required activity? I am prepared to argue that the problem (a) itself is not effectively solvable; and that, therefore, even though the behavioral problem (b) is, in principle, solvable in the class of systems we are dealing with, we cannot be sure we can always bring our universal Turing machine to the correct initial state, in which it must be before the conditioning can begin.

In practice, this would mean that the reinforcement schedule required to condition, say, a pacific rather than an aggressive response must be prefaced by a separate schedule that will bring the organism being conditioned from whatever internal state it happens to be in to the correct internal state. This separate prefatory schedule is, in general, a function of the organism's initial state, and to determine which initial state the organism is actually in may be a difficult problem. One can see that applying a fixed reinforcement schedule when the organism is in the wrong initial state will not, in general, result in the desired behavior, and may actually generate the opposite behavior from what is desired.

2) Let us suppose that the questions raised in the preceding paragraph could be disposed of. Now suppose that, instead of conditioning for a single behavior, we wish to condition two or more behaviors in such a way that they do not interfere with each other. Can this always be done for arbitrary behaviors? Not in general. Inasmuch as any reasonable behavioral technology must seek to condition a variety of behaviors essentially simultaneously, it follows that the technology can only be successfully applied in circumscribed situations, which we cannot be sure include all the cases of interest.

3) All of the considerations presented thus far pertain to a single system. We have seen that, if the given system is in an arbitrary state, the program required to condition a particular behavior must be "custom-tailored" to the initial state. But in any realistic situation for a behavioral technology, we must deal not with a single machine but with a population of machines exhibiting a distribution of initial states. Does there exist an input sequence that can be presented to every machine of the population that will simultaneously bring them all to the required initial state at the end of a definite time? I do not believe that this kind of question has been investigated, but I strongly suspect that the answer is "no," at least in the sense that such an input sequence cannot be effectively determined.

4) A behavioral technology must not be concerned so much with conditioning definite behaviors as it is with seeing to it that certain kinds of behavior never occur. Thus, the question above may perhaps be rephrased in the following way: Does there exist an input sequence that can be provided to every machine in a population exhibiting an arbitrary distribution of initial states such that particular behaviors are excluded for all time in every machine of the population? In effect, can we make every machine in such a population "forget" the presence of

certain of its internal states, or, equivalently, those portions of its programs that involve those states? This is a rather less stringent requirement than (3) above; again, questions like this do not appear to have been investigated in detail, but I would conjecture that the answer to this question is a qualified affirmative.

The upshot of the above considerations is that the kind of "behavioral technology" envisaged by Skinner is liable to be highly circumscribed in the kinds of things it can do, even under the best of circumstances. It should be pointed out, however, that this envisaged technology employs a correspondingly circumscribed set of operational techniques. Using the Turing-machine metaphor, the operations available to this technology involve only a manipulation of the inputs (that is, the environment) of the machine; the set of internal states and the program that determines the machine's activity (which correspond roughly to the specific wiring of the structures inside the machine) cannot be reached by such techniques. If we could widen our repertoire of operations on the machine to include modifications of the state set and the internal program, we would have at our disposal a much more flexible set of techniques than simple conditioning schedules can provide. Such techniques might involve, for example, the use of chemical agents to selectively modify neural pathways, or the modification of underlying genetic determinants. I would conjecture, on the basis of the preceding analysis, that a technology based on conditioning alone is most unlikely to accomplish the good results that Skinner expects of it, and that these results can be accomplished only by an appropriate combination of a "behavioral technology" with other technologies that involves a direct rewiring of the machinery inside the behavioral "black box." And the problems connected with these technologies are, if anything, orders of magnitude greater than those raised by "behavioral technology" itself.

Postscript

Much of the heat generated by Skinner's book, it seems to me, arises less from the substantive claims made by Skinner concerning operant conditioning as a causal agent in behavior than from Skinner's further assertion that the realities of operant conditioning *force* us to give up the idea of autonomous internal mental states as a cause of behavior. Thus, he says (in effect) that we can only begin to implement operant conditioning in a systematic way *at the expense of* traditional myths of "freedom and dignity." I should like briefly to argue that this whole argument raises a false issue, which has distracted attention from the real substantive matters raised by Skinner.

Briefly, it seems to me that the language of operant conditioning, and the language of "freedom and dignity" (that is, of real internal states of mind as a causal agency in behavior), pertain to two different and distinct discursive levels of explication that arise in the discussion of behavior. It is perfectly possible to use both of them in a meaningful fashion, without ambiguity or conflict, provided we do not mix them up, or pretend that they both refer to the same explicative level. The existence of such different levels of explication, employing apparently contradictory modes of discourse, is characteristic of complex, hierarchically organized systems; such systems constantly appear in biology and human sciences, but are unfamiliar in traditional discussion of systems drawn from physics and engineering.

A few examples may clarify this point. One can, for example, argue against Skinner, in the same way that he himself has argued against the level of "freedom and dignity," as follows: Every event occurring in the world has a material, physical basis, and is, therefore, governed by the laws of physics. These laws are essentially causal laws (even in quantum mechanics) and, therefore, every event in the world is totally predetermined by the way in which the physical universe was created. Thus, it is meaningless to talk of "creating contingencies of reinforcement"; in this kind of determinism, internal states of mind—and also the possibility of any event being different from what, in fact, it is—is denied. Yet one can accept such a thoroughgoing determinism at the very lowest level without giving up the capacity for usefully talking about phenomena occurring at higher levels—indeed, science does this all the time. Thus, the fact that contingencies of reinforcement generate behavior does not imply that we cannot usefully talk about internal mental states when it is convenient to do so, any more than Newtonian Mechanism implies it.

A second example, drawn from physics itself, may also be relevant here. It is well known that there are at least two different ways in which we can talk about a fluid. Originally, fluids were considered to be primitive entities, without substructures, and infinitely divisible. With the growth of the atomic theory, an alternate description became possible: a fluid is an assembly of elementary particles whose aggreagate behavior is responsible for its gross properties. Clearly, these two descriptions are contradictory. But the micro description (the description in terms of elementary particles) and the macro description (the description in terms of a structureless fluid) can each be applied meaningfully to appropriate properties of the fluid. At the macro level, for example, it is useful to talk of properties like pressure or temperature, even though these concepts become meaningless or nonexistent at the micro level. Indeed, to attempt to deal with pressure and temperature at the micro level, though possible, is cumbersome and unsatisfactory for most purposes. On the other hand, we can find micro properties of the fluid (such as Brownian motion) for which the macro description is inappropriate and misleading. But as long as we know what we are doing, we can use the two languages separately and usefully, without any conflict, or without any necessity for claiming that one of the languages must be absorbed into the other.

Once this is recognized, we can see that we can talk about operant conditioning and setting contingencies of reinforcement without involving ourselves at all in "the literature of freedom and dignity," and vice versa. To deny that operant conditioning can be used until the traditional ideas of freedom and dignity (that is, the language pertaining to the level of internal states of mind as causal agents in behavior) is given up is analogous to a physician refusing to prescribe a medication to a patient until the patient forswears a particular view of physiology. Just as the act of medication in this example is unrelated to any particular prejudice on the part of the patient, so too is the possibility of a behavioral technology independent of whether or not it is ever useful to talk about internal states of mind; the confusion of the two languages is an irrelevancy that merely serves to distract from the substantive issues.

10

How Good Is
Current Behavior Theory?

John Wilkinson

*John Wilkinson is a senior fellow at the Center for the Study of
Democratic Institutions. Wilkinson is the author of numerous papers on
physics and the philosophy of science, especially the philosophy of
mathematics, and is the American translator of Jacques Ellul's*
The Technological Society.
   *Wilkinson's chapter continues the effort to evaluate operant
conditioning from the standpoint of the mathematician and logician.
It serves as a bridge between the preceding systems analysis of Robert
Rosen and the explicitly mathematical treatment of L. A. Zadeh.*

The history of the sciences, grossly considered, is simple enough: as
each young science, having developed appropriate principles and methods to manage a more or less clearly demarcated subject matter, broke
loose and became autonomous, it was bombarded by canonical abuse
from its parent disciplines, which were collectively called Philosophy.
Psychology was one of the last of the academic disciplines to take this
step, and it begins to look as though the rejection of the father was
premature. Freud's work, for example, is in tatters, and other large
areas have been swallowed whole by more firmly grounded disciplines,
such as pharmacology and biology. The malaise one senses when

speaking with psychologists is overpowering. Only one variety, the one
that passes by the name "behaviorism," is widely thought to be "scientific," even though most psychologists deem it "narrow" and even
manifest a certain revulsion toward it. How good, really, as science, is
the current behaviorism made controversial by B. F. Skinner? The
observations that follow apply to behavioral theory and not to the more
restricted science and technology of operant conditioning.

The meagerness of behavioral theory, its total inability to make
feasible prognoses coupled with a nearly Assyrian contempt for the
infinite variety of the things in its jurisdiction that need explanation,
make arguments in its defense as meaningless as those in condemnation
of it; and one is tempted to speculate about the need felt by so many
to take a stand at all. This need may derive from weak ideologies that
possibly prompt bad consciences but seldom appropriate actions.

Behaviorists must have had occasion, in their holy places like Cambridge or in travelling the lecture circuit, to hear all the objections to
their speculations that could be raised; and they have sought to anticipate
and to defend against them by denying them, in the way a seminarian
prepares himself not only to combat the too enthusiastic immediacy of
expectation of the true believer, but also to counter the equally weak-
minded expostulations of the village atheist, without much conviction
of dampening the ardor of either. These decanti and cantori have generated such a wide variety of opposing themes that behaviorism has
become, like theology, more operatic than scientific, and Skinner's
theories would sound better set to music, a procedure that often makes
us tolerant or unaware of bad libretti.

The rule of requisite informational variety in argumentation, first
proposed by Descartes in his "existence" proofs, and later brought to a
high degree of definition by information theory and cybernetics, means,
among other things, that weak reasonings can overthrow weaker ones;
whereas to establish "strong" universals requires the examination, or
algorithmic calculation, of a sufficient variety of complicated systemic
properties of wider and wider universes of discourse. Very often, to cast
down a "weak" theory requires only that a single disconfirming fact
be found, or that one necessary condition be shown not to hold. Negat-
ing procedures of this kind demand much ingenuity; and no one could
assert that behaviorism lacks this qualification, nor that its arguments,
as far as they are able to go, are, in the main, true. Its conceptual apparatus, however, offers no *sufficient* variety for erecting a science of
human behavior considered in all the complexity of its natural and
cultural setting. The behaviorist's extension, to the survival of cultural
patterns, of the biological "survival of the fittest," operating through
some inexplicable and unlikely analogy of mutation and selection, is,

like Darwinism itself, able to clean out a venerable closet of weak theories that, by being repeated, have become inveterate. But, like Darwinism, which could easily dispose of Bishop Wilberforce, the behaviorists have proposed no theory strong enough to account for the occurrence of "cultural" mutations, or to explain their "ends," much less to describe the "origins" of whatever it is they believe themselves to be describing. The causalities that appear in evolutionary theories of both sorts probably operate only locally—say, in "explaining" why flies quickly become resistant to pesticides, or why one method of irrigation, but not another, received religious sanction in Babylon. But, they probably have no reference at all to complex biological evolutions over incomparably longer periods, or to erecting or controlling whole cultures. Because *ends*, for example, cannot be descried, it becomes agreeable for latter-day social Darwinists to assert that they are meaningless entities of speculative philosophy or religion, although most scientists involved with the consideration of systems have been persuaded that the richer variety of feedback theory had once and for all revived ends-in-view, and even whole hierarchies of ends, as rational concepts.

In general, "refutations" of behaviorism by the utilization of weak dogmas drawn from Marx, or from those even weaker "hidden hand" ideologies of the liberal bourgeois intelligentsia, are contemptible and, paradoxically, even demonstrate some small degree of what behavioral conditioning they seek to discredit. Knee-jerk liberals—conditioned to slaver over "liberty" and "dignity"—generally mean that everyone else should have the courage of *their* convictions, and they usually cover up the most heinous crimes with denunciations of scientists like Skinner. Not long ago, for example, we heard much of these liberals' "New Frontier"—in practice, the Bay of Pigs was its first landfall and Vietnam was its second. This is not so much an argument *ad homines* as a simple illustration of the way in which weak theories overthrow weaker ones.

The important question is whether or not "liberty," "purpose," and "mind," must be revived in "richer" theories, hierarchically arranged in the way that richer "metalanguages" are always related to their "object" languages. One must, for example, ascend to the metalanguage "grammar" before such useful symbols as "noun" and "verb" are generated. These latter classes are clearly different in kind from the objects—such as "chair," "Skinner," and so on—that are classified. Metalanguages involve higher levels of organization and explanation, and it is usual to find that *only* through their use may any clarity at all be introduced into the discussion of the subordinate levels, or outright contradictions be recognized and avoided. In the concrete "structuralist" logic of primitive thought that convulsed the fashionable salons of Paris until the events of 1968 removed their attention to Chairman Mao and

Sartre, "things" may seem to have that superior reality testified to by Samuel Johnson when he refuted one version of Idealism by kicking a stool. But in the technological society, in which we have come to dwell almost exclusively in symbiotic contact with classes of artifacts of our own making, "classes of classes" have greater theoretical reality, and we cannot avoid inquiring into whatever it is that rational discourse about them involves. That means that we have come to possess an inescapable "freedom" denied to savages; for *we* possess an infinitely greater variety of "options" (a good metalinguistic term) that neither pigeons nor savages ever had much opportunity to think about.

The state of behavioral psychology, and its frequent need to justify itself to a run-down intelligentsia, has led it to water its theses to such a degree that, as in the closely related literature of systemic "city planning," what emerges is not so much an analysis of the variety and complexity of human behavior in its psychosocial environment as it is a weak and inadequate "metaphysic" of these things. These theories, nevertheless, represent a clear advance over those weak-minded and incompetent speculations about cultural matters that are currently fashionable. Take, for example, explanations of the alienation of the young. The translation, into behavioral language, of the mental condition of an alienated youth, who has just graduated from a "university" into a rapidly changing world for which "education" has ill prepared him, is admirable, at least in comparison with the foolish way such topics are most often spoken of in academic departments of the modern political, religious, and social-scientific sort.[1] Now, all words of natural language, and certain "scientific" ones, are what some mathematicians have begun to call "fuzzy" sets. But minor triumphs of behaviorism should not lead us to perpetuate or to increase fuzziness; the least that may reasonably be demanded of dialogue and theory is that their use *not* render the things that they attempt to explain even fuzzier. The "semantic fields" of behaviorist terminology should operate, as they obviously do not, not only to invalidate nontheories of psychology and social science but to generate information by the only method possible— that is, by increasing requisite theoretical variety in an appropriate metalanguage, rather than by increasing the ambiguity and the sheer number of "observable" facts. Good metalanguages avoid an entropically increasing fuzziness of argument by obviating the commonest sort of "explication"—that is, the sort that operates by inventing mnemonic devices and metaphors on the lowest level of discourse, devices that, unfortunately, always cope with increasing object com-

---

[1] See Skinner's *Beyond Freedom and Dignity* (Alfred A. Knopf, 1971), pp. 156 ff.

plexity with less and less precision.[2] Control and stability, another pair of closely related terms, become progressively more difficult to build into a system too weak to use them.

A scientist or philosopher, then, seeks to evade (often successfully) these and other problems of complex systems, never by increasing any merely mnemonic machinery, but by inventing a larger, richer, super-ordinated and controlling vocabulary of terms—both operationally better defined and algorithmically more easily calculable—to the end that unmanageable confusions of fuzzy object languages achieve a meaningful (and less fuzzy) translation into the chosen metalanguage or "metaphysic," but not inversely. Successful constructions of languages to talk about experimental observables introduces truly useful variety into theory. Pattern recognition and learning are essential parts of this process, abilities that, for the moment, are reserved to human minds. Whatever secures better understanding, by putting less strain on our mnemonics, is always a preferable way of proceeding in science. Behaviorism has made a feeble attempt to create—or, better, to talk about —hierarchical superordinated control theory in psychology, but, unfortunately, with no recognition at all of the complexity of the object and its environment. The test of requisite variety applied to behaviorist "metaphysic" suggests that it is deficient, and irremediably so, and that what it is really experimenting with belongs to purely associational mnemonics that merely "preserve the contours" of a proper theory.[3]

Part of this failure is the result of cutting itself off, right at the beginning, by denouncing those very unobservables that would serve it best, were it ever to elevate itself to the condition of a really interesting theory. One might have thought that E. L. Thorndike's failures, those that inhered in his dictum that "everything which exists exists in quantity and can be measured," might have been exemplary. Skinner, like Thorndike, throws out a mass of necessary terms, adds a few dubious mathematical flourishes, and comes up with what George Miller calls a "null" hypothesis, a hypothesis of the sort that makes him hope that he will be unable to disprove it by facts that are, in effect, random to it. What Skinner calls a "probabilistic schedule-of-reinforcements" that condition operatively is little more than a brute attempt to catalogue certain facts by neglecting whatever he chooses. Behaviorism has no half-way adequate theory of probability, and it contents itself with disarming critics by agreeing that it *needs* one, while rejecting any

---

[2]The best mnemonic devices are high-level theories like Dmitri Mendeleef's periodic table of the elements, a display that allowed some marvellous predictions to be made.

[3]Behaviorists dislike the description of their theory as a "metaphysic." But "metalanguage" seems to mean the same thing and raises fewer hackles.

suggestions that are made. As far as the multiple states of a complex system are concerned—that is, for those conditions that are supposed to be reinforced (or the reverse)—we get "schedules" that look rather like "Thirty days hath September . . . excepting February. . . ."

The lesson one quickly learns from the history of science is that the sole way of getting requisite variety is by establishing more encompassing theories with information-generating constraints. The "variety" of such a theory (an adequate explication of its "strength") measures relevant information by specifying the number and the probability of transition between the independent states in which the system under examination can exist. Thus, in ecology, greater variety (more available "niches") usually, bit not always, means greater stability—that is, survival value. An actor who is able to play a large number of roles is less likely to be unemployed and, in this important sense, is more stable than the actor whose abilities are limited to one sort of role.

In general, information and control are possible only by specifying a "band"—that is, upper and lower limits to the probable states of a system. This band between the too little and the too much *is* "variety." If one were to ask "How many genes are involved in what we measure as 'intelligence'?" and if we were able to specify what percentage of this useful commodity were estimated to be the result of genetics and what of environment, the width of this band could be calculated to be "not less than 25 and not more than 100." This exemplifies the sort of information we need about systems, and this is exactly the kind that current behaviorism never possesses.

The results of the debates about the foundations of logics, mathematics, and the physical sciences (in particular, quantum theory), and related measurement and experimentation, that began in the 1920s and are not yet concluded, are compelling. It is unfortunate that the usual obscure formulation of these matters renders them unavailable to most intelligent people; but they are not, on that account, less absolutely constraining of *any* theory. "Variety" and information arise always by imposing constraints on a much wider spectrum of *a priori* possibilities of states of a system, even though we often naively see constraints as acting as a bar to information.

Rudolf Carnap and the Vienna Circle of positivists originally propagated strongly the thesis of "physicalism," according to which *all* theory (if clarity and freedom from metaphysical "obscurantism" were to be gained) had ultimately to rest on physical observables. This thesis is the complete theoretical equivalent, in the physical sciences, of behaviorism. The positivist program of the 1920s, called *Logischer Aufbau der Welt*, had then to rely completely on observables, by constructing from them the world through long chains of inference of a logical nature.

Almost immediately, however, the physicalists were constrained to invent new logical categories and structures. Simultaneously, among related groups, a discussion began concerning the applicability of physicalism, or some version of it, to quantum theory. Because of the omnipresence of nonintuitive and unavoidable limitations on observing data in our interpretation of the microphysical world ("uncertainty"), a long debate began that issued at last in conclusions that must be stated here perhaps too summarily. It turned out that the logic of quantum states could not be described with that two-valued logic that was, in its essence, an embroidery of the logic descended from the Greeks. A "complementary" multivalued logic (that postulates, among other things, that a greater number of values than "true" or "false" attach to propositions) seemed clearly to operate in the quantum domain. On the other hand, conventional logic, and classical descriptions making use of it, appeared not only justified but necessary in designing and protocolling experimental behavior in the laboratory. The irremediable differences between the two logics was resolved (by Reichenbach and others) by deciding that the necessary rejection of classical logic in the quantum domain, and its simultaneous acceptance in the experimental, turned, in great part, on a distinction between two sorts of entities—namely, the unobservable and the observed. In particular, the "law of the excluded middle" described above had to be put on ice, with respect to many of these "unobservables."[4] This compromise led to a major modification of the original physicalist thesis, principally by giving a definite meaning to these "unobservables." This is not too strange a hypothesis if we reflect that all the entities we habitually call "observables" are, in fact, shaky inferences, involving long logical chains, from what we may be said only *conventionally* to observe; and, further, that many inferred entities indispensible to science, and called "observations," have never actually been "observed" and possibly never will be. The quantum theory is a strong metalanguage with respect to billiard-ball mechanics, inasmuch as it contains conceptual entities that this latter does not, and includes it as a case limiting our day-to-day experience.

The presence of hierarchically superordinated, but unobservable, metalinguistic constraints in quantum theory was, I believe, an important, universal, historical development that happened to be studied first because physical systems are "simpler" to investigate and replicate and easier to manage. Because, in the psychosocial sciences, observational

---

[4]Other suggestions—for example, those of von Neumann—are even less intuitive and less grateful to positivists or behaviorists. I use the expression "put on ice" because it turns out, rather astonishingly and completely counterintuitively, that this basic "law" of ordinary logic (that states that a proposition must be either false or true and that a third possibility does not exist) is not affirmed, but that it is always false to deny it.

uncertainties arising through the interaction of the observer and the observed are even more ubiquitous than in quantum theory (think of the traffic cop who observes fewer violations than anyone else), the conclusion must be that the richer metalanguage we need to explain what we crudely observe with the eye and certain coadjutant mechanisms will necessarily contain some symbols that are neither observed nor observable, nor tractable with the use of ordinary homespun logic. Some functional equivalent of "mind" must form a part of psychological science and the behaviorism of the future, even though it escape the sufficiently mysterious procedure of *direct* observation. Thus, we reasonably speak of a "state of mind" without supposing gratuitously (and probably falsely) that such a state is completely explicated by reference to the wiring of the brains' neurons. Perhaps even "God" may get back into the ultimate description of sufficiently complicated behavior. In Descarte's meditations, with the use of the principle of necessary metaphysical "variety" (called by him "reality"), that is exactly what happened through one version of the so-called "ontological" argument. The fact that unmeasurable concepts are as intuitively repugnant to most behavioral scientists as they were long ago to the Positivistic program (bravely called, at first, *Überwindung der Metaphysik*) may signify as little as Rudolf Carnap's original neglect of them. Caution is advisable with the notion of "freedom," too. We very usefully speak of "degrees of freedom" in describing any complex system, although we must always share behaviorism's distaste for those unobservables when they are used by liberals and Fascists alike to confuse our discourse or to conceal their crimes.

The most powerful tool available to human intuition in handling the complexity and diversity of even moderately complicated psychological or social systems is high-speed digital simulation *plus* graphic display. These devices are already "mental," in the sense that they are complicated enough that it is impossible even for their inventors or programmers to "observe" *all* that they can do. It would be the worst possible mistake to suppose that computers can only process numbers. Their best use is in connection with symbolic processes in general. J. W. Forrester, Richard Bellman, and a few others have made a beginning. The same scurrilous rabble who attacked Forrester have mobilized their decrepit ideologies to attack a competent behaviorism. Forrester's "world" dynamics is a strong metalanguage of human behavior in its global environment. It has begun to tease out of the raw data a "variety" that is half-way commensurate with a theoretical rendering of society. He takes as his primitive logical entities a simple but nevertheless incredibly complicated systemic network of feedback mechanisms. It agrees with behaviorism at least in one important point—namely, that the indispensable conditional value for any rational account of society is that it be "stable," and, one forlornly hopes, "just." Stability of systems is a concept that seems to intersect greatly with Skinner's and Darwin's survival of species, cultural and biological. Only a beginning has been made by Forrester, but there is a well-founded hope that this simulation method, perhaps after it has been successively refined through many adaptive additions and iterations, may be able to predict, as unaided human intuition cannot, the effects of secondary changes arising from "policy" manipulations, or those of adaptive control processes within the social order. It is on the level of so-called "adaptive control processes" that an effective human science must operate, and it is on this level that the requisite varieties of theories are to be compared. It should be noted that the "secondary" effects that always appear in manipulating complex systems are only "secondary" in the sense that we don't want them and didn't previse them. Further, they usually have the disagreeable property, through being almost totally *counter*intuitive, of running in the opposite direction to whatever was primary, or "planned," and, what may be worse, in displaying these effects after long delay. Behaviorist theories are far too weak to be compared with the hypersophisticated digital, analogue (or hybrid), computerization techniques that alone seem to be able *to aid the human mind* in coping with sheer complexity of data and the logical relations among these data. By speed of operation, they allow the mind to foreshorten or compress the time dimension, and so to allow the framing of policies indispensable to rational control of cultures that are evolving with accelerating rapidity.

The import of these secondary effects, here, is that a behaviorist might well find himself in the position of reinforcing, and being himself reinforced, through the operation of initially encouraging but finally disastrous effects of manipulation. What will a behaviorist do if secondary and effectively random results produce more aggressiveness in human beings than the rather frightening quanta of this disagreeable quality we have recently observed? Or what if he produces an organism that possesses too little? Should he then proceed to eliminate his mistakes? After the manner of cattle breeders, or that of nature "red in tooth and claw"? Moreover, controlled breeding usually eliminates both variety and variability, simultaneously introducing instability of one or another unexpected kind. If behaviorism were to succeed in turning cultural conditioning into biological breeding (and probably more than half of all children—the "good" ones—are thought to be biologically docile and to manifest nonaggressive behavior almost immediately after birth), the reduction of variety would paradoxically have the effect of making a bad theory possessing little variety into a "good" one, but only by following the path that would have led men to declare Hitler's race theories "good," had he succeeeded in his design of establishing the 1000-year Reich by eliminating all opposition.

It would clearly be infinitely more acceptable first to simulate the system to approximate its behavior over condensed periods of time, and then to get the behavior modifiers or planners, by jiggling the computer's knobs, to change the psychosocial parameters that control the rates that regulate the state variables, in order to be able to conjecture for themselves and demonstrate for others the possible effects of different proposed policies. One can reasonably be persuaded (without harboring any excessively strong conviction) that most men have already been conditioned, by nature and nurture acting in concert, *not* to choose too readily to commit suicide. But, whatever they choose, they are capable of exercising through such simulation a greater degree of freedom that has been allotted to men in history by *any* culture from the remotest recoverable antiquity.

The behaviorist is right in pointing out that all of us already live in systems, like the capitalistic, in some sense almost totally invented by men; but he is certainly wrong in assuming that the inventors of these systems either control or understand even the grosser workings of their inventions. Mr. Nixon's economic advisors, were they to become candid, could easily testify to that. Systems, for want of something better, have an inherent logic (or a collection of local logics) of their own, which certainly involve "unobservables." A primitive agnosticism concerning these unobservables, on the part of behavioral scientists, *must* stand in the path of any elaboration of feasible policies of human behavior or any conditionings based on these policies.

There is one forlorn hope. Weakness is sometimes strength; and even if behavior modification, applied to large or complex systems, rests upon a weak theory, the unpredictable secondary effects of its cultural culling process of trial and error may conceivably turn out to be more beneficial than fatal. Biological evolution, for example, could probably never have "selected" for survival value the ability to create, or enjoy, Beethoven's Ninth Symphony. Because genes are highly polyvalent, only incidentally can they have enabled men, through mutation and selection, to accomplish more than merely to survive. "Culture" may be just that totality of secondary effects that have accrued to us as a bonus above and beyond survival. Skinnerian behaviorism is less rational than many other presently available and richer theories of adaptive control, none of which are without their difficulties. There always exists the possibility that, by being brutally conditioned for psychic and social survival, cultural goods may incidentally be added unto us. The arts have most often flourished under the patronage of one or another despot, who most often patronized the artist at the expense of everyone but himself. This is hardly an acceptable version of "democracy." But evolution, learning, control processes, and stability all are achieved only at very high costs, no matter what theory or practice is involved. Variety always exacts a price in time, money, suffering, or resources; and one thing that is clear about most democracies—which are, in their very nature, pluralistic—is that they are seldom, if ever, willing to pay the price for excellence, or even for survival. Our comfort must probably be that real "freedom," expensive and peremptory though it may be in its own way, would probably cost much less than behavior modification.

Summary

A theory is "weaker" or "stronger" if it possesses lesser or greater "variety." Variety is a function of certain probabilities and measurable data embedded in a complex system. Only a commensurably stronger theory can serve to explicate the facts or predict the future of a given universe of discourse. Behaviorism, if strong on some levels of explication, is weak on others. The construction of a stronger theory here, as elsewhere, will involve the addition of "unobservables"—that is, things unobservable at the level of the weaker theory, and perhaps even unobservable in principle. Improvements of psychological theory, in this way, will result in the addition of terms that are functional equivalents of "freedom," "dignity," "mind," and so forth. A particularly important addition is the concept of stabilizing "feedback." Large-scale combinations of social and cultural feedbacks often result in unpredictable, costly, and destabilizing effects at long term. So, "schedules of reinforcement" may incur the danger of actually reinforcing instability and promoting the disequilibration—even the disappearance—of the system. This is clearly of especial danger in a period of very rapid and accelerating cultural change.

11

A System-Theoretic View
of Behavior Modification

L. A. Zadeh

L. A. Zadeh, professor of electrical engineering and computer sciences at the University of California, Berkeley, is co-author of Linear System Theory *and editor of the* Journal of Computer and System Sciences.
This evaluation is of special value in that it considers Skinnerian behaviorism from a mathematical point of view. Zadeh employs the formalism of the theory of "fuzzy sets" that he developed in evaluating operant conditioning. He concludes that "the time is coming, if it has not come already, when the society will have much more effective means at its disposal for manipulating . . . its members." Zadeh concludes that operant conditioning lends itself to formulation in a mathematical model, which would facilitate computer analysis.
The work on this paper was supported, in part, by National Science Foundation Grant GK-10656X.

To someone like myself, steeped in the quantitative analyses of inanimate systems, the principal ideas in Skinner's *Beyond Freedom and Dignity* are difficult to translate into assertions that are capable of proof or refutation. Nevertheless, I find them highly interesting and thought-provoking.

It is a truism that human behavior is vastly more complex than the behavior of man-conceived systems. This is reflected in the fact that such basic concepts as control, reinforcement, feedback, goal, constraint, decision, strategy, adaptation, and environment, which are central to the discussion of human behavior, are much better understood and more clearly defined in system theory—which deals with abstract systems from an axiomatic point of view—than in psychology or philosophy. Unfortunately, high precision is rarely compatible with high complexity. Thus, the precision and determinism of system theory have the effect of severely restricting its capability to deal with the complexities of human behavior.

Essentially, inanimate systems are amenable to quantitative analysis because their behavior is sufficiently simple to admit of characterization by equations containing numerical variables (that is, scalars or vectors whose components are real or complex numbers). Typically, the state of an inanimate system S at time[1] t, $t = 0, 1, 2, \ldots$, is an n-vector, x_t, of low or moderate dimensionality, whose components are real numbers. For example, if S is a point of mass m moving in a three-dimensional space, then its state has six components, of which the first three define its position and the last three its velocity.

If S is subjected to a sequence of inputs, $u_0, u_1, u_2, \ldots$, each of which is a numerical variable, then the behavior of S is usually characterized by two equations:

$$x_{t+1} = f(x_t, u_t), \tag{1}$$

$$y_t = g(x_t, u_t). \tag{2}$$

The first equation defines the next state (that is, the state at time $t + 1$) as a function of the present state, x_t, and the present input, u_t. The second equation defines the present output, y_t, as a function of the present state and the present input. Thus, the behavior of a deterministic discrete-time system may be characterized by two functions f and g, which define, respectively, the next state and the output of the system.

In the past, attempts to describe human behavior by equations of the form of (1) and (2) have met with little success because human behavior, in general, is much too complex to admit of description by numerical variables. However, as suggested by Zadeh (1971) and Bellman and Zadeh (1970), a possible way of dealing with the problem of complexity is to employ *fuzzy* variables—in place of numerical variables—in (1) and (2). The values of such variables are not numbers but labels of fuzzy sets[2]—that is, names of classes that do not have sharply defined

---

[1]For simplicity, we assume that time varies discretely. Dependence on t will frequently be assumed but not exhibited explicitly.

[2]Roughly speaking, a fuzzy set is a class with unsharp boundaries. More precisely, a fuzzy set A in a space $X = \{x\}$ is a collection of ordered pairs $A = \{[x, \mu_A(x)]\}$, in which $\mu_A(x)$ is the *grade of membership* of x in A, with $0 \leq \mu_A(x) \leq 1$. A more detailed discussion of fuzzy sets may be found in Zadeh (1971) and Bellman and Zadeh (1970).

boundaries. For example, the terms *green, big, tired, happy, young, bald,* and *oval* may be viewed as labels for classes in which the transition from membership to nonmembership is gradual rather than abrupt. Thus, a man aged 32 may have partial membership—represented by a number, say, 0.6—in the class of *young* men. The class of young men, then, would be characterized by a membership function μ_{young} (x) that associates with each man x his grade of membership in the class of young men. For simplicity, membership functions are assumed to take values in the interval [0, 1], with 0 and 1 representing nonmembership and full membership, respectively.

The use of fuzzy variables to describe human behavior is, in effect, a retreat into imprecision in the face of complexity. This, of course, is what has been done all along in psychology and philosophy. However, the use of fuzzy variables in conjunction with equations such as (1) and (2) may make it possible to deal with human behavior in a more systematic and somewhat more precise fashion than is customary in psychology and related fields.

In what follows, I shall sketch the rudiments of this approach and relate it, in part, to human behavior modification. In my brief discussion of the equations characterizing human behavior, I shall not attempt to specify the functions of fuzzy variables that enter into these equations, nor shall I concretize the meaning of the variables representing state, input, environment, and so on. Thus, my very limited aim in this paper is merely to suggest that some of the aspects of behavior modification discussed by Skinner may be formulated, perhaps more systematically, through the use of equations and functions employing fuzzy, rather than numerically-valued, variables. It should be understood, of course, that the detailed task of characterizing the functions entering into these equations by tables or flow charts of labels of fuzzy sets would normally require a great deal of psychological testing and data analysis.

Our point of departure is the assumption that the behavior of a human —who, for convenience, will be referred to as H—can be represented, in part, by the following two pairs of equations:

$$x_{t+1} = h_1(x_t, u_t, e_t, t), \tag{3}$$

$$y_t = h_2(x_t, u_t, e_t, t); \tag{4}$$

$$s_{t+1} = g_1(s_t, u_t, y_t, t), \tag{5}$$

$$e_t = g_2(s_t, u_t, y_t, t); \tag{6}$$

in which

x_t = state of H at time t, $t = 0, 1, 2, \ldots$,

u_t = action taken by H at time t, with u_t chosen from a constrained (possibly fuzzy) set of alternatives,

e_t = input representing the effect of the external influences not under the control of H (for example, the effect of the environment, both physical and social),

y_t = response of H to action u_t and external influences e_t,

s_t = state of environment at time t, and

h_1, h_2, g_1, g_2 = fuzzy and, possibly, random functions.

It is understood that some or all of the variables in the above equations are fuzzy, which means that their values are labels of fuzzy sets (for example, x_t = tired, u_t = taking a nap, e_t = hot and humid, and so on). Thus, a typical entry in a table characterizing (3), say, would read: If, at time t, the state of H is a fuzzy set described by a label α (for example, α = tired), the effect of the environment is a fuzzy set described by a label β, and the action by H is a fuzzy set labeled γ, then, with high likelihood the next state of H will be a fuzzy set labeled δ, and possibly, but much less likely, the next state will be ϵ.

In effect, the first pair of equations, (3) and (4), serves to describe, in a very approximate (and yet systematic) fashion, the response of H (or some particular aspect of the response of H, represented by y_t) to the external influences (represented by e_t) and the action taken by H (represented by u_t). In a similar fashion, the second pair (5) and (6), describes the effect of the behavior of H on the environment. Generally, the effect of H on the environment is much smaller than the effect of the environment on H. This is not true, however, in the case of operant conditioning, where the changes in environment serve to reinforce a particular mode of behavior of H.

To make the description of the behavior of H more explicit, we need an additional equation that describes the decision principle employed by H in selecting an action u_t from a constrained set of alternatives. To this end, it is expedient to make use of the notion of the *maximizing set* of a function, which is an approximation to—or, in our terminology, a fuzzification of—the notion of a maximizing value.

Suppose that $f(x)$ is a real-valued function that is bounded both from below and from above, with x ranging over a domain X. The maximizing set of f is a fuzzy set, M, in X, such that the grade of membership, $\mu_M(x)$, of x in M represents the degree to which $f(x)$ is close to the maximum value of f over X, that is, $\sup f$ ($\sup f$ = supremum of $f(x)$ over X.) For example, if $\mu_M(x_1) = 0.8$ at $x = x_1$, then the value of $f(x)$ at $x_1 = x_1$ is about 80% of its maximum value with respect to some reference point. In effect, then, the maximizing set of a function f serves to grade the points in the domain of f according to the degree to which $f(x)$ approximates $\sup f$.[3]

Now let $R_t(u_t)$ denote the estimated total reward[4] associated with action u_t at time t, with the negative values of R_t representing loss, pain, discomfort, and so forth. Then we postulate that the decision principle employed by H is the following: For each t at which a decision has to be made, H chooses the u_t that is the maximizing set for the estimated reward. It is understood that, if the membership function of this set does not peak sharply around some particular action, then H first narrows his choice to those actions that have a high grade of membership in u_t and then uses some random or arbitrary rule to select one among them.

To gain better insight into the operation of the decision principle, it is advantageous to decompose the estimated reward function into two components, one representing an immediate reward or gratification and the other representing estimate future reward (or penalty, if the reward is negative). More specifically, we assume that R_t is a function of two arguments: immediate reward function $IR_t(u_t)$ and estimated future reward function $FR_t(u_t)$. Thus, in symbols,

$$R_t(u_t) = G_t[IR_t(u_t), FR_t(u_t)], \qquad (7)$$

where G_t represents a function[5] of IR_t and FR_t, playing a role analogous to that of an objective function in control theory. Note that implicit in

---

[3]In more precise terms, the membership function of the maximizing set of a real-valued function $f(x)$, $x \in X$, is defined by the following equations (in which inf $f = $ infimum of $f(x)$ over X):

$$\mu_M(x) = \frac{f(x)}{\sup f},$$

if inf $f \geq 0$;

$$\mu_M(x) = \frac{\sup f + \inf f - f}{\inf f},$$

if $\sup f \leq 0$; and

$$\mu_M(x) = \frac{f - \sup f}{\sup f - \inf f},$$

if inf $f \leq 0$ and $\sup f \geq 0$. If f is a fuzzy function—that is, if, for each $x \in X$, $f(x)$ is a fuzzy set with membership function $\mu_f(x,y)$—then the maximizing set for $f(x)$ is defined by the preceding equations with $f(x)$ replaced by $\sup_y \mu_f(x,y)$. Although the definitions given are precise, it should be understood that, in dealing with fuzzy variables, maximization and other operations performed on functions of such variables are highly approximate in nature.

[4]It should be understood that expressing the total reward as a function of u_t alone is intended merely to single out the dependence of R_t on u_t. In general, R_t will depend, in addition, on the strategy used by H as well as on x_t, s_t, y_t, e_t, and, possibly, other variables.

[5]As in the case of R_t, it is tacitly understood that G_t may depend on x_t, s_t, y_t, t, and, possibly, other variables.

FR_t is a goal (or subgoals) in terms of which the consequence of choosing u_t may be estimated.

We are now in a position to make the description of the behavior of H more explicit by adding to (3), (4), (5), and (6) the equation

$$u_t = \text{maximizing set for } G_t(IR_t, FR_t). \tag{8}$$

In words, this equation means that H chooses the action u_t that maximizes a specified combination of the immediate reward IR_t and the estimated future reward FR_t, with IR_t and FR_t understood to be known functions of the actions. It should be remarked that the description of the behavior of H by (3), (4), (5), (6), and (8) is consistent with the point of view taken in Skinner's work.

If the variables appearing in equations (3), (4), (5), (6), and (8) were assumed to be numerically valued, the task of characterizing the functions h_1, h_2, g_1, g_2, IR_t, FR_t, and G would be impossibly complex. The crux of this idea is to regard the variables in question as fuzzy variables ranging over labels of appropriate fuzzy sets.[6] Equations (3)–(8), then, would represent approximate (that is, fuzzy) relations between fuzzy variables. These relations could be characterized by (a) tables in which the entries are labels of fuzzy sets, or (b) algorithmically—that is, by a set of fuzzy rules (like a computer program with fuzzy instructions) for generating a fuzzy set from other fuzzy sets. In this way, the description of the relations between the variables characterizing human behavior could be greatly simplified—at the cost, of course, of a commensurate loss in precision. In this perspective, the approach sketched above may be viewed as a systematization of the conventional verbal characterizations of human behavior (Zadeh, 1973).

When human behavior is described by equations of the form (3), (4), (5), (6), and (8), a modification in human behavior may be viewed as a change in the functions h_1, h_2, G_t, IR_t, and FR_t. Of these, the changes in G, IR_t, and FR_t play a particularly important role because they influence, in a direct way, the choice of actions taken by H. Thus, in terms of these functions, Skinner's operant conditioning may be regarded as a form of modification of behavior resulting largely from a manipulation of IR_t through its dependence on the environment.

To clarify the role played by FR_t in relation to IR_t, it will be convenient to make a very rough approximation to G_t by a numerically valued convex linear combination,

---

[6]It is understood that the fuzzy sets in question would, in general, be defined in an approximate fashion by exemplification (that is, ostensively). For example, the fuzzy set *very likely* would be defined by a collection of examples of probability values together with their grades of membership—for example, {(1, 1.0), (0.9, 0.9), (0.8, 0.7), (0.7, 0.4), (0.6, 0.1)}—in which the first element is a probability value and the second element is its grade of membership in the fuzzy set *very likely*.

$$R_t = \alpha\, IR_t + (1 - \alpha)FR_t, \qquad\qquad (9)$$

in which α is a weighting coefficient, $0 \leq \alpha \leq 1$. Thus, (9) signifies that the reward at time t is a weighted linear combination of the immediate reward and the estimated future reward at time t, with the latter multiplied by the factor $\rho = (1 - \alpha)/\alpha$ in relation to the former.

Though not a constant, the *anticipation coefficient* ρ constitutes an important personality parameter of an individual. In this connection, it should be noted that, in a given individual, ρ will be small when the uncertainty in the estimate FR_t is large. To put it another way, the influence of the immediate reward tends to be predominant when there is considerable uncertainty about the future consequences of an action.

As an individual matures and learns from his own experience as well as that of others, his knowledge of the IR_t and FR_t functions improves and his anticipation coefficient trends to increase—that is, he tends to become more far-sighted. Nevertheless, it is probably true that, judged over a long period of time, the ρ of most individuals is not as large as it should be for their own good, as well as for the good of others. The acceptance of this premise naturally raises the troublesome question: To what extent should society attempt to coerce its members to increase their anticipation coefficient if they are unwilling to do so on their own volition? Obviously, it is this question that is at the heart of problems relating to such practices as smoking, drinking, and drug-taking.

It is important to observe that the effect of increasing ρ (for negative FR_t) can also be achieved, for fixed ρ, by decreasing IR_t. In other words, if an individual tends not to give sufficient weight to long-term harmful consequences of an action that gives him immediate pleasure, then one way of inducing him to modify his behavior is to make IR_t sufficiently negative by adding to it an immediate penalty. For example, one possible way of controlling affinity for excessive drinking might be to implant an electronic monitor in a person who is in need of external reinforcement of his will power. Such a monitor could be programmed to produce an acute sensation of pain or some other form of discomfort when the level of alcohol in blood reaches a predetermined threshold. In this way, the immediate pleasure derived from having one or more drinks would be offset by the nearly simultaneous feeling of pain, with the net immediate reward becoming negative when the amount of alcohol consumed exceeds a set limit.

Behavior-modifying monitors of this type are within the reach of modern electronic technology. Clearly, the potential for abuse of such devices is rather high: through remote signalling, they could be used by a totalitarian government as a highly effective means of punishment and control.

The *temporal* decomposition of the reward function into two components, one representing the immediate reward and the other representing the estimated future reward, serves to exhibit an important facet of the decision-making process—namely, the way in which an individual, H, balances short-term gains against long-term losses. In a similar way, we can perform what might be referred to as a *relational* decomposition of the reward function into components that represent the rewards to other members of a group of individuals who interact with H. Specifically, suppose that we have a group of N individuals $H^i, \ldots, H^N$, with the reward function and action associated with H^i denoted by $R_t^i(u_t^i)$ and u_t^i, respectively.

As a very rough approximation, we assume that $R_t^i(u_t^i)$ admits of the following decomposition:[7]

$$R_t^i(u_t^i) = w_{i1} R_t^{i1}(u_t^i) + w_{i2} R_t^{i2}(u_t^i) + \ldots + w_{iN} R_t^{iN}(u_t^i), \quad (10)$$

in which

$R_t^{ij}(u_t^i)$ = reward accruing to H^j at time t as a result of action u_t^i taken by H^i,

w^{ij} = weight attached by H^i to the reward accruing to H^j as a result of action u_t^i, with $w_{i1} + w_{i2} + \ldots + w_{iN} = 1, 0 \leq w_{ij} \leq 1$, and

$R_t^{ii}(u_t^i)$ = self-reward = reward accruing to H^i at time t as a result of the action u_t^i taken by H^i.

The basic assumption underlying (10) is that the behavior of H^i is governed not only by the self-reward function R_t^{ii}, but also by a weighted combination of the rewards accruing to other members of the group as a result of the action taken by H^i. More precisely, this implies that when H^i is faced with a decision, he chooses the u_t^i that maximizes R_t^i, as expressed by (10), rather than the u_t^i that maximizes R_t^{ii}.

As in the case of the anticipation coefficient ρ, the relational coefficients $w_1, \ldots, w_N$ constitute important parameters of an individual's behavior and personality. In what way does an individual weigh the reward to himself in relation to the rewards to his family, close relatives, friends, enemies, coworkers, members of the same religion, residents of his community, fellow countrymen, and so on? Clearly, the answer to this question would be very different for a typical member of a primitive society than for a person of high level of culture and enlightenment. Indeed, the evolution of a society is directly related to the changes in the relational coefficients of its members, with an individual learning from his own experience, as well as from that of others, that it is in his

---

[7]As in the case of (7), implicit in $R_t^i(u_t^i)$ is the possibility that R_t^i may depend on other variables and actions in addition to u_t^i.

long-term self-interest to assign greater weight to the interests of others—not only those who are close to him, but also those who are remote.

In essence, then, once the reward functions IR_t, FR_t and R_t^{ij} have been identified, the behavior modification would involve, in the main, changes in the anticipation coefficient ρ and the relational coefficients w. In the past, changes in ρ and w were induced primarily by experience, education, religious training, political indoctrination, and other environmental influences. As implied by Skinner, the time is coming, if it has not come already, when the society will have much more effective means at its disposal for manipulating the ρ and w of its members, perhaps electronically or through systematic psychological conditioning on a mass scale.

To give a simple example of electronic manipulation in a small group, consider a group comprising just two members: $H^1 = $ husband and $H^2 = $ wife. Suppose that each has a device with a push-button such that, when the button is pressed, the other party experiences acute pain or discomfort induced by a probe implanted in or attached to the body. Thus, if H^1, say, takes an action that makes H^2 unhappy, then H^2 can retaliate by pressing her button, and vice versa. To limit the extent of retaliation, both H^1 and H^2 have a quota that varies from day to day in a random fashion and is not made known to H^1 or H^2. This rule is intended to induce H^1 and H^2 to use their push-buttons rather sparingly.

The point of this example is that the availability of means of retaliation is likely to have the effect of increasing the values of relational coefficients w_{12} and w_{21} in the reward equations

$$R_t^1(u_t^1) = w_{11}\, R_t^{11}(u_t^1) + w_{12}\, R_t^{12}(u_t^1) \tag{11}$$

and

$$R_t^2(u_t^2) = w_{21}\, R_t^{21}(u_t^2) + w_{22}\, R_t^{22}(u_t^2), \tag{12}$$

which govern the behavior of H^1 and H^2. However, excessive retaliatory capability or its misuse may, of course, result in a rupture of the relationship between H^1 and H^2.

The use of electronic means (rather than some other means) of retaliation in the preceding example is intended merely to make retaliation more convenient to apply and, hence, more effective as a modifier of behavior. The basic point, however, is that, whether in small groups or in large ones, the threat of retaliation plays an essential role in tending to increase the values of those relational coefficients that would be small in the absence of retaliatory capability. This is particularly true of the modern technologically based society, in which the degree of communication and interdependence between distant individuals and groups is far greater than it was in the past.

It has been experimentally observed of inanimate systems that, as the degree of interaction (feedback) between the constituents of a system increases, the system eventually becomes unstable. The same phenomenon may well be at the root of the many crises confronting modern society, particularly in race relations, pollution, mass transit, health care, power distribution, monetary systems, employment, and education. These crises seem to grow in number and intensity as technology—in the form of TV, radio, telephone, communication satellites, computers, data banks, jumbo jets, and the automobile—rapidly increases the degree of interaction between individuals, groups, organizations, societies, and countries. The "culprit" may well be the very basic and universal human desire for freedom, which makes it distasteful for most of us to accept the degree of control and discipline that is needed to maintain societal and interpersonal equilibrium in the face of rapid growth in the degree of interdependence brought about by technological progress. Thus, we are witnessing what may be called the *crisis of under-coordination*—a crisis that, in the main, is a manifestation of insufficient planning and control in relation to the extent of interaction between the constituents of our society.

We may be faced with the necessity to curtail our freedoms—perhaps rather extensively—in order to achieve survival in a technologically based, highly interdependent world of tomorrow. Perhaps this is the crux of Skinner's thesis in *Beyond Freedom and Dignity*.

In conclusion, it is quite possible that deliberate, systematic, mass-scale behavior modification employing Skinnerian techniques of operant conditioning, electronic monitors, computers, devices to alter brain function, and other paraphernalia of modern technology may become a reality in the near future. I, for one, do not look forward to that day.

12

Questions

Fred Warner Neal

Fred Warner Neal, an associate fellow of the Center for the Study of Democratic Institutions, is a professor of international relations and government at Claremont Graduate School. The most recent of his many books is War and Peace and Germany.

Here, a political scientist raises a series of questions concerning the social implications of operant conditioning. Neal feels Skinner left a number of important problems untouched in his book. "Skinner could now perform a very great service," Neal concludes, "if he would spell out how his theory could be applied to society, in concrete ways, to enhance the freedom and dignity of man. If he, or his adherents, fail to do this, the theory of operant conditioning could become a part of the literature of nonfreedom and nondignity."

If I understand Skinner correctly, what he is urging is a sort of systems analysis of the total environment, of which man is an integral part, to show us the way to make the human condition "better," if not ideal. This is an interesting and potentially useful exercise—made more so, possibly, by the unusual, if not esoteric, use of certain words. It puts a peculiarly twentieth-century American Protestant touch to a long line of concepts about man and society, starting, perhaps, with William of

Occam and including the French Encyclopedists, the later French sociologists, the nineteenth-century English and American utopians, and Kark Marx and his various apostles. The fact that human society now faces starkly the impact of exponential change lends both poignancy and urgency to considerations of this sort.

Skinner's main contribution, as I see it, is that he has posited a general theory about the absolute dependence of human behavior on environmental factors and the ability of man so to alter the environment as to produce desired kinds of behavior. The debate ensuing over this general theory may have enormous consequences.

At once, a comparison comes to mind between Skinner's theories and Marxist concepts. The main difference in underlying thought seems to be that, although Skinner generalizes about the need and possibility of altering human behavior through altering the social environment, Marx is specific about it in terms of application. Marx saw private ownership of the means of production as the basic negative reinforcing contingency—to utilize Skinner's language—responsible for all aversive controls and blocking all positive reinforcers leading to human betterment. Men themselves, once they understand this, according to Marx, could change the total social environment by eliminating private ownership and, hence, produce totally different—and better, if not ideal—human behavior.

Indeed, the absence of any suggestions for applicability of the "Skinner approach" to man and society was, for me, the most striking feature of *Beyond Freedom and Dignity*. The enunciation of a concept and the popularization of it can, of themselves, be significant. The lack of specifics of applicability in *Beyond Freedom and Dignity* does not, therefore, necessarily negate its value, even if it may limit its usefulness. But surely applicability, the possibility of applicability, of a social theory has to be involved in any consideration of the theory. After reading *Beyond Freedom and Dignity*, I turned with eagerness to Professor Skinner's earlier and more detailed work, *Contingencies of Reinforcement*. Here, even though this book is subtitled *A Theoretical Analysis*, I hoped I would find some indication of the author's ideas about how his theory might be used to bring about the utopian conditions he asserts are possible. Again, I was disappointed. Although he spells out in more scholarly details some of the experimental work underlying the general concept, and deals with the concept itself in a somewhat broader way, nothing is said or suggested about how we might utilize it in terms of the social environment. We are simply told, in both works, that we *can* do so.

The question arises as to whether the proponents of operant conditioning as a means of bringing about human betterment are not obligated, at some point, to deal with this matter. It has been characteristic of the physical scientist simply to fool around with natural laws and properties in the hope of discovering something new about them. The traditional attitude of the physical scientist, when the results of his experiments are translated into some terrible social product—nuclear weapons, for example—is to say, as Tom Lehrer quotes Wernher von Braun as saying, "That's another department." And in one way, of course, the physical scientist is right. The social uses of his experimentation are "another department." But a social scientist is in a different category, especially if, as is true of Skinner, the purpose of his theories is to change man and, further, to change him in certain specific ways.

Man, after all, cannot be changed—and especially changed in particular ways—simply by setting forth theoretical concepts, even if they are "scientifically" developed and their potential applicability tested by both "micro-logic" and "micro-laboratory" experiments. Indeed, to rest the effort here would seem to be procedurally faulty, inasmuch as the objective is "macro" in nature—that is, the environment of society as a whole. Because the objective is, more specifically, "human betterment," is there not a gap between Skinner's claim that his concept is broadly applicable to a society and his failure to deal with the question of how a society operates *qua* society? I have no quarrel with the idea that experiments on pigeons and dogs can tell us much about human behavior. Maybe such experiments can even tell us everything about the behavior of humans as individuals, although such a conclusion still must rest on faith rather than on scientific proof. Even if it were true, however, does it necessarily follow that contingencies which reinforce an individual man will also reinforce, in the same way, a large group of men, a human society? May there not be laws according to which a society moves which are different from those governing the behavior of individuals? Might not a society, once it starts moving, develop a momentum of its own which would, or might, create contingencies different from those envisaged by the "culture designers"? I don't know, nor, I think, does Skinner. Maybe the answers are unknowable. But does not the matter have to be dealt with? Is it not necessary to raise the questions and deal with their implications? There is, of course, a considerable literature dealing with the difference between individual and social psychology, but it does not, as far as I know, give us answers which could be utilized in conjunction with Skinner's theories.

Aside from methodology, the absence of treatment of applicability involves serious risks. I am sure Skinner is cognizant of them. If operant conditioning can be utilized for human betterment as he defines it— and I suspect most of us would be in general agreement with his definition—could it not also be utilized for human betterment according to some other definition, a definition which might not be to our liking at all? Could it not, in fact, be utilized for selfish aggrandizement by a powerful few? Obviously, both questions must be answered positively.

The last question takes us back to the question of the nature of societal development. We are all creatures of our environment, to an important degree. This is the essence—or one essence, at least—of Skinner's concept. How much are we prisoners of our social environment? Here, the time factor may be significant. Assuming that it is possible, theoretically, to tinker with the social environment so as to produce reinforcing contingencies beneficial to all mankind, at what point do the environmental changes so dominate the society that new directions are irreversible? The operant-conditioning theory posits that the existing social environment is flawed because it has produced undesirable reinforcing contingencies. These, in turn, produce various modes of undesirable behavior on the part of individuals, not because these individuals are "evil" in themselves but because they are responding to certain kinds of reinforcing contingencies. As I understand the theory, once the right kind of reinforcing contingencies are established, the right kind of human behavior will be produced. But this is not an overnight process. The possibility of instant social revolution is not asserted. Skinner himself implies that it would be a gradual process. Is it not likely that, long before man were made over, individuals representing the old man, reinforced by contingencies in the old society, would be tempted—if not absolutely impelled—to utilize, for their own ends, whatever operant-conditioning techniques were being utilized?

This is one problem the modern-day Marxists have to contend with, both conceptually and practically. Practically, the desired human behavior anticipated from a new general contingency—an end to private ownership of the means of production—has not materialized universally (within the Marxist-oriented societies). The social lag—if one may call it this—has been so persistent that it has, up until now, been an impediment in the development of the desired new contingency itself. Moreover, to make sure the desired contingency obtains, those who believe in it have been forced to take many steps which gravely distort the nature of the new society. This, if one assumes Stalin was a sincere Marxist-Leninist, can be considered a Skinnerian explanation of Stalinism. If one assumes that Stalin was simply a self-seeking ogre, then do we not have an example of an individual reinforced in the old ways taking advantage of the new contingency to prevent the goals originally anticipated. Either way, something unforeseen happened and produced unforeseen results.

Of course, it can be said—and it is true, to some extent—that the whole Soviet experiment, the whole socialist experiment, is so compara-

tively new that what has happened in the Marxist-oriented countries is
no basis for generalization. It could be argued also that the Soviet
Union abandoned Stalinism (although some would dispute this) and is
again back on the slow but correct road of developing the new reinforcing contingency in the proper way. There is another difficulty,
however, both of a theoretical and practical sort. The Marxist-Leninist
definition of socialism—the system produced, or produceable, by the
new reinforcing contingency of state ownership of the means of production—envisages political equality but economic inequality; that is, to
each according to his ability, which is, in part, the pattern of the old
contingency. Lenin wrote, for example, that it was necessary to utilize
the desire for personal gain developed under capitalism in order to
create the economic plenty needed for Communism, the end social result
of the new reinforcing contingency. But some students of socialism,
including certain Marxists, have queried whether this does not build up
and "reinforce" in individuals the very kind of behavior—individual
rather than group-oriented—which the system is attempting to overcome. Vladimir Bakaric, the Yugoslav Communist leader, has argued
that patterns of behavior which had one effect in a "capitalist environment" would have a different effect in a "socialist environment." Maybe.
Perhaps probably. But that the problem can be posed argues for the
necessity of dealing with it in connection with a theory of social engineering like Skinner's.

In addition to the confusion engendered by Skinner's methodology
and his neglect of specifics, I find also a problem in his idea about the
survival of a "culture."

Is a "culture" something beyond a social environment? Does it involve
certain values? If so, what values? For Marx, for example, culture seems
to be ultimately a part of the superstructure. Not only should it not
survive, it *could* not survive once the infrastructure—that is, the material
basis of society—changed. What does Skinner mean by culture? Is it
not a part of the social environment? Does it not have to be changed
fundamentally, if behavior is to be changed fundamentally? If it is
changed fundamentally, can it be said to have survived? How cultural
survival and changes in the social environment necessary to affect human
behavior can both be goals is not made clear. The difficulty might be
cleared up if culture were defined, in some way, as separate and different
from environment, or if the types of environmental change considered
necessary or desirable were spelled out. Or, it could be that only a
behaviorally designed culture—that is, one with the right kind of contingencies—can survive. In the absence of clarification about these
points, are we not left with some confusion between cause and effect?

The matter is important, as far as Skinner's concept goes, because so much emphasis is placed on "cultural survival."

Skinner sees the idea of "autonomous man" and the "literature of freedom and dignity" as impediments to conscious social engineering to produce human betterment. He makes an impressive case against the concept of the autonomous man. But does he really dispose of it? For example, if man can consciously alter his environment in desired ways, is this not an example of autonomousness? It is man's role as a thinking creature that is at question. In *Contingencies of Reinforcement*, Skinner deals with Descartes' dictum "*Cogito ergo sum*" as follows: "Descartes could not begin, as he thought he could, by saying, '*Cogito ergo sum.*' He had to begin as a baby—a baby whose subsequent verbal environment eventually generated in him . . . certain responses of which '*cogito*' was an example." Is Skinner here saying that the thinking process itself is determined by environmental factors? Or is he only saying that the results of the thinking process—the behavior—is determined by environmental factors? If the latter, does he mean that the thinking process has no independent function under any circumstances? If so, is this the same as saying that all humans will think—and react— in the same way, provided they are subjected to the same stimuli? If he is, indeed, saying this, then does not his conclusion rest largely on faith? And, if so, is not another conclusion resting on a different faith equally valid?

It is beside the point, it seems to me, to hypothesize about a Robinson Crusoe marooned as a baby. What we are concerned about is man in society, not a man on a desert island. Given society, there is an *ipso facto* social environment to which his thinking apparatus responds. But this is not the same as saying that, once stimulated, man's thoughts are absolutely controlled by environmental factors. Maybe they are. Maybe they are not. I can appreciate Skinner's concern that myth and superstitition, arrogating to man a special place in the nature of things and clothing him with values supposedly free of environmental influence, may stand in the way of man trying meaningfully to improve his condition. But even if we could prove this, it would not necessarily prove the totality of environmental dominance or the manageability of it.

Finally we come to the question of freedom and dignity. Here, it seems to me that Skinner is beating a dead horse—or at least the wrong horse. He himself is not opposed to freedom and dignity but to the misuse of these concepts in the "literature." I doubt if one can generalize about this. The "literature of freedom and dignity" can be divided into at least three kinds. One is the use of these concepts in a reactionary, if not dishonest, way. Selfish interests, desiring to perpetuate the status quo in their own interests, throw up the ideas of freedom and dignity as a method of preventing social change. A second kind is well-intentioned but emotional, if not mystical. It is claimed that there is a "divine spark" in man which sets him apart from all other beings and gives him, as an individual, the potential to rise above all environmental factors, at least spiritually. One can see how both of these kinds of freedom-and-dignity literature oppose social engineering of the kind proposed by Skinner. A third kind of this literature, however, is not necessarily opposed at all, as far as the general idea is concerned. It sees both value and limitations in man but believes that it is environmental factors which keep him from fulfilling his potential. It defines freedom and dignity as something really to be attained only when the noblest ideals of man are put into practice and made applicable to mankind as a whole. If this kind of freedom-and-dignity literature looks askance at Skinner's ideas, it is more because of fear or uncertainty about their applicability than because of dissent on a theoretical plane. Not only does it not oppose changing the human environment so as to affect behavior, it insists on such a course—but only to preserve and enhance human values. The writings of T. H. Green, among others, come to mind as an example of this kind of literature of freedom and dignity.

This third kind of freedom-and-dignity literature occupies a much more significant part of the total product than is apparent from reading Skinner. Indeed, his own works could be a part of this third kind, if they were more closely and explicitly tied in with the human values its exponents uphold and seek to enhance. One of the reasons why I would hope that Skinner will develop the practical side of his theory, and consider its pitfalls, is that, if he would do so, he could have this third kind of literature of freedom and dignity as an ally, rather than as an opponent.

Skinner could now perform a very great service if he would spell out how his theory could be applied to society, in concrete ways, to enhance the freedom and dignity of man. If he, or his adherents, fail to do this, the theory of operant conditioning could become a part of the literature of nonfreedom and nondignity. In that case, it may have done nothing more than open Pandora's box and help usher in a more nightmarish future than the one which Skinner fears will come about if things go on as they are.

13

Skinner and Human Differences

Arthur R. Jensen

Arthur R. Jensen is a professor of educational psychology at the University of California, Berkeley, and a contributor to many journals and books. Jensen is perhaps most widely known for his theories about the impact of genetic factors upon intelligence.

With this chapter, a developmental psychologist not entirely unfriendly to operant conditioning explores Skinner's behavioral assumptions. Jensen separates Skinner's views from those of his over-enthusiastic disciples and establishes that Skinnerism is far from incompatible with views widely accepted by nonbehaviorists. This is a useful corrective to the generalizations and inaccuracies about Skinnerism that have been published both by its supporters and by its critics.

If a thinker wants to guarantee that he will be misunderstood and misinterpreted to the world, he should have many disciples and followers. It also helps to have plenty of critics. They are often most expert at inventing and spreading misconceptions about the things they criticize. Among living psychologists, B. F. Skinner has had, by far, more than a fair share of disciples, followers, and critics. (In this respect, he is scarcely rivaled only by Jean Piaget, who also pays a similar price.)

So we have to distinguish carefully between the real Skinner and the Skinnerism of disciples and critics. I wonder how many others have noticed, as I have, that it is much easier to find fault with Skinner on the basis of writings *about* him—and I mean even the most sympathetic accounts—than on the basis of Skinner's own writings. My own disagreements with Skinner, on analysis, turn out to be merely disagreements in emphasis rather than any essential disagreement with his views of behavioral science or of man. I had long hoped that sooner or later I would get the chance to connect Skinner's work with some of the kinds of psychological and educational problems I have become involved with in recent years. Fortunately, his latest book, *Beyond Freedom and Dignity*, gives a number of direct leads for tying him to some of my own concerns.

My strategy here is to rectify (as I believe Skinner has not done loudly enough himself) what seems to me one of the most entrenched popular misconceptions of Skinnerism; and, to the extent that I may be wrong, I trust this will be rectified by Skinner himself. I am referring to the notion that all individual differences in human behavior, with the exception of those produced by brain damage or pathological conditions, are solely a result of differences in individuals' histories of reinforcements. That is to say, persons differ in their behavior wholly because of differences in their past environmental contingencies. I have had to argue against this notion with a number of true-blue Skinnerians. Skinner himself, as far as I am aware, has never made this claim. I do know that he has, in numerous writings, explicitly stated the contrary, but, until *Beyond Freedom and Dignity*, it has been in such hushed tones and surrounded by so much other seemingly contradictory material that, I admit, it is not hard to see why so many of his less critical readers have misunderstood him on this point. Skinnerism has been grasped by many ideological environmentalists as their scientific rationale, and I think the case could be argued that much that is made of Skinner's relevance to educational practices and policies really derives, not from the analytical applications of his laboratory research to the technology of teaching, but to his misconstrued environmentalism. The famous "Hollow Organism," which is so often ascribed to Skinner but is actually an artifact of Skinnerism, is, of course, also empty of genes, or at least any genes that could make for intraspecies behavioral differences. Thus, human differences can be viewed as amounting to no more than the individual's history of environmental contingencies, as accidental and imposed externally, thereby preserving the illusion of inherent equality. The apparently supreme importance of this belief to many persons may be based on what I maintain is a mistaken conception—namely, that "inherent equality" (like "autonomous man") is a fundamental premise for the validity of the "equality" referred to in the phrase "All men are created equal" in the Declaration of Independence.

I hope that Skinner has not been too reinforced by the obvious signs of comfort that some persons seem to have derived from misunderstanding him on this point. I have discovered a most interesting thing about humans' reactions to individual differences. It may even have a more profound significance for understanding the human condition than I am yet fully aware of. This is the fact that other persons warm up to us whenever we do or say anything that ignores or minimizes individual differences. And this is very reinforcing, believe me. Like all reinforcement, it shapes our behavior. But it is an interesting thing to observe, when one becomes conscious of it; it seems to be almost an instinctive human emotion (my apologies to Skinner). I wonder why? One can see it (and feel it) on a large scale in lecturing to an audience; one's statements that point up human differences or try to analyze them evokes glum, tense expressions. But then say something that minimizes differences and you feel a rushing glow from the audience— such reinforcement, and such inducement to continue in the same vein! Tell them that Einstein, as a child, was a late talker, and that he didn't do too well in grammar school, either, and the audience will love you. So we have to watch it, and be careful not to let our beliefs about reality be shaped by such scientifically irrelevant reinforcers. This interesting human tendency probably accounts, at least in part, for the relative unpopularity of differential psychologists, whose business it is to study human differences, when they try to be objective scientists. And popular prejudice casts "hereditarians" as the "bad guys" and "environmentalists" as the "good guys." Thus, many who preach popular Skinnerism are in for certain rewards that may not be accorded to Skinner himself or to those who take the trouble to read him thoroughly.

The most insistent message running through nearly all of Skinner's works, one that he keeps hammering away at in many forms at every conceivable opportunity, is the abolition of "autonomous man" from behavioral science, indeed, from all our thinking. Skinner's position is nicely epitomized in the following statement:

> What is being abolished is autonomous man—the inner man, the homunculus, the possessing demon, the man defended by the literatures of freedom and dignity.
>
> His abolition has long been overdue. Autonomous man is a device used to explain what we cannot explain in any other way. He has been constructed from our ignorance, and as our understanding increases, the very stuff

of which he is composed vanishes. Science does not dehumanize man, it de-homunculates him, and it must do so if it is to prevent the abolition of the human species. To man *qua* man we readily say good riddance. Only by dispossessing him can we turn to the real causes of human behavior. Only then can we turn from the inferred to the observed, from the miraculous to the natural, from the inaccessible to the manipulable [pp. 200–201].[1]

Because I seem to have grown up with this view, it does not appear startling to me. And I think it is a view that is now taken more or less for granted by perhaps the majority of psychologists of my generation. It is part of the mainstream in the history of American psychology coming through Watson and Thorndike and Skinner. But the gross Skinnerian misconception that so many psychologists have derived from this view is that, by getting rid of autonomous man, we can explain all of human behavior in terms of *external* (that is, environmental) circumstances in the individual's personal past history and his current situation. I emphasize *external* because it is deemed "Skinnerian" to eschew the "inferred" in favor of the "observed," and the "manipulable" in favor of the "inaccessible," in describing the causes of human behavior. I doubt that Skinner would knowingly endorse the kind of gross sensory-motor positivism that some of his followers have read into these kinds of statements. Other sciences that are more highly developed than psychology have not found it profitable to eschew inference or that that is inaccessible to direct observation by our unaided senses, least of all nuclear physics. So I see no reason for imposing any such restrictions on behavioral science.

The fact is that all of human behavior, and particularly individual differences, need not be explained and cannot be explained solely in terms of external contingencies in the environment—at least not the external environment of the individual. If we want to bring in the environmental contingencies that have shaped the evolution of the species through genetic selection, that is another matter. "Autonomous man" is, of course, no more acceptable to the evolutionist's or the geneticist's view than to Skinner's. In fact, what I am about to point out is that these views are all essentially the same. We might call them the biological view of man. As far as I can see, it is the only conception of man and behavior that we can say or do anything about scientifically. We find buried inconspicuously in one of Skinner's earlier works the following hint of his recognition of genetically conditioned behavioral differences. He points out interspecies differences in capacity to be rein-

---

[1]Throughout this paper, page numbers in square brackets refer to pages in Skinner's *Beyond Freedom and Dignity* (Alfred A. Knopf, 1971).

forced by certain kinds of events—"What is reinforcing to a horse need not be reinforcing to a dog or a man" (Skinner, 1953, p. 75). These are clearly seen as inherited characteristics. About intraspecies differences, Skinner (1953, p. 196) wrote:

> Differences in hereditary endowment, which are too conspicuous to be overlooked when we compare different species but presumably are also present to a lesser extent between members of a single species, account for other differences in repertoire, as do differences in age . . . or in development. . . .

Skinner finally surfaced completely on the issue of the genetic aspect of behavioral differences in his article "The Phylogeny and Ontogeny of Behavior" (Skinner, 1966), but apparently the substance of this rather difficult essay was not enough like Skinner's other writings to have become assimilated as an integral part of Skinnerian behaviorism. This is unfortunate, because the view put forth in that article, I think, affords a proper perspective for human behavior genetics and the study of human differences.

In a still more recent work, Skinner (1968, p. 241) is quite explicit in what he says about individual differences, acknowledging but minimizing their genetic aspect:

> Differences in speed of learning and forgetting, and as a result in the size of the repertoire which may be acquired and maintained, have political and other implications which have made them the subject of continuing debate. These are presumably the main differences shown by measures of intelligence. Their nature is not clear. Speed of learning is hard to define. It can easily be shown that the behavior of a pigeon changes as the result of one reinforcement, and the human organism can presumably not learn more rapidly than that. There remain, however, great differences in such aspects as the extent of the change which may take place upon a single occasion, the speed with which complex repertoires may accumulate, the extent to which they can be maintained without mutual interference among their parts, and their durability. The practical question is not so much whether these differences are genetic or environmental as whether environmental contingencies may be designed to reduce their scope. . . . If the differences are genetic, different methods of instruction may be needed, but a great deal can probably be done to reduce the range of differences of this kind through environmental measures.

Now, in *Beyond Freedom and Dignity*, Skinner gives full, though not detailed, recognition to genetic behavioral differences, and he lists the denial of a genetic basis of behavioral differences as one of the misrepresentations of behaviorism [p. 166]. The "environmentalism" of

Skinner is essentially no different from that of modern genetics, inasmuch as Skinner traces genetic variability to differential environmental influences through genetic mechanisms in the evolution of the species. In a sense, an organism carries with it, in the genetic code and gene frequencies, the effects of distant environmental contingencies in its evolutionary past. In Skinner's words, "As a science of behavior adopts the strategy of physics and biology, the autonomous agent to which behavior has traditionally been attributed is replaced by the environment—*the environment in which the species evolved* and in which the behavior of the individual is shaped and maintained" [p. 184, emphasis added]. Skinner extends this view to include "cultural" differences:

> A culture, like a species, is selected by its adaptation to an environment: to the extent that it helps its members to get what they need and avoid what is dangerous, it helps them to survive and transmit the culture. The two kinds of evolution are closely interwoven. The same people transmit both a culture and a genetic endowment—though in different ways and for different parts of their lives. The capacity to undergo the changes in behavior which make a culture possible was acquired in the evolution of the species, and reciprocally, *the culture determines many of the biological characteristics transmitted* [p. 129, emphasis added].

This theme has been greatly elaborated upon with a wealth of examples by a leading British geneticist, C. D. Darlington (1969). Though it is probably no surprise to Professor Skinner, we may wonder how many Skinnerians could have imagined that "environmentalist" Skinner and "hereditarian" Darlington would be found espousing essentially the same view on fundamental issues. And when Skinner writes as follows, there are shades of Sir Francis Galton and the British eugenicists who followed him, to say nothing of William Shockley!

> The designer of a culture is not an interloper or meddler. He does not step in to disturb a natural process, he is part of a natural process. The geneticist who changes the characteristics of a species by selective breeding as by changing genes may seem to be meddling in biological evolution, but he does so because his species has evolved to the point at which it has been able to develop a science of genetics and a culture which induces its members to take the future of the species into account [p. 180].

At this point, I am reminded of the concluding paragraph of a most interesting essay by sociologist Kingsley Davis (1964, p. 204):

> If and when it does come, the deliberate alteration of the species for sociological purposes will be a more fateful step than any previously taken by mankind. It will dwarf three of the previous most revolutionary steps: the

emergence of speech, the domestication of plants and animals, and the industrial revolution. The reason is simple: whereas these other changes were socio-cultural in character and thus subject to the limitations of man's capacities, the new development would be both socio-cultural and biological. It would, for the first time, enable man to overcome the sole limit on socio-cultural evolution, the limit set by his innate capacities. These capacities would change very slowly, and quite probably in a downhill direction, under present conditions of inadvertent selection. On the other hand, deliberate control, once begun, would soon benefit science and technology, which in turn would facilitate further hereditary improvement, which again would extend science, and so on in a self-reinforcing spiral without limit. In other words, when man has conquered his own biological evolution he will have laid the basis for conquering everything else. The universe will be his, at last.

So now that I have established Skinner's bona fides in the genetic-behavioral analysis of human differences, I should like to push the matter a bit further in order to force some consideration of problems that I think are important and quite germane to the topics of *Beyond Freedom and Dignity* but that are rather shirked therein.

Individual differences in behavioral characteristics are a central fact, both to psychologists and to people in general. Differences are fundamental data, in the sense that all people have always noticed them and wondered about their causes, and they are conspicuously related to the reward systems of every society we know anything about—which, of course, makes them very important to everyone. Note that it is not just the *particular* behavior that is important (though it may be important, too), but the fact of human differences itself that is important. This is true, whether we like it or not. One type of differences that are of such importance in many societies are those behaviors and all their correlates that are measured by what we happen to call "intelligence tests." Skinner (1953, p. 198) has expressed his disappointment with the IQ as a behavioral datum because it does not describe or quantify any behavior per se, and this, of course, is true. The score yielded by a test has meaning only in reference to a population; it is a comparative index, not an absolute measure of the individual's behavior. Skinner correctly likens it to the scale for expressing the hardness of minerals, which are ordered in terms of which mineral can scratch but not be scratched by another mineral when they are struck together. The degree of hardness of any one mineral is meaningless without reference to another. In fact, the notion of hardness might not even occur to us in this context if we did not first notice differences in hardness between minerals. But Skinner says that "such a scale is unquestionably useful for technological purposes, but it does not greatly advance the study of the hardness of minerals," as would, for example, an explanation of hardness in absolute, noncomparative terms, by reference to molecular structure and the like. True, an explanation of hardness must probably resort to some form of description at the molecular level. But I think this misses the point and mistakenly belittles the comparative scale. For the observed *differences* is where the question of hardness began in the first place, and the differences are every bit as much a basic datum as the molecular structure of any particular mineral. Moreover, the explanation of hardness at the molecular level must, in the final analysis, accord with the findings of our comparative scale, or we might conclude there is something wrong with the explanatory theory. In short, the fact of observed differences and our comparative scale of measuring them not only poses the question of their explanation but provides the criterion for the validity of the answer. I believe this is a good parallel to the whole problem of ability testing and the study of individual differences in general.

If we are concerned mainly with controlling behavior by operant techniques, we quickly realize that practically any bit of behavior responds to reinforcement contingencies. This is impressive raw fact: reinforcement contingencies change behavior. But the next step, taken by so many Skinnerians, is not fact: that is, when we observe a behavioral difference between two organisms, we may say the difference must be due to different histories of reinforcement. And one can always point to circumstantial differences in individual histories, which adds to the plausibility. But this second step, we know, is both logically and factually wrong.

Concern with shaping behavior by means of reinforcements understandably gives the investigator in this field a rather particularistic view of behavior. Having this particularistic view of behavior is probably one of the more common characteristics by which we might identify psychologists who turn out to call themselves "Skinnerians" or one of the impersonal synonyms that mean much the same thing. We find that these persons have little or no use, usually even a dislike, for more general behavioral terms like "traits," "abilities," "aptitudes," and so on—terms that figure so prominently in the technical vocabulary of the differential psychologist. It is usually in terms of traits and abilities that psychologists describe and measure individual differences. Behaviorists originally decried these terms, probably because they identified them with the "mentalistic" inner homunculi they were trying to get rid of in the study of behavior. But most present-day differential psychologists, it should be noted, are behaviorists, too. I, for one, have no use for mentalistic homunculi, any more than Skinner has. Yet I think it is beating a dead horse to eschew traits and abilities, which are probably the most valid and useful terms for the description of individual differences. All we mean by such terms, essentially, is that we are dealing with behaviors that have a high degree of *reliability* (that is, in the same circumstances, the individual's behavior is consistent from one time to another) and *generalizability* (that is, the individual's behavior is consistent in a wide variety of circumstances). These characteristics of behavior can be treated in ways that, in principle, are just as empirical, just as operational, as is change in response rate under a schedule of reinforcement. So behaviorism really has no justification for excluding differential psychology, other than the legitimate grounds of a division of scientific labor, or for presupposing that all the subject matter of differential psychology can simply be subsumed under the study of reinforcement contingencies. Hardly anyone disputes the idea that skills, abilities, aptitudes, and all their behavioral correlates are acquired (that is, learned) in an environment and depend upon various contingencies of reinforcement or feedback—this is granted. What are not entirely attributable to environmental contingencies—and, in some kinds of human behavior, are hardly attributable at all—are differences in rates of acquisition, in the age at which rate is maximal, in the relative effectiveness of reinforcing contingencies, and in the asymptote of performance. All of these may be influenced by environmental contingencies, but they are also attributable to organismic factors—that is, causal factors that are not referrable to the subject's personal experiential history. Interspecies differences in these respects are obviously so great as to require no further comment, and they are acknowledged throughout the writings of Skinner and other behaviorists. From these writings, however, one might easily gather that the magnitude of intraspecies differences of this sort is so minute, by comparison with interspecies differences, as to be practically insignificant, and minute also in comparison with the differences that are attributable wholly to environmental contingencies. This, I believe, is a mistaken belief. It may be true of a particular behavior or a particular subject. As a general rule, however, it is most doubtful. At Berkeley, for example, it has been possible, by selective breeding, to obtain different strains of laboratory rats that differ in maze-learning ability by four times as much as any differences the investigators have been able to induce by a combination of environmental means, including direct training on mazes.

There are wholly objective, operational means for determining whether differences are attributable to external contingencies or to genetic factors and for determining how much each source contributes, on the average, in a given population. These are the methods of quantitative genetics. We have learned from the application of these methods to the study of human behavioral differences that, in the case of some traits and abilities, among these being the kinds of behavior we classify as intelligent, a large part of the variance indeed is attributable to genetic factors. If a particular class of behavior has what is called high heritability, which can be objectively ascertained by some specified set of operations, we know that a large part of the observable differences in that behavior is caused by genetic factors rather than by differences in the external environment. Though differences in the external environment may actually exist, they are not, in such a case, the major cause of the observed behavioral differences. Genetic variation is the rule in nature. Without it, there could be no biological evolution; it is the mechanism by which natural selection operates and by which environmental contingencies leave their mark on future generations. The elimination or denigration of human diversity is inconsistent with evolution and negates the possibility of biological adaptation to the changing demands of the environment.

Apparently, however, there is some price to pay for behavioral variability, especially in those behaviors deemed important by society, such as intelligence, and we have not yet learned really how to handle this problem. Individual differences in socially valued behaviors have always been too conspicuous to ignore. But, in a sociopolitcal sense, they are benign, as compared with *group* differences in such behaviors. Groups are the result of classification—whether in terms of geographic origin, physical characteristics, economic status, occupation, sex, or whatever— and can be quite arbitrary. Although group mean differences in any characteristic are really just an average of *individual* differences classified by some particular rubric, they can, when viewed in this collective form, be social dynamite, if the behavior in question is socially valued and economically rewarded and if the mean differences between groups are large relative to individual differences within groups. The problems are magnified when group membership is rigidly imposed and the group identity of individuals is highly visible, as in the case of physical characteristics associated with racial classification. Yet there is no fundamental distinction, in a genetic or behavioral sense, between group differences and individual differences; the former are produced by some arbitrary classification of the latter. If there are a number of correlated characteristics and we classify on the basis of one, we thereby automatically classify also to some extent on the basis of the others. We can urge doing away with classification and groups, we can make laws against discrimination in educational opportunities, employment, and housing on the basis of group membership, we can insist upon equality before the law, and we can advocate considering only persons' individual characteristics rather than their group membership as a basis for social relations. All well and good. What we may not accomplish by these means is equality of performance in those behaviors that are deemed valuable by society and are rewarded accordingly. If we repeatedly look for the causes of differences in ability to acquire a socially valued skill (such as reading, for example) in the external environment and are hard put to find a convincing explanation there, but we also refuse to consider any factors other than external ones as possible causes of these differences, perhaps we sow the seeds of a kind of social paranoia—a need to find an external cause to blame for the observed differences, a cause on which to vent the frustration and aggression that arise as a consequence thereof.

General intelligence—a large class of correlated behaviors—is the most embattled of psychological concepts just because of its important social consequences and because individual differences in intelligence are so large and so obvious to the pragmatic man in the street. If intelligence tests had never existed, it would not make the least bit of difference socially. That is why it always seems so fatuous to talk about doing away with IQ tests, as if it would make any real difference. How else to explain the fact that the average correlation between the IQs of marriage partners is almost as high as the correlation between various standard intelligence tests? (Husbands and wives are more alike in IQ than brothers and sisters reared together in the same family.) And how else to explain the fact that, when people are asked to rank-order various occupations in terms of their own subjective impression of their "prestige" and "desirability," they come out, on the average, with a ranking of the occupations that correlates between .70 and .90 with the rank order of the actual mean IQs found for members of those occupations? Let's face it: we are dealing, here, with a prime reality.

A division of labor in science is necessary, and it would be foolish to criticize Skinner or any of his followers for concentrating their attention on a particular aspect of the study of behavior. But when what began as a division of labor gets generalized to the broad aspects of social philosophy, as we see happening now with Skinner's work, the comparative lack of emphasis on those important phenomena of behavioral science that are subsumed in other divisions of labor becomes uncomfortably conspicuous. I would propose that people's realistic perceptions of individual differences (and perhaps group differences, too) have extremely important behavioral consequences. They can act as positive or negative reinforcers or as punishment. Here, I venture, is grist for Skinner's mill that he has not yet begun to grind. Assuming that my analysis is not altogether amiss, I would hope his creative intellect will sooner or later go to work on it. Let me mention some of the specific issues that I think need to be considered in this hoped-for extension of Skinner's thinking.

Differential psychologists speak of behavior as having *structure*. It is something more than a mere cumulation of everything one has learned, something more than a history of operant contingencies. Structure means there are relatively stable patterns of correlations among many behaviors, and many previously unobserved behaviors may be predicted probabalistically from a knowledge of this structure. Moreover, all behavioral correlations are not merely a product of common learning—that is, the overlapping of numerous smaller units of behavior with common reinforcement histories, or a result of transfer due to "identical elements." There are four main causes of correlations among behaviors in the domain of skills, abilities, aptitudes, and so on, and these causes are not at all mutually exclusive: (1) dependence of the behavior upon common sensory or motor capacities (this is trivial in most so-called mental tests); (2) part–whole functional dependence—that is, one behavior may simply be a subunit of some other behavior, such as (*a*) shifting gears smoothly being a subunit of (*b*) passing a driver's test consisting of driving your car around in city traffic with an examiner present; (3) hierarchical functional dependence—that is, one behavior is prerequisite to another, or, conversely, one is functionally dependent upon the other, as skill in working problems in long division is dependent upon skill in multiplication; and (4) genetic correlation among behaviors, apparently due to common assortment of their genetic underpinnings through selection and homogamy, and to pleiotropism (one gene having two or more seemingly unrelated phenotypic effects). Methods are available for distinguishing purely functional correlations from genetic correlations.

Factors derived from the methods of factor analysis no more deserve to be dismissed as mere "mentalistic fictions" than the physicist's unobservable pi mesons and neutrinos can be dismissed as "physicalistic fictions." A factor is not any specific observable bit of behavior, and I'm not sure anyone would know how to go about reinforcing factors, but I imagine one could, to some extent, change a factor structure or create new factors through operant techniques. It is surely possible to do so through genetic techniques. One can, for example, selectively breed in or breed out factors in a given population, or markedly increase one factor and decrease another, which shows that some factors (but not all) have a strong genetic basis—that is, the behavioral intercorrelations from which they are derived have a substantial genetic component. The well-known *g* factor (*g* for general) of human abilities is quite clearly of this nature. One of the most impressive phenomena to the differential psychologist is the high degree of correlation found between seemingly quite different behaviors, each of which, presumably, must have developed under exceedingly different histories and types of reinforcement contingencies—for example, the high correlation found between such seemingly diverse and unrelated behaviors as defining the meaning of words in a vocabulary test, completing such number series as 2, 5, 8, 11, _?_, and copying geometric forms, such as those shown in the accompanying figure (The Gesell Institute's Figure Copying Test). All of these disparate tests, when factor analyzed among many other tests, have their largest loadings (that is, sources of variance or differences among persons) on the *g* factor.

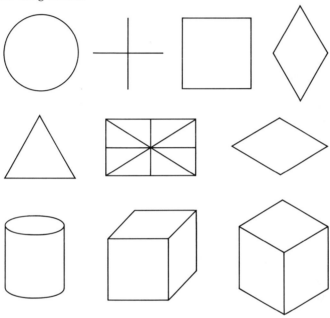

The ten simple geometric forms used in the Figure Copying Test. In the actual test booklet, each figure is presented singly on the top half of a $5\frac{1}{2}'' \times 8\frac{1}{2}''$ sheet. The circle is $1\frac{3}{4}''$ in diameter.

Another thing: there is something about the behaviors on such tests that can lead one who studies them to have such seemingly heretical, nonbehavioristic, not to say antibehavioristic, thoughts as "behavior is the medium, not the message." Now I may really be getting into trouble with Skinner; but I think this has to be cleared up. I think there are structures *inside* the organism, presumably in the brain, that may get laid down in conjunction with particular operant contingencies, but that then become quite independent of them. For example, we find that a child can spontaneously perform up to a certain level on the Figure Copying Test illustrated here, but then practice on the test, and even direct instruction, will not much improve his performance; merely getting six months or a year older will do a lot more. Is this because he has picked up more skill at drawing, through practice and environmental feedback, in the intervening months? I doubt it. More likely, some autonomous growth process has taken place in his brain. It is an interesting thing that drawing skill—that is, the sheer behavioral act of copying these figures—seems to be the "medium, not the message," in the sense that the essential of the child's performance remain the same if he copies with his nonpreferred hand (with which he has had so much less practice in drawing) or even with the pencil held between the toes of his foot. The artistic or draftsmanlike quality suffers, to be sure, but the essentials of the drawing do not. If a child can't copy the diamond with his foot, he can't do it with his preferred hand, either. The behavior, in other words, seems to be guided by a central program; it is *conceptual* rather than just behavioral. Shaping the behavior by operant techniques may shape the "means" but not necessarily the "message." All untutored children who can copy the cube, for example, can also copy the diamond without any trouble. But take a child who can't draw the diamond (he won't be able to draw the cube, either) and train him (if you can) to draw the cube (it will be fantastically more difficult than your most pessimistic expectations), and then see if he can copy the diamond. The child usually can't do it, when this sort of thing has been tried. An older child does not have to be taught any of this. If he learns it (beyond learning how to work a pencil), we do not known when, where, or how. I think most behaviorists have not paid sufficient attention to these kinds of behaviors (I hesitate to call them "cognitive"), which are not so readily shaped by operant contingencies.

Similarly, I think the behavioral handicaps of the retardate or the psychotic are not merely a product of their reinforcement histories, and, although some of their behavior may be shaped to conform to certain standards by operant conditioning (often a valuable thing, indeed), they will not become "normal" persons through these behavioral techniques. Their problems are essentially structural or biochemical—inner, autonomous mechanisms gone awry. Again, the behavior is the medium, not the message.

This brings me to the whole subject of mental development. (As a behaviorist I have no more dread of saying "mental" than has the astronomer in saying that the sun "rises," even though he knows all school children are taught that the sun doesn't "rise," but that the earth revolves.) I believe that behavior has a kind of biological integrity, such that, in the long run and to a large extent, it is not at the mercy of a capricious environment. Genetic mechanisms are a kind of gyroscope for stability in the long-range course of development. From moment to moment, day to day, perhaps even week to week, behaviors are wafted hither and thither by environmental contingencies, but, in the long haul, the most important behaviors (which usually turn out to be those strongly conditioned by genetic factors) show an increasing stability and predictability that there is good reason to doubt can be attributed to a consistent piling up of a reinforcement history. The genetic endowment that the individual starts out with in life is a capricious thing, the total parental genes having acted as a pure random lottery from which the offspring got its shake (of one-half the parental genes), for better or worse. But beyond that point, genetic capriciousness ends. From then on, the environment is the capricious factor in the individual's development, and, in most cases, he can thank his lucky stars for the long-range stability of the course of his development laid down by the genes. This is true, to a large extent, of physical growth and also, I believe, of behavior. It is interesting, for example, that children who are subjected to a period of famine, such as the year or two of extreme famine in Poland and Holland near the end of World War II, show a retarded growth rate and stunted development, but then quickly catch up when adequate food rations become available; and, as adults, these children are indistinguishable in statute from those who never underwent starvation (Harrison et al., 1964, chap. 21). There are parallels in behavior. The most dramatic illustration is the famous case of Isabel, the girl who was reared, for the first six years of her life, by a deaf-mute mother in a semidarkened attic and had no other human contacts until she was found by the authorities at the age of six (Davis, 1947). She had no speech, no language, and the behavioral development of an infant, with a Stanford-Binet mental age of less than two years and an IQ of about 30. Removed to a normal home where she was cared for by a nurse, she gained about six years of mental age (an enormous gain in behavior repertoire) in only two years. This is a rate of gain in behavior repertoire that would be found in a normal environment only in a child having an IQ of at least 300! The gain lasted, but the fantastic rate did not persist: at eight years of age, Isabel was able to keep up with her age-mates in school; from there on, she simply progressed at the rate of an average child.

In Head Start programs, we typically see the other side of this phenomenon; workers in compensatory education call it "fade-out." That is, quite often the dramatic short-term accelerated gains in behavioral repertoire induced by especially intensive instruction and environmental manipulation simply "fade-out" in the course of the next year, and the children are soon found to be right back on the same mental or scholastic-achievement "growth" curve that is found for the control group, which received no induced behavioral spurt some months earlier. It is interesting to me that achievements (that is, scholastic-behavior repertoire) measured at regular short intervals throughout the course of the children's schooling, when intercorrelated, form a matrix of correlations that fit beautifully what is called a simplex model. That is to say, the growth in achievement, when measured at many points along the way, can be interpreted in terms of the cumulative addition of *random* increments—so capricious are the short-term environmental influences affecting rate of gain over short intervals. But, for the individual growth curves to fan out and approach quite different asymptotes, another feature must be added to the model: the random increments, i, before being added into the cumulative total at each point, must be multiplied by a constant, c, which has a different value for different individuals. It might be called a coefficient of consolidation—that is, how much of the gain from point 1 to point 2 actually "sticks" or gets "consolidated" so as to have a discernable influence at point 3. "Mental age" is indexed in terms of behavioral repertoire; it is ci plus the i of the immediate past. The c, in this case, is the individual's IQ. Notice that I said "gain from point 1 to point 2"; I did not say "from time 1 to time 2," because time along a linear scale is merely incidental in this context. The essential underlying continuum, of which points in chronological time are merely a correlate in the individual's development, is increasing complexity of behavior, or of "cognitive structures," as Piagetian types might prefer to say. The asymptotes toward which the processes tend in these kinds of behavior are quite strongly conditioned by genetic factors; this we now know with considerable certainty.

I think there can be little doubt about the fact of "readiness" for acquiring behaviors of various degrees of complexity, and I doubt that all differences in readiness are due to differences in prior histories of reinforcements or other external environmental factors. The degree to which it is, for any given class of behavior, is an empirical question to be answered by evidence, not debate. I wonder about the effects on a child lacking readiness for acquiring a certain complex behavior of subjecting him to environmental contingencies designed to shape up the desired behavior. The behavior may appear to be shaped up today, but will it be consolidated in such a way as to be available tomorrow, to transfer to the acquisition of still more complex behaviors? I don't know. But I think I have seen, in some school learning situations, what look to me very much like experimental extinction, conditioned inhibition, experimental neurosis, and the emotions of frustration and aggression that often are a part of these phenomena. The more enduring consequences of repeated early failures are not so much of an intellectual nature as they are emotional and motivational. "Turn-off" occurs, and then further learning does not take place at all in a particular domain. The subject learns, instead, to avoid the very contingencies that would make for successful learning. "Intelligent behavior," in some spheres, might be extinguished.

There are great individual differences in readiness in acquiring such complex behaviors as reading, for example. The extent to which this is viewed almost as a national calamity is seen in such lofty pronouncements as the U.S. Office of Education's "Right to Read" campaign. Many people wonder why the countless millions spent on research on reading instruction has not been more effective—meaning why don't all children learn to read more or less equally well when taught (as the majority are) at about six years of age? (Fewer people ask this question in the Scandinavian countries, where reading instruction is postponed till age seven; yet, as far as we know, Scandinavians finally read as well as the French, who begin at age five.) Some people can't understand why the schools can't teach all children to read at about the same age just as easily as all children learn to talk at about the same age. Surely, speaking a language is very complicated behavior, too; yet virtually all children learn it between two to three years of age, merely through exposure and without any special instruction. Only a very few children suffering from severe brain damage or rare single-gene or chromosomal defects fail to acquire language. But I think there is an important difference—a difference one would not suspect, if he viewed all behavioral repertoires equally as the cumulative result of operant conditioning. If some children have so much more trouble learning to read than they had in learning to talk, the argument goes, we must be doing a rotten job of teaching reading. In fact, some children do learn to read as readily as they learn to talk, and it is partly because of this, perhaps, that so few questions were asked about reading until the enforcement of universal education. In bygone days, only the good readers survived long in school. But with universal education and a social order that is avowedly intolerant of illiteracy, learning to read becomes a critical matter, and a large spread of individual differences, for those in the lower quarter of the distribution, becomes a calamity.

Vocal language, on the other hand, seems to be a species-specific characteristic. It does not need to be built up or shaped laboriously through the conditioning and chaining of myriads of behavioral units. Language is learned, to be sure, but learning a species-specific form of behavior is quite different, in terms of individual differences, from the learning of many other kinds of behavioral repertoires. In species-specific behaviors, learning capacity for a class of behaviors has been more or less maximized and individual differences have been more or less minimized; there is little genetic variation, but so much genetic determination for the ease of acquisition of certain behaviors that capricious environmental contingencies, within very wide limits, have little effect on the acquisition of the behavior. (We often therefore tend to call it "development" rather than "acquisition.") Lenneberg (1969, p. 638) has reported studies of language acquisition in monozygotic and dizygotic twins, permitting analysis of genetic influences. The age and rate of language acquisition, and the specific types of problems encountered, show a high degree of genetic determination. [To those who have read Skinner's *Verbal Behavior* (1957), I recommend also Lenneberg's *Biological Foundations of Language* (1967).] I suspect the same is true for reading, although the range of individual differences is much greater. Some children pick up reading as easily and inconspicuously as most children learn to talk or walk. Others must be carefully and laboriously tutored and coached. The difference can be much like teaching speech to a child who has suffered damage to Broca's area: he must learn with another part of his brain, a part that is much less adpated for language learning. Some teachers comment that children who have to be explicitly *taught* to read, rather than learning it from rather casual exposure, seem to have to learn something different from what is learned by the child who doesn't require careful teaching. The final behavioral result may, of course, be rather indistinguishable. But the effort involved surely is not, nor are the chances for extinction and frustration. The problem of teaching reading to all children at the same age is that the contingencies that work so well for some pupils do not seem to work much at all for others, or they work so poorly that the job they must do cannot be accomplished in the little time available for such instruction. "Human freedom and dignity" become a question, too, when we ask about how much time a child should be forced to spend in order to acquire a particular behavioral repertoire by a certain age. What price equality of performance? we might ask. We might also ask whether instructional time schedules and methods that evolved to some reasonably satisfactory degree of effectiveness in one culture, or in a limited range of genotypes for certain abilities, can be transplanted wholesale to other cultures or populations and still be effective for the majority of subjects. With universal education, there are only a few fields in which teachers can simply look for pupils who can learn practically without being taught (they are called "talented") and can let the others fall by the wayside— music, the arts, higher mathematics, and chess. Arthur Rubinstein, the famous pianist (who was also a child prodigy), made an interesting comment in a recent interview. He said, "To become a great pianist, you have to practice a great deal. But there is really nothing to *learn*. So there's nothing much you can teach anyone about it. You have to practice only in order to develop your talent." Many music teachers say similar things; the elite among them simply drop or won't accept those pupils who need to be taught. Fortunately, society doesn't demand that everyone become a musician. It does demand that everyone acquire the content of the basic curriculum of the school and that they spend ten to twelve years or more of their lives expressly for this purpose. Anyone who reads the daily papers knows of the problems this generates.

In *Beyond Freedom and Dignity* [p. 6] Skinner asks the rhetorical question: "Was putting a man on the moon actually easier than improving education in our public schools?" The answer will seem obvious to the many who interpret the question to mean that education must be quite lacking, for what should be so difficult about improving education as compared with the astounding feat of putting a man on the moon? But I think the answer is really not so obvious. Putting a man on the moon, at least, is a clearly defined criterion, of which the failure or success of attainment is easily assessed. As for "improving education," it is not clear to me just what criteria Skinner has in mind.

What most educators, government officials, and writers in the popular press who talk about the present problems of education are, in fact, referring to is not dissatisfaction with some *absolute* level of achievement, but rather with the large group *differences* in educational attainments that show up so conspicuously in our educational system—the achievement gaps between the affluent and the poor, the lower-class and the middle-class, the majority and the minority, the urban and the suburban, and so on. It is differences, not absolute level of performance, that seems to be the cause of all the concern. Skinner, in his concern with the control of individual behavior per se, hardly faces this problem at all. Yet the problem of differences is, apparently, where the action is, where the billions of dollars in educational funds are being spent, where the heat is on, and where the schools are being torn apart. A careful study of today's popular literature of injustice and inequality, it might be noted, shows that it appeals not so much to demonstrated inequalities of rights and opportunities as to inequalities of *performance*, from which, usually, inequality of opportunity and other injustices are inferred. This seems especially true today in education. What has behavioral technology à la Skinner to offer to the solution? I would not be surprised that it might have a great deal to offer—but it may not be obvious, so I wish Skinner would spell it out, if only programmatically.

When teaching machines and programmed instruction, backed up by Skinnerian rationale, made their appearance in the 1950s, it seemed to me that they generated great enthusiasm. (I was an enthusiast myself, though I never got into the mainstream of their development.) This approach, teaching machines and programmed instruction, was hailed by some as the solution to our educational problems. From what I have seen, they *do* work, they *are* an effective and efficient means of teaching—certainly more effective than most ordinary classroom instruction—and children like them and seem to learn more effortlessly from them. These techniques are not used enough, certainly far less than their merits would warrant. But as far as I am aware, their applications have given no hint that they are capable of solving the problems connected with *differences* in educational performance. Where I have seen teaching machines and programmed instruction in apparently competent and systematic use in school settings, it slightly raises the overall level of achievement and greatly magnifies the spread of individual and group differences. It appears that any new instructional technique that proves good for the educational "have nots" proves even better for the "haves." One of its main virtues, however, may be that it permits children to learn on their own at their own pace, with little or no knowledge of what their classmates are doing, so that the child's learning behavior is not afflicted by the punishing contingencies of perceived differences in performance.

One might simply dismiss the whole issue, urging that performance differences are inevitable. If there is no solution, there is no problem: there is simply a state of affairs. But this attitude just won't do. Society sees this as one of its major problems, a crucial one, and is in turmoil over it. A large part of the trouble is that individual differences so often get tabulated so as to show up as group differences—between schools in different neighborhoods, between different races, between different cities and regions, and so on. They are then a political, not just a psychological, matter. To reduce the social tensions that arise, we see proposals to abolish aptitude and achievement testing, grading, grade placement, special classes for the retarded and the gifted, neighborhood schools, the classroom as the instructional unit, the academic curriculum, or even the whole school system. There is probably a good deal of merit to some of these proposals. But I think they are too often aimed at covering up problems rather than at coming to grips with them.

Inasmuch as whatever instructional technique aids learning for the "slow learners" usually turns out to do even more for the "fast learners," the particular philospher's stone now being sought by many educational psychologists, myself among them, is what has come to be called Aptitude X Training Interactions, or ATI for short (also called aptitude X instruction interaction.) What ATI means, simply, is that no single instructional method is best for everyone; that optimal performance will result only by matching a diversity of instructional methods with the diversity of individual aptitudes. If Bill and John are both taught by method *A* and Bill does much better than John, perhaps there is a different teaching method, *B*, that will permit John to learn as fast as Bill. That is the hope of ATI researchers. The only trouble, so far, has been that, when you find a method *B* that boosts John's performance a little, it usually does so even more for Bill. Hence, back to the drawing board. Bracht (1970) recently reviewed a large number of studies in the ATI field that met certain methodological and statistical criteria to permit rigorous evaluation, and he found that, out of 90 studies that were specifically designed to yield aptitude X treatment interactions of the kind that would solve the performance difference between Bill and John, only five actually yielded such an interaction, and none of these aptitude differences was of the IQ variety—they were personological variables unrelated to intelligence. Bracht (1970, pp. 636–638) says a number of interesting and important things:

> When a variety of treatment stimuli, especially conditions not controlled by the experimenter, are able to influence performance on the dependent variable, it is unlikely that a personological variable can be found to produce a disordinal interaction with the alternative treatments. . . . Success on a combination of heterogeneous treatment tasks is predicted best by measures of general ability [i.e., IQ tests], and the degree of prediction is about equally high for alternative treatments. . . . The degree of task complexity may be a major factor in the occurrence of ATI. Although the treatment tasks for most of the 90 studies were classified as controlled, the treatments were generally relatively complex tasks. Conversely, four of the five experiments with disordinal interactions [ATI] were more similar to the basic learning tasks of the research laboratory. . . . Despite the large number of comparative experiments with intelligence as a personological variable, no evidence was found to suggest that the IQ score and similar measures of general ability are useful variables for differentiating alternative treatments for subjects in a homogeneous age group. These measures correlate substantially with achievement in most school-related tasks and hence are not likely to correlate differentially with performance in alternative treatments of complex achievement-oriented tasks.

In view of these conclusions, unless we come up with something drastically different from anything that has yet been tried, the prospect of substantially minimizing the overwhelming influence of IQ differences (whether measured or not) on scholastic achievement seems quite dim. Of course, scholastic differences get reflected in the occupational market, and IQ does even more. As Harvard psychologist Lawrence Kohlberg recently put it, "Scholastic achievement merely rides on the back of IQ."

In terms of society, the absolute level of "have-not-ness" does not constitute the most aversive contingencies; it is rather the perception of *differences* between the "haves" and the "have nots" that leads to frustration and aggression. Punishment is *relative* poverty, not absolute poverty. A society that truly creates equality of opportunity and encourages a high degree of social mobility in accord with individual

abilities and drives but allows very unequal rewards for unequal performance may find itself in serious trouble. Yet how much can rewards be
equalized without risk? If high abilities are a rare and valued resource
to a society, can it afford not to provide every inducement to attract
scarce ability into those pursuits in which it is most needed for the well-
being of the society? Is our culture's system of rewards and punishments all wrong? Should we attempt to decrease the spread of some
kinds of human differences, and, if so, which ones and how? Or must we
accept them and learn to live with them, and, if so, how? Is perhaps a
complete reorientation of societal values in order, a new orientation
that somehow takes the sting out of differences in the abilities to com-
pete and achieve? What will be the resolution? The answers are not
clearly inferable from *Beyond Freedom and Dignity.*

Now that B. F. Skinner has taken the mantle of social philospher as
well as that of behavioral scientist, we should like know how he thinks
about these questions. What he might have to say is likely to be enlightening and worthwhile.

14

Skinner's New Broom

Alexander Comfort

Alexander Comfort, an associate fellow at the Center for the Study of Democratic Institutions, describes himself as a "medical biologist, writer, and pamphleteer, dividing time equally between science, literature, and politicosocial agitation of various kinds, chiefly connected with anarchism, pacifism, sex-law reforms, and application of sociological ideas to society generally." He is the author of a number of novels, poems, plays, essays, and texts.

Comfort, whose special interest is gerontology, contributes an evaluation of operant conditioning that, among other things, finds it compatible with certain assumptions characteristic of philosophical anarchism. He credits Skinner with constructing an important generalization about human behavior and with presenting it in a scholarly and "forbearing" style. Nonetheless, Comfort feels Skinner has failed to deal satisfactorily with a number of facts of human life, and he uses a computer technology to make clear some of his objections to behaviorist theory. He concludes by stressing the importance of understanding the value of Skinner's "real insights," without losing sight of other causes of human behavior that he feels are not dealt with in Beyond Freedom and Dignity.

Rebuking the "excesses" of classical behaviorism (oversimplification, extrapolation from rats in boxes) has become something of a formality for writers about human behavior. Skinner's book is highly salutary, because it reminds us that the excesses were not of his sponsoring. The reservations on the totality of his model are real enough, but they do not spring from narrowness of view. We need to begin with a clear idea of the reservations; but when we have made them Skinner still confronts us with an important generalization for which a place must be found. Not many possessors of so wide a generalization present it in so scholarly or forbearing a style.

The reservations in regard to human behaviorism are Freudian in form but biological at root: they are, essentially, that Skinner tends to overlook the substratum or "wiring" on which memory-based reprogramming is imposed. In other words, he tends to assume, though obviously he doesn't think, that the system is being programmed from scratch, and infers that all of the software of human behavior is added by simple experiential stimuli, aversive or reinforcing. (More accurately, he nowhere infers that it is not.) To this, one has to point out that:

1) Certain behaviors are probably laid down in the hardware—by way of the epigenesis of the nervous system—and since this hardware includes a developmental clock, they may be exposed serially or turned on and turned off, rather as animal sex behaviors are turned on or turned off by simple hormones.

2) Part of this ongoing program may well be the inclusion of programmed "spaces" in which experience writes in further program preferentially—like the gaps in a printed workbook which the student is expected to fill in for himself. "Ethical" behaviors other than altruism in defense of mate or progeny, the substratum of Haldane's "moral biology," are practically confined to social animals: they occur in dogs, for example, but not in cats. (Dogs relate to other conspecific individuals, and to man, who is an honorary member of the club, in a way that cats do not, though by intensive training they might well come to do so.) This could be because social animals are subjected throughout life to special reinforcement of these behaviors; or because genetic selection has short-circuited this learning process by printing out much of the required "text" in the animal's hardware, leaving spaces which are especially readily filled, at a particular moment in development, by minimal reinforcement. This is a special case of "evolution making organisms more sensitive to the consequences of their actions." In other words, Skinner ignores the possibility of imprinting—special, high-speed learning at a particular point in development and facilitated by built-in arrangements—and of archetypes, or preferred patterns of association. Had he worked initially with ducks rather than rats I think this element would have bulked larger in the Skinnerian view. The male duckling

imprints maternal plumage with minimal experience and uses the response later in mate slection: if male hormone is given to an adult female, she will then imprint like a newborn and androgenless male. Human imprinting is less easily pinned down by reason of complexity (this is much the same problem as that which agitated our predecessors over human instincts), but the early fixity of abnormal human sex objects, and the presence of the Oedipal anxiety period as a temporary organ like the tadpole's tail, when aversive stimuli are extra effective, if not endogenous, make any biologist highly suspicious that such programmed critical periods do exist.

3) A hardware–software interplay as complex as that in man may carry a fair amount of its behavioral conditioning in an internal form—that is, wholly endogenous mental events can be aversive or reinforcing by continuous playback, once they are set in motion. A well-developed system of this sort in man, and the special neurology of pleasure or reward centers, may well explain why one critical aversive experience plays back and generates anxiety, the name we give to the introspection of the playback process, and could explain the Freudian consequences of infantile programs persisting out of time.

4) In disposing of gremlin-type mentalism, which sees us as a spirit thinking thought and initiating behaviors, Skinner underplays the importance of the identity sense, which is an experience even if it is an illusion (or rather, it is a potential but society-generated mental "organ," like the body image), and the human capacity to scan part of the program and its printout, as it were, downwards. It is not certain, as Skinner asserts, that the intelligent man doesn't experience his intelligence or the disturbed teen-ager his disturbance; I would have thought that they did. Rejection of the autonomous "I" also raises difficulties over the exact meaning he attaches to "environment," but this is a matter for arbitrary definition.

I worded this preamble in this way on purpose. Both the reservations on Skinner and the great importance of the issues he raises can be expressed without falling foul of biologically based, as opposed to metaphysical, neo-Freudianism, and this is the pattern Freud himself, as a pretty hardheaded biologist, would certainly have preferred. Accordingly, if we take in the reservations, Skinner's new broom can do nothing but clear the fairies out of depth psychology, a task which primatologists, and biologists generally, have long waited to see undertaken. The reservations and the importance of the issues can also be discussed in computer terminology, though Skinner avoids this. It is the analog model most suited to this kind of basic and operational analysis of a learning system. Moreover, it emphasizes the first major Skinnerian proposition—which was there before, but needs hammering into arts graduates and biologists who haven't done too much thinking about thinking, or who like Aristotelian entelechies. This is, quite simply, that if we could construct a fully mechanical system which exactly replicated the complexity of human mentation, either it would show all of the attributes (conation, spontaneous behaviors, free will, neurosis, the lot) which exist in the biomechanical system that is writing this piece, or there are fairies at the bottom of our garden. Accordingly, a mechanistic evaluation of behavior at some level, provided it isn't naive and is based on a knowledge of what mechanical analog systems can already do, is intellectually obligatory, and we had better come to terms with it. All of the major hangups of philosophy (free will, values, aesthetics, and so on) must be incorporable into, and soluble by, a sufficiently subtle recognition of the interplay by which existing, and developing, mental circuitry, incorporated into our genes and nervous systems, programs experiential exposure and is in turn further programmed, and altered, by it. Skinner doesn't to my mind stress this complex model nearly enough. He is so concerned with the effect of the input on behaviors from the environment that he treats experience as a mold impressing itself on wax rather than as a dialogue between hardware and input which both alters the hardware and generates programming. Both the hardware's capacity for generating initiatives which the environment "answers" and its serial character (it asks appropriate experiential questions at appropriate moments, and has a space to write down the answers, which modify its future wiring plan) seem to be left out. This neo-Pavlovianism is already out of date in dealing with our own relatively simple mechanical systems. The more sophisticated model is harder to handle but far more rewarding—there is nothing difficult, if we use it, about the idea that values represent a "space" in the program of social animals, which evolution selected because it shortens learning, and which is filled by conditioning; or that "free will" can represent a process of selection (partly programmed, partly conditioned) acting on a process of random variation. Nobody need now get sleepless over how a process can be both indeterminate and programmed—any electronics buff will make a simple Skinnerian free-will system to order for the confused philosopher to play around with. On the other side, it is the answer, though Skinner doesn't make sufficient use of it, to the perfectly valid objection that what is aversive or reinforcing in man can be pretty complex, because of the virtuosity of a two-way system in converting pain to pleasure or pleasure to pain by avoidance, equivalence, symbolism, and an evening-out of tensions.

Freud recognized the "acceptance of pain in the devious pursuit of pleasure," and this is not confined to the man who can only get an orgasm by being beaten or insulted. (It is also the answer—a Sherringtonian one—to the old psychoanalytic argument over hedonism: for "pleasure" read "balancing up central excitatory states for minimum tension"; most animal psychologists would read "libido" as "the pursuit of a minimum-tension, rather than a maximum-tension, economy," and the reward mechanisms are superimposed on this, "drives" of various kinds being endogenous, programmed states which tilt the balance and initiate further equilibrative behavior. This, at least, is how one would build an experimental analog.)

One extremely important aspect of operant conditioning, not fully discussed on this occasion, is its use in enabling subjects to control involuntary body processes (heart rate, blood pressure, alpha rhythms, penile erection, peristalsis) by voluntary effort. The subject cannot verbalize the nature of the operation—all that is necessary is that the "feedback loop" is completed by providing a visual or sound display which indicates to him when the desired change is taking place. It has been claimed that, in yogic meditative states, internal sensing suffices without any external cyb-org sensor. If the change, whenever it occurs, is reinforced, the subject becomes rapidly able to control the "involuntary" process at will. The medical potential of this use of body image to manipulate the body has not yet been assessed (it has already been used to control brain potentials and prevent resistant fits), but it may be large. Any development in this field would tend to bring operant conditioning into still greater clinical use and familiarity—even, if successful, into controlling states such as tension or insomnia, into competition with drug therapies, and, possibly, into military or political abuse.

The system in this type of physiological control, which is a special use of operant conditioning, is really analogous to that used in a simple demonstration given by Skinner, in which a dog is taught to jump by marking lines on the wall and rewarding it whenever its head rises above the lowest line. The function of the display loop is simply to make the subject continuously aware of changes in the variable and of the direction of those changes. In the case of the dog, the feedback loop is provided by the experimenter; in the case of heartbeat control, the subject must be given a scaled indication of change on which reinforcement can operate. In the use of operant conditioning to treat impotence, the subject may desire a particular physiological end result which would be reinforcing if it occurred, but has no moment-to-moment index of the appropriateness of his own internal states, so that he inhibits erection by anxiety, and the result is self-defeating through aversion. Introduction of a mechanical readout of, for example, skin tension or penile blood flow provides a continuous monitor on which operant conditioning can act to reinforce appropriate inner behaviors and bypass central interference. Erection at will or control of alpha rhythms are permanent physiological maneuvers, once learned. It is still arguable how far control of, say, blood pressure could be made permanent if continuous monitoring were provided.

Physiological states are not commonly classed as "behaviors" and controversy over their control (uses, abuses, hazards) is likely to follow the same lines whether drugs or training methods are employed, although training methods have both the advantages and drawbacks of not being time-limited by natural breakdown. Most controversy about the use of operant conditioning in society is likely to arise over the alteration of behaviors recognized as behaviors, and its uses and risks are those of education, of which it is a form, but from which it appears to differ in being specifically more effective. I am concerned in this paper solely with the more usual application—that is, the alteration of behaviors ranging from alcoholism to commuter travel habits—but the more practical, physiological use is worth stressing because, if it proves effective, the change in techniques of dealing with physical dysfunctions will accelerate both research and acceptance, and affects any technological forecast. In behavioral contexts, operant conditioning is likely to spread if it first proves efficacious and side-effect free in psychiatry and criminology. In both of these contexts it will be tested against longstanding irrational attitudes, as it would be in more political contexts.

So much for the biology—I have gone through it telegraphically so as to avoid a long paper, but the point of it is that Skinnerism *is* reconcilable with the totality of present knowledge, though Skinner, even in a highly scholarly book, doesn't here do the extra expounding which is needed to reconcile it. If we built a man-analog incorporating all of the models I have outlined, it would probably work in a human manner.

In the analysis of all less complex social interactions, Skinner's basic extrapolation, though simple, is highly valuable. It goes beyond a new angle on "God is Love." It is the universal experience of all studies in empirical human relations—education, penology, pyschiatry, manageagement—that reward works and punishment does not, that reinforcement is more effective than aversion and avoids its ill effects. But all our institutions, except the consumer economy, are designed on the reverse assumption. People with knowledge in this field and people with power are basically two different tribes—one can pardon Blake for wondering if they were not two different species. Skinner is not alone in failing to come to terms with the biology and psychopathology of the extraordinary human phenomenon of power-seeking. It is far more complex than simple dominance behavior, and may well, as Freud thought, express programming derived from the family situation. The fact that Skinner goes on to make social assumptions, to foresee the end of "autonomous man," and to make suggestions which will at least be interpreted as proposals for social management, makes only too evident the gap left in his psychology by the absence of a perception of the structured nature of human irrationality. A pessimist view would read the future differently than he. Some of the humane insights of what he has to say may get (are already getting, by other routes) an expression in such things as management and education: in wider contexts—society in general, political life— they risk being applied only to misuse, because organizational power lies only with professional mismanagers, who reward the short-term nondisturbance of their own roles, and might be able to manage a nonaversive velvet-glove facade. In spite of his attack on other utopians, Skinner is the daddy of them all. The crunch is real enough. On the one hand, we must both be social and accept planning of nonindividualistic kind in order to survive; on the other, given the selection of psychopaths to office and of office by psychopaths (pardon, by people conditioned to kick other people around and manipulate them for antisocial or frankly deranged ends), there is no more likelihood that such planning will be rational or constructive than there was that constitutions would be written by philosopher kings, or, when written, observed by their officials. This being the case, Skinner could be seen as the philosopher of repressive tolerance, of keeping them happy for the public good. There are two possible ways out of this difficulty. First, there is the fortunate fact that individuals subjected to nonaversive patterns in education, the family, and their own life style will *also*, and in a more marked degree, respond to coercive authority by extreme aggression. This may indeed be already happening. Second, nonaversive techniques, being purposive, select against self-destructive personalities and power-seeking psychopaths, while our present techniques actively favor, if not create, them. Punishment, for prohibitive persons, is an end in itself. Skinner stresses the seriousness of a situation in which a high proportion of youngsters refuse military service. I myself would stress the far greater seriousness of the situation in which they did not. Unless the antiaversive sieve is fully effective, however, it is really no letout to say that we should concentrate our insights on the circumstances in which nations go to war. Can he see Brezhnev or Kissinger actually backing this? And is not his behavioral technology more likely to be enthusiastically researched by them for ways of keeping conscripts from mutiny, voters from protest, and underdeveloped countries from resenting exploitation? Just as, at the biological level, Skinner, for all his range, has bitten off a fraction more than he can chew, so with his social extrapolations, humane as they are, he might eventually be aghast at the operational outcome of what he writes, and its takeover by that irresponsible old harridan, Laura Norder, because his capacity for intuitive (that is, nondiscursive) intake of social events is basically poor. He lacks the aptitude of the primitive wizard and the mystically unscientific psychotherapist to respond to complex social signals, and, since theories, even when true, are the product of personality, one must wonder if a Skinnerian generation wouldn't lack the same aptitude and if this wouldn't basically alter the character of man. This capacity for highspeed nondiscursive intake, or sensing of society, is another faculty of social animals, and an analog capacity of the human computer program, which Skinner's book almost wholly lacks (which is possibly why it didn't convert its critics, or disarm them, by reinforcement). It is hard to say which came first, the chicken or the egg, but the theory both reflects the lack and could perpetuate it—theory and deficiency reinforce each other, though Skinner, like his creation Frazier, is not a product of *Walden Two*. Anyone with psychoanalytic training will be deeply impressed, here, by the interplay between the man and the construct—and not simply *ad hominem*, because Skinner gives depth psychology a rough ride; what is urgent, since they are dealing, from different aptitudes, with the same material, is some kind of dialogue between them directed to the exchange of insights.

At the same time, Skinner survives both ignorant misrepresentation and rational reservations by sheer force of intellect and genuine and unparanoid humanity of intention. By devoting this paper to possible reservations, I neither can, nor wish to, dismiss what he says. His chapter on values is memorable in particular. As an anarchist, I find the time-stressed need for planning, and for getting events and people into shape to plan, as much my nightmare as anarchy is the nightmare of administrators. I cannot answer the original-sin problem any more than he. The difficulty is not that man is "sinful" as an innate attribute, but, more probably, that having evolved in a small-group, food-gathering culture, his organizational needs have outrun his adaptations. They probably did so at the time, less than one thousand generations ago, when he invented cities and kings, when adaptations designed to stop male infant primates falling foul of their fathers combined with dominance-behavior to create institutional and basically aversion-maintained power. A traditionalist, and this includes Skinner, often makes the unspoken assumption—far closer to "original sin" as originally taught, but at variance with the rest of the book—that men, being as they are, cannot afford to dispense with institutional power, at least at the manipulative level. The anarchist view is that men, being as they are or are likely to be, cannot afford *not* to dispense with it. The anarchist, like Skinner, is dedicated to a socially oriented autonomy, and he also regards the experience of sociality as itself highly reinforcing, once it can be attained—that is, he hopes, like Skinner, that a truly social society would be self-maintaining through its own feedback, if only enough of us experience it (compare *Walden Two* with Aldous Huxley's *Island*). That men have survived so long is partly due to the effect, that Skinner mentions, that aversive and coercive techniques generate revolutionary aggression. Human countersuggestibility, though it is itself learned, is an adaptive character. We have survived so far through sheer bloody-mindedness and the fact that, if the managers dig holes in Irish roads to stop gunrunning, people fill them in overnight. We are not rationally committed to the defense, at all costs of "our"—possibly lethal—culture. There is nothing in this book which tends to the abolition of man. A one-shot revolutionary would probably say that our culture would come into its own after the revolution: those who believe that revolution is a continuous process with no further side, including both the conservation of a culture and its radical reform, have to undertake the more difficult task of integrating its very real insights with the things it leaves out.

It is hard to know what aspect of the academic environment is to blame for the fact that Skinner on paper is aversive to some, while Skinner the man is not. Fear, no doubt, plays a part. So does Skinner's wry sense of humor. Some readers found the book abrasive. I must say I do not. It could be argued that Skinner is reinforced by criticism and tends to invite it. If he had substituted the word "education" for "control," or even the word "training," he might have lubricated the acceptance of his ideas. It is worth pointing out to quaking traditional liberals that, though he himself is not an anarchist, the society he postulates could be truly in line with anarchist (not totalitarian) insights, and his data explain why nonviolent experiments have tended to work until suppressed by society. Anarchists are opposed, in principle, to aversive government, not to education, and they favor the inner-directed man, substituting mutual aid for free competition and direct action for centralism. In essence, Skinner is answering the libertarian or anarchist dilemma—how to educate men to be social without the use of a coercive apparatus generative of abuse and of acting out. In being antiaversive, his pattern includes an important and unique sieve mechanism against precisely the abuses which anarchism rejects in democracy. Operant conditioning is no diabolical device invented by Skinner. It is only the mechanism by which many human behaviors have always been programmed (whether it is a sufficient paradigm for all behaviors is beside the point: it is a useful one for some of those most socially important). What he offers is the attempt to make their use insightful instead of random.

The problem of normation remains. *Walden Two* described an agreeable society, reminiscent of the Amish and dedicated to the propagation of Skinner's own personal life-style. Another community adopting the same techniques could have adopted another style—one more sexualized, for example. Were operant education to be confined to community-sized experiments, the individual could choose, but such communities would be bound to diverge and encounter communication and inbreeding interface problems, since, if the techniques worked, they would be homeostatic for their differing mores and society might become tribalized. I don't, however, see this as a likely model. A more likely one is the application of Skinnerian, noncoercive methods of socializing behavior first to psychiatry (chiefly among groups about which society is in despair—the anomic, the autistic, the alcoholic); then to practical problems such as patterns of commuter travel. (What reinforces our insistence on the one-man private car? If it is enclosure, isolation, and sense of control, plus door-to-door convenience, then modular, not mass, transit, is a thinkable answer.) Then to the key problem of coercive societies, the self-defeating and self-propagating penal system; and finally to the abolition of play-therapy-type politics. Such politics can solve no existing urban problems; a technique which could would have an overriding necessity behind it. Population is another educational field where government is traditionally unable to think beyond aversive forms of social instruction. I have set out a possible technological forecast for the time-scale of changes that a comprehension of these factors in forming behavior might generate. I have omitted the intriguing idea that the constituency, or a scientific part of it, faced with psychopathic acting-out in office, might try to zero in on particular leaders by operant techniques going beyond sending a box of Cuban cigars to the President every time he withdraws more troops from Vietnam. The forecast assumes a 75 percent correctness (the approximately likely limiting value for a single experimental insight, however far-reaching) for the idea that the operant paradigm alone will modify human behaviors.

Operant Conditioning—A Possible Scenario

(*Note:* Bear in mind that we commonly overrate effects of 5- to 10-year applications and underrate effects of 15- to 20-year applications.)

Years	*Effects*
>5–<10	Psychiatric, educational, and industrial experiments on an increasing scale.
>7–<15	First semimacro experiments in civic use, up to city, but not to state, scale (for example, reform of commuter traveling habits). First examples of abusive use (for example, for military or commercial ends).
>10–<20	Wider abuse, exciting protest from a scientific and public constituency increasingly alerted by success in constructive use. Control mechanisms evolving. Launching of environmental and antiaversive "parties" or movements, themselves using operant nonaversive methods. Vogue of nonaversive and operant child-rearing. Operant Dr. Spocks and Ralph Naders become prominent. Operant-reared persons begin to become common.
approx. 20	Conflict stage: Attempts at takeover by opposing interests; attempts at employing suppression; simultaneous acute intensification of resistance from those responding to operant methods leads to failure of such attempts. Operant New Deal, based on an educated, environmentalist, scientific, and libertarian–anarchist constituency (libertarian here meaning those who oppose aversive conditioning, favor education and inner-direction, and oppose conventional power structures). Hahn–Strassman point for macro use equals end of conventional penal system (this is probably the test change in attempting to dynamite the conventional establishment). International applications outside the scope of this forecast, but relations with U.S. clients will already have shifted by *force majeure* from backing military-fascist regimes. People least impressed may well be a growing cadre of urban guerrillas who see operant conditioning as bourgeois revisionism.
>20–<25	Early macro experiments, state and federal scale, starting with population, education, and penology. Massive growth of decentralization, ad-hocracy (that is, officials appointed ad hoc for a particular contract and removable in terms of success/failure). Integration of new style into frame of conventional U.S. democracy.
>25–<50	Transition of present political structures to a new operant-conditioning–anarchosocial style.

Likelihood: Reasonably strong (10-year forecast, 75 percent probability; 50-year, 90 percent; 100-year, 97 percent). I base this on the following consideration:

A critical point of operant conditioning is that it substitutes reinforcement for hostility. If operant conditioning worked well, it would be the answer to the "anarchist bind" I foresee between the need for intensive, planned, group action to avoid major systems failures, the growth of a public which is ungovernable by aversive, coercive, or malarkey techniques, and the tendency of present institutions to reinforce antisocial behaviors in office. It could get its constituency by a fusion of growing environment threats, anger over irresponsible policies of industry and politics, mutiny against overseas war, unmanageability of urban problems, the basic wish of Americans to avoid unproductive civil violence, and the now emergent "libertarian" (antipolitical, antiaversive, concerned) style. If operant techniques worked, they could end or limit acting-out in public life. I suspect that there will be less rewriting of constitutions and democratic rituals than reinterpretation of their meanings. Legitamacy and democracy will persist and mean something different, being experienced differently with a different life-style of the culture, as British monarchy now is something diametrically opposite in sense to British monarchy in the time of Washington. The British monarch is now a bung or blocking piece to prevent any other person or persons from occupying a position of power—for example, Commander-in-Chief, source of appointment and dismissal of judges. Institutions can be preserved and titles maintained to guarantee a power vacuum, and this may occur in the U.S. In fact, there is only a limited number of public contexts in which an ideological devotion to operant conditioning is likely to pay off, and these (which aim chiefly to substitute cooperation or "mutual aid" for coercion and "free enterprise," and intelligent purpose for play therapy in office) will need blocking-off mechanisms to prevent an abusive counterrevolution from emergent new sources of power.

Marxism is right in saying that, on most past occasions, this sort of change has involved an emerging class. This new class will be a constituency of those now getting aversive vibrations, not Skinner's fixers. Whether you call these neoproletarians (who have nothing to lose but everything) "workers" or "intelligentsia" seems beside the point. They represent a new dispossessed constituency which is acquiring power.

Psychoanalytic critics might ask why operant planning would be less likely to be irrational than any other. My forecast is based on the following consideration: The attraction of an operant scenario is that it should exclude many acting-out opportunities and personalities from public roles via the antiaversive "sieve." This point is critical. Whether anti-

antiaversive education and child-rearing would also exclude the genesis of neurotic behaviors in the long term remains to be seen. It should, at least, reduce them. I want to stress this point, since I accept both depth psychology and behaviorist paradigms as simultaneously relevant to the forecast.

15

Beyond B. F. Skinner

Lord Ritchie-Calder

Lord Ritchie-Calder, a senior fellow at the Center for the Study of Democratic Institutions and formerly a professor of international relations at Edinburgh, is the author of 32 books, most of them on science or its social implications.

Lord Ritchie-Calder continues the exploration of the social and political implications of operant conditioning. He would "bracket together Ellul (the means swallow up ends), McLuhan (the medium becomes the method), and Skinner (the end of autonomous man) as latter-day determinists who are 'hooked' on technology. . . . Their forebodings, given the weight of scientific findings, become predictions that confirm trends, inasmuch as policy-makers start planning for, and not away from, the conditions they foresee." Lord Ritchie-Calder considers this a bleak proposition and finds comfort in the observation that young people and many others are "questioning the . . . technological system. . . . This is a return to real (human) values, as against artificial (machine) values."

At the Paris Conference on Information Processing in 1959, Dr. Edward Teller expounded as follows: "If you give a machine a large enough memory, and give it enough random trials, it will remember those trials which are successful. It will thus learn. I believe that the machine can be given the powers to make value judgments and, from that, I construct, mathematically, a model for machine emotions." I intervened to ask him whether his machines would ever make love, and he replied, "Yes—dispassionately."

In this banter (if one can connect that word with Edward Teller), it was pretty clear that the "value judgments" he had in mind were logical conclusions that a self-educated machine might arrive at independently of its human programmers—but scarcely the values of morals or ethics, or of freedom or dignity, or of passions, good or bad. Now that B. F. Skinner proposes to abolish these, Teller can get down to the drawing board.

Frankly, I should rather have his version than Skinner's—machines thinking like humans rather than humans thinking like machines. "What is needed," says Skinner, "is more 'intentional' control, not less, and this is an important engineering problem." That is the understatement of the megalennium: "important engineering problem" refers not to transistors, circuits, and feedback but to persons, societies, and cultures; and the answer is to be found in the "technology of behavior," although, as he admits, behavioral science on which such technology could be based is a poor foundation because it "continues to trace behavior to states of mind, feelings, traits of character, human nature and so on." He says,

> It will not solve our problems, however, until it replaces traditional pre-scientific views and these are strongly entrenched. Freedom and dignity illustrate the difficulty. They are the possessions of autonomous man of traditional theory and they are essential to practices in which a person is held responsible for his conduct and given credit for his achievements. A scientific analysis shifts both the responsibility and the achievement to the environment. . . .

In the pigeon-loft of my persona, the aversion conditions and reinforcements seem to have produced a perversity that may justify Skinner's worst misgivings about "autonomous man." I cannot understand how shifting the responsibility redeems the human predicament.

As Harvey Wheeler remarked in a discussion of Ellul's *The Technological Society* at the Center, "He [Ellul] leaves the reader with a strong feeling of methodological paranoia. . . ." For me, Skinner does the same with *Beyond Freedom and Dignity*. It is eloquently written and vigorously argued. It is aggressively defensive, as it must be when its very title deliberately "asks for trouble" and periodically troubles the author. In the end, to assuage the wounded vanity of man, the self, he says man can "promote a sense of *freedom and dignity* by building a sense of *confidence and worth*." Which brand washes whiter?

I would bracket together Ellul (the means swallow up ends), McLuhan (the medium becomes the method) and Skinner (the end of autonomous man) as latter-day determinists who are "hooked" on technology. They chose a field. They analyze selectively. They write persuasively. They produce *obiter dicta* that become slogans for the credulous. Their forebodings, given the weight of scientific findings, become predictions that confirm trends, inasmuch as policy-makers start planning *for*, and not away *from*, the conditions they foresee.

In a previous symposium at the Center, the one on Ellul, we examined the bleak proposition that technology had become a closed circle and that the answers to the problems created by technology would have to be found within technology. Technology had become an autonomous force, invading not only our working lives but our entire society. Technology, which was to produce the means to free men from drudgery and the material means to better well-being, was in process of robbing workers of their jobs and decision-makers of their power to make decisions. Ellul's examples were disquieting, and all of us could think of many more, including the President of the United States being left with a computer-dictated decision about nuclear war. One consolation I finally derived from our discussions was that technology was not a closed circle—it was a spiral, moving so fast that it looked like a closed circle, but still open-ended. Similarly, it is easy to be impressed by McLuhan's examples, and by common experience, that the communications systems, by their technical ingenuity and pervasiveness, were ritualizing our behavior and usurping our powers of self-determination. This was the new mythology, the submission to depersonalized powers. Now we have Skinner arguing that the man-made environment has taken over and that the individual will have to submit his personality (freedom and dignity) to a synthetic culture and become a creature of his own creation. In this sense, "environment" has become a Humpty-Dumpty word ("When I use a word it means just what I choose it to mean—neither more or less"). He is concerned with that "part of the social environment called culture." He goes on to say,

> Our culture has produced the science and technology it needs to save itself. It has the wealth needed for effective action. It has to a considerable extent a concern for its own future. But if it continues to take freedom or dignity, rather than its own survival, as its principal value, then it is possible that some other culture will make a greater contribution to the future.

The "our" and the "other" are revealing. Some of us are concerned about the fate of the human species if "our" culture continues to impair or destroy the physical environment, the biosphere, but he is concerned with the survival of "our" culture, in which the Ellulian prediction can fulfil itself, provided that the "literatures of freedom and dignity" do not encourage a "lethal mutation."

"What is being abolished," he says, "is autonomous man—the inner man, the homunculus, the possessive demon, the man defended by the literatures of freedom and dignity. His abolition has long been overdue. Autonomous man is a device used to explain what we cannot explain in any other way."

As Tolstoy wrote in his postscript to *War and Peace*:

> If the concept of freedom appears to the reason as a senseless contradiction, like the possibility of performing two actions at one and the same instant of time, or the possibility of effect without cause, that only proves that consciousness is not subject to reason. It is this unwavering, certain consciousness of freedom—a consciousness indifferent to experience or reason recognized by all thinkers and felt by everybody without exception—it is this consciousness without which there is no imagining man at all, which is the other side of the question. . . . Only in our conceited age of popularization of knowledge—thanks to that most powerful engine of ignorance, the diffusion of printed matter—has the question of freedom of will been put on a level on which the question itself cannot exist.

Those latter-day determinists invoke "scientific analysis" to give cause-and-effect inevitability to their findings, with what Sir Frederick Gowland Hopkins called "the lusty self-confidence of 19th Century scientists." Then, scientists were reinforced by Newtonian certainty, which gave them a sense of Scientific Predestination, of unalterable processes leading inexorably from one event to the next. This sense affected social thinking. Malthus, by projecting his analysis, predicted that the population would inevitably increase beyond the capacity of the soil to feed the people and this, in turn, determined the "inevitability of poverty." Karl Marx could predict the "inevitability of socialism" based on what his follower Rosa Luxemburg described as the "granite foundation of objective historical necessity." Herbert Spencer (not Darwin) applied causality to "the survival of the fittest" and, as an economist, used it to sanction the extreme form of *laissez faire*. Science was travelling on the rails of certainty.

Twentieth-century science (if not all scientists) is much more humble: chance is back, probability is perfectly respectable, and indeterminacy is not a confession of faltering. In the nucleus of the atom, we find *uncertainty* in a philosophically insoluble form. It is impossible to predict how an individual electron will behave, and it never will be possible; it is not a question of improving methods or instruments, it is unknowable. What scientists would want to know with certainty is what the position and velocity of any electron is; only therefrom might they predict what its path is likely to be. They never can. If they use X rays or other intensive rays, they are so energetic that they will displace the electron, thus changing its speed or its position and, possibly, its direction. Thus, it is impossible to predict its future behavior. The mere act of observation thus changes the behavior. But it is possible, by observations of millions of particles, to discover that the behavior of an *average* electron will be.

This seems a fair analogy with the nature of autonomous man. Reason, reconciled to indeterminacy, can remove "the senseless contradiction of the possibility of performing two actions at one and the same instant of time." The contradiction, in terms of modern science, is no longer senseless; and, when Skinner says that "it is the nature of the experimental analysis of human behavior that it should strip away the functions previously assigned to autonomous man and transfer them one by one to the controlling environment," it is rather like saying that we will abolish the electron, which is inconveniently unpredictable, and call it electricity, which we can control with a switch.

The human predicament is sufficiently discouraging without the dystopians claiming scientific inevitability for their scenarios. Fortunately, we are not all literate ignoramuses—Tolstoy's dupes of the printed word—nor human cassettes imprinted by Skinner's learning machines, nor simpletons brainwashed by McLuhan's medium.

There is now plenty of evidence of powerful forces running contrary to the trends that would justify these predictions. It is not without significance that young people are reasserting the human values that Skinner is seeking to abolish and are concerning themselves with the individual's place in the total environment, not just with the technology-dictated cultural environment. And not only young people: many others are strongly reacting to the Ellulian determinants, the technological means that are usurping our ends. They are the heretics who are questioning the "economic growth-rate" that is the mainspring of the technological system that relies on production for its own sake. (Even *The Times* of London, the organ of economic orthodoxy, had a leader headed "Can We Afford to be Rich?") This is a return to real (human) values, as against artificial (machine) values. This is a case of Skinner's "daemon" breaking out before he can suppress it.

Two hundred years ago, the philosopher David Hume argued that a radical distinction should be made between the "is" and the "ought," between "fact" and "value." Science is the "is." Moral philosophy, not the technology of behavior, must decide what is the "ought."

16

Skinner and
"Freedom and Dignity"

Nathan Rotenstreich

Nathan Rotenstreich, professor of philosophy at Hebrew University of Jerusalem, is the author of various books in Hebrew and English, the three most recent being On the Human Subject: Studies in the Phenomenology of Ethics and Politics, Jewish Philosophy in Modern Times: From Mendelssohn to Rosenzweig, *and* Tradition and Reality.

Rotenstreich resumes the philosophical attack on behaviorism and criticizes Skinner for failing to come to grips with problems raised in philosophical systems (particularly those of Spinoza, Kant, and Pico della Mirandola) whose formulations depend upon the concepts of freedom and dignity. He confronts Skinner's theories with some of these problems and, after detailed analysis, concludes that Skinner has not been able to resolve them satisfactorily.

The direction of Skinner's argument in *Beyond Freedom and Dignity* seems to be clear: "A scientific analysis shifts both the responsibility and the achievement to the environment" [p. 25].[1] But what sort of

---

[1]Throughout this paper, page numbers in square brackets refer to pages in Skinner's *Beyond Freedom and Dignity* (Alfred A. Knopf, 1971).

environment does this imply? Is it the cosmos, nature, society, culture, or mores?

In order to present his argument, Skinner uses two or three categories: those of freedom, dignity, and, possibly, values. These are philosophical categories, but their systematic connotation is by no means clear. Skinner refers several times to the "literature of freedom" [pp. 30, 31]; he also refers to the "literature of dignity" [p. 54]. But to what literature is he actually referring? It seems that, when he refers to the "literature of freedom," the reference is to the various pamphlets of what he calls the freedom movement; it is less clear what the literature of dignity may be. I would expect to be directed to Spinoza, and the question of necessity and freedom in his system; to Kant, and the problem of decision and predetermination by a universal law; or to Pico della Mirandola's "Oration on the Dignity of Man," for a delineation of the scope of the concepts employed. But no such direction is to be found. Is it a mere oversight, or is it professional bias on my part to evaluate a text employing certain concepts with the classic formulation of these concepts in mind? One need not necessarily subscribe to the direction of those classical formulations to believe that a real attempt to deal with the issue has to come to grips with the problems raised in those philosophical systems whose very formulation depends upon these concepts.

Let us start, following the structure of the book, with the concept of freedom. Insofar as it is possible to find a systematic explication of the concept, freedom, in Skinner's presentation, connotes a release from harmful contacts [p. 26]; as a release, it may be viewed as an escape from, for example, the heat of the sun [p. 27] or an escape from an attack [p. 30]. In general terms, "Escape and avoidance play a much more important role in the struggle for freedom when the aversive conditions are generated by other people" [p. 28]. What is not clear is whether the act of escape is itself an act of freedom, or whether the act of escape takes place in order to feel free: Skinner states that, once a man feels free and "can do what he desires, no further action is recommended and none is prescribed by the literature of freedom, except perhaps eternal vigilance lest control be resumed" [p. 32].

These quotations make me wonder to what extent preference or choice is taken into account. To be sure, when Skinner refers to the protest that would arise if prisoners were forced to participate in a dangerous experiment [p. 39], he presumably means that those who protest are expressing a preference. In other words, they would prefer not to be forced. But preference is an act of ranking or, from another view, it is an act of selection from among choices. As such, preference is, despite Skinner, a state of mind, and his objection [p. 42] to defining freedom in terms of states of mind does not hold good. This is so not only because, as Skinner has it, our language is imbued with mentalistic terms, but also because the phenomenon of preference involves pondering, weighing one situation against another, and possibly making a choice. Making such a choice is not only an overt act; it also acknowledges the choice as being preferable, gives assent to a proposition, or admits something as being valid. Even when it is freedom that is desired, that choice is *selected.*

In Skinner's discussion of freedom, there is no mention of the notion of a norm in general, or of a norm of freedom in particular. A norm is a standard, and is thus different from whatever is being evaluated by that standard. The standard may be freedom as an ideal, or equality, or the removal of human aggression, or even harmony between man and his environment (which seems to be Skinner's underlying norm). Yet, by its very definition, a norm is abstract, and there is no way yet to grasp abstractions except by thinking, cognitive activities—precisely the activities that Skinner questions.

In his random presentation of the concept of freedom, Skinner mentions purposefulness as one of its aspects [p. 20]. He is correct in doing so, because freedom is shown not only in running from a situation, but also in anticipating something to come, something to be created. This being so, Skinner is bound to assume that man anticipates the future. But can he consistently do so, in view of his questioning of cognitive activity because of its mentalistic bias? Skinner speaks of culture and its evolution; he speaks about new practices furthering the survival of those who practice them [p. 134]. To speak of survival is to refer to a time that is not the present; it is, to some extent, taking into account future generations. In addition to that, it involves comparison: there are practices that further survival, practices that do not, and—within each of these two categories—practices of varying degrees of efficacy, such as child hygiene and nutrition. Could man take all these factors into account without the cognitive activity proper, not merely the "cognitive" activity called thinking [p. 193]?

Does it blur the lines of the analysis to refer to anticipation and the cognitive activity even though we started with freedom? I do not believe so. Freedom is rooted fundamentally in the cognitive activity, and two characteristic features of cognitive activity are: negatively, it is not a continuation of the object taken cognizance of; and, positively, the cognitive activity has its own momentum, by which it directs itself to its own objects, and thus is self-directed—which is but another expression of the concept of freedom. It is to this aspect of freedom, totally neglected by Skinner, that we referred at the beginning of our presentation to Kant.

The major point in Kant's analysis and presentation is precisely the notion that freedom is a correlate of objectively determining grounds; or, as *Prolegomena*, paragraph 53, has it, "freedom in which reason possesses causality according to the objectively determining grounds." It is in freedom that one's determinedness by circumstances is overcome and one's determinedness by norms emerges. The whole idea of reinforcement can make sense only in the context of compulsions and overcoming of compulsions, but does not face up to the notion of norms. That is why reason proper is the agent of freedom in Kant: only reason can entertain universal notions or grasp abstractions. Now, again, reason is a mentalistic term. Possibly such terms should be removed when they are inessential or confusing, but, in cases where we use them to point to phenomena that should not be disregarded, there is no way to escape them without ignoring factual evidence.

For these reasons, we cannot follow Skinner when he stresses what he calls "the inner man," or agree with him that "the function of the inner man is to provide an explanation which will not be explained in turn. Explanation stops with him" [p. 14]. Freedom proper, in Kant's sense, is not what he calls "spontaneity" (*spontaneitas*) in one of his precritical writings. Referring to spontaneity as an action performed because of what he calls "internal principle," he suggests a distinction between liberty (*libertas*) and spontaneity, liberty being determinedness by the representation of the best (Kant, 1755, p. 409). The distinction suggested here is a telling one, because freedom is not presented as being identical with a smooth outpouring from one's internal life, but rather as an opting for the best (and "best," being a superlative, can only be grasped by a comparison—that is to say, through the medium of reflective acts).

Indeed, Skinner seems to be perplexed about the phenomenon of reflection, if we take reflection to mean thinking about the thinker or perhaps about the act of thinking itself. He does not deny, from the outset, the existence of reflection; in fact, he speaks about the role of the environment as being particularly subtle when what is known is the knower himself [p. 190]. Nonetheless, he lists several instances that make me wonder whether he really attributes to reflection the status that he most certainly does not deny in another context. For example, "The possessed man does not feel the possessing *demon* and may even deny that one exists. The juvenile delinquent does not feel his *disturbed personality*. The intelligent man does not feel his *intelligence* or the introvert his *introversion*" [pp. 15–16]. (We do not quote Skinner on grammatical rules; the problem of language is a very controversial issue, and one may refer here to Chomsky's critical writings.) Do the phenomena listed here have a family resemblance? The *demon* and the *disturbed personality* are to some extent generalizations of obsessions or states deviating from the normal or regular; one does not necessarily have to assume that, when one is driven by an anxiety or attracted by something that does not conform to normal standards, one is necessarily aware of the deviation and its generic name (although one certainly could be and still refrain from identifying the deviation with disturbance). We can see exactly this situation in homosexuals who are aware of their deviation but who do not grant that they are disturbed. This makes their case a borderline one, inasmuch as they reflect upon themselves but do not acknowledge the standard allegedly to be followed. There is reflection here, there is even acknowledgement or consent, but these do not lead to acknowledging the prevailing standard.

But *intelligence* is certainly of a different character. One applies intelligence whether one knows it or not, and it is not by chance that intelligence knows itself: one of its functions is to deal with new situations or to invent rules; these activities certainly force intelligence to mobilize itself, to direct itself, and even to rely upon itself. All these are only different expressions of the reflective character of the cognitive activity; they demonstrate that reflection cannot be disregarded, regardless of whether or not it fits any given vocabulary. It is not enough to say, as Skinner does [p. 180], that

> The geneticist who changes the characteristics of a species by selective breeding or by changing genes may seem to be meddling in biological evolution, but he does so because his species has evolved to the point at which it has been able to develop a science of genetics and a culture which induces its members to take the future of the species into account.

One may grant that a branch of science develops in a certain climate of opinion or in spite of certain cultural conditions; but the science of genetics is not a continuation of the subject matter of genetics. The science of genetics presupposes a general cognitive or interpretative attitude, which may or may not focus itself on certain subject matters, themes, or technologies. The cultural environment may explain the focus of interest, but it cannot explain the emergence of the interpretation itself. And the same applies to the reactions of young people who drop out of school, refuse to take jobs, and so forth [p. 15]. They react or respond because of their interpretation of what can or cannot be done. The reaction is not a continuation of the situation. The statement "The inner man has been created in the image of the outer" [p. 15] is a *bon mot*, but it cannot be accepted as an adequate account of the position of man in the environment (man is an interpreter, whether or not he is aware of it), nor does the phrase give a generic or categorical formulation of man's condition.

Let us now turn to the concept of dignity. Again, it is not easy to define the concept as it is employed in Skinner's book. Still, dignity seems to be used, by and large, in a social context. That is why Skinner speaks of blaming or punishing a person when he behaves badly and of giving credit to him and admiring him for his positive achievements [p. 21]. That is why he connects such expressions of applause as "Again!" "Encore!" and "Bis!" [p. 45] to the concept of dignity, as well as (in a negative way) to loss of status [p. 46]. He equates dignity with credit [pp. 47–48]: "We recognize a person's dignity or worth when we give him credit for what he has done" [p. 58]. Only by establishing these relationships could he make the far-reaching statement that dignity concerns positive reinforcement [p. 43]. (It goes without saying that positive reinforcement is the leading concept in the theory before us.) Moreover, the total shift toward a social context is made most explicit in a discussion of what can be viewed as the most sensitive issue of all:

> "You should (you ought to) tell the truth" is a value judgment to the extent that it refers to reinforcing contingencies. We might translate it as follows: "If you are reinforced by the approval of your fellow men, you will be reinforced when you tell the truth." The value is to be found in the social contingencies maintained for purposes of control. It is an ethical or moral judgment in the sense that ethos and mores refer to the customary practices of a group [pp. 112–113].

It is rather easy to start the critical analysis from this point, where truth is defined as a custom in a social context, and telling the truth is defined as a customary practice within a group, a practice whose validity lies in reinforcing contingencies. The flaw in Skinner's logic is so obvious that I hesitate to point it out. After all, the author of any book of this sort strives to describe a situation adequately, and is thus, willy-nilly, tied up with truth as a principle or as a norm, regardless of reinforcing contingencies. The reason we quote this far-reaching statement of Skinner's at all is because of our didactic concern to bring the exclusiveness of the social context into prominence when we speak about dignity, in Skinner's sense, as credit *qua* reputation, honor, or commendation.

To be sure, the etymological roots of the term "dignity" do lie in the social context (in addition to the rhetorical or stylistic context): *dignitas consularis* means "being worthy of the office of Consul," and *dignum est* is sometimes understood as "being fit." But the concept of dignity of man went far beyond these ornamental connotations, and that fact cannot be disregarded. Pico della Mirandola saw the dignity of man as lying in the indeterminedness of his nature. God assigned man a place in the middle of the world and told him that "neither a fixed abode nor a forum that is thine alone nor any function peculiar to thyself have we given thee, Adam . . ." (Pico della Mirandola, 1486, pp. 224–225). For this reason Pico referred to man as a being of "varied, manifold, and inconstant nature" (ibid., p. 227). Paradoxically, Skinner—in placing the dignity of man in a social context and disregarding the traditional cosmic context of man's indetermined nature—is bound to presuppose that cosmic aspect. After all, were it not for the fact that man's nature is inconstant, he could not be managed or controlled, directed or reinforced. Only a flexible being can be open to the technology of control. But Skinner, who presupposes the indeterminedness of human nature, takes this simply as a fact or as a point of departure, not as something evoking esteem or respect in itself. In the traditional approaches to the notion of the dignity of man, we find a combination of discernment of man's unique characteristics and evaluation of those features as they concern dignity or stimulate respect. Skinner presupposes the uniqueness but gives away the esteem. It is essential for him not to disregard a notion that has significance in the history of ideas. The objective dignity of man in terms of his characteristics would not justify this, nor would Skinner's subjective response to those characteristics in terms of the perhaps unconscious reverence he betrays for the objective dignity of man. Here again it is apposite to refer to Kant, who, as is well known, combined dignity with purpose or worthiness, eventually assuming that dignity, absolute value, and the end in itself are identical. Skinner seems to be concerned with the position of man—otherwise he would not seek his improvement—but we don't know why he makes this effort; he presents his case only in the context of social interaction (again, see the telling example involving truth). There is no room for the phenomenon of respect in the presentation before us. It is rather interesting that Kant says ("Metaphysik der Sitten," paragraph 24) the principle of respect (*Achtung*) demands limiting our own self-esteem so we can recognize the human dignity of the other person. These concepts are totally missing in Skinner's presentation. And this is not a historical but a conceptual criticism that takes advantage of the reservoir of motives to be found in classical literature.

One last point relating to freedom and dignity before we move on to the notion of values: the statement that "one of the great problems of individualism, seldom recognized as such, is death—the inescapable fate of the individual, the final assault on freedom and dignity" [p. 210] is factually incorrect. If we take only the contemporary *Existenz* philosophy, we cannot but notice that it is both individualistic and very much concerned with death. But more important is the relevance of death to the notions of freedom and dignity as features of human nature. Freedom and dignity refer to man as he is in his finitude. One may resent finitude and wish that death were not one of its expressions, but it remains just that and no more; it certainly is not an assault on freedom and dignity. One may say that man is free and has dignity in spite of his finitude, but this does not mean that freedom and dignity are inconsistent with death. The ontological position of man is not identical with his freedom and dignity, even though they may be among his assets. The cosmic uniqueness of man does not free him from the chains of nature, and no traditional philosopher who has spoken of the dignity of man has said that it does. The contrary is true. Kant, for instance, stressed freedom precisely because he had seen the sensuous or natural character of man. Only an identification of both freedom and dignity with limitlessness, in terms of endurance in time, could be viewed as relevant in the context that Skinner describes.

We have, thus far, deliberately confined our analysis to *Beyond Freedom and Dignity*, but two issues make it appropriate to refer to a nontechnical book: Richard I. Evans's *B. F. Skinner: the Man and his Ideas*. The reason will become clear as the argument goes on. One issue is that of creativity. Evans (1968, p. 86) quotes Skinner in the dialogue as saying: "If I were to try to isolate the events in my own behavior which have led to original behavior, I would look for them in certain techniques of self-management." Who, we must ask ourselves, is the self involved in self-management? And what is the difference between self-management, which has somehow a professional sound, and self-control, which is rather a common term? Of course, the question arises out of curiosity, but, in addition, it relates to a very important substantive issue. There is no way to attribute responsibility to man without assuming a kind of self, be the interpretation of the latter notion what it may. And Skinner, in advocating control and management, proposing reinforcement as a means, must face the issue, willy-nilly, of whether or not there is an agent to be reinforced. Either that, or we are involved in an infinite regression from one reinforcement to another, ultimately not only missing the addressee, but not even intending to reach him. Here the questions dealt with before—that is, those of cognitive activity, spontaneity, norm, and freedom—re-emerge. Let us refer again to Kant, with the proviso that we do not consider any system—and Kant's is a system—as an embodiment of truth but rather as a carrier of the formulations of problems. Kant makes this point in one of his "Reflexionen" (4220): (1) the expression "I think" itself shows, with respect to the representation (*Vorstellung*), that I am not passive, that the representation is ascribed to me by myself; and (2) the capacity to think *a priori* and to do is an absolute condition of the possibility of all other phenomena. The ought (*das Sollen*) would not have any meaning whatever ("Reflexionen" 5441). What we notice in these two "reflections" is a kind of continuity or convergence between "I think" and "I do." Any ascription presupposes the "I," whether the ascription has a cognitive or a moral meaning in terms of accountability (though perhaps the German term *Zurechnung* is more apt than the usual English word *accountability*). Skinner struggles with the question of human responsibility—he cannot avoid doing so in suggesting the control of human behavior. To be sure, he says that "the problem is to induce people not to be good but to behave well" [p. 67]. And we know, from the religious vocabulary, that this is called *orthopraxis*. Yet he still says: "We give him instruction in safe and skillful driving. We teach him rules" [p. 69]. The question we cannot escape is: Who is being taught here, and why should those who are taught be taught rules? Rules can be grasped only insofar as they have intrinsically abstract content. If we assume that there is somebody to be taught or somebody to be controlled, we surmise his qualities by ascribing ideas to him, or representations, or merely rules. But once we allow for a cognition in relation to rules, we are bound to allow for the "I" engaged in the cognition, and who will tell us which direction the "I" will take in his cognition? Don't we come back to the "I" through the back door?

We are led, at this point, directly to the question of values. "Under a 'perfect' system no one needs goodness" [p. 67]. We take the quotation marks accompanying the term "perfect" to be a kind of understatement or self-criticism but, just the same, the underlying notion of the whole system seems to be that there is indeed an overriding value—that of harmony between man and what is expected from him—and that this harmony can be achieved by a shift toward environment: "A scientific analysis shifts both the responsibility and the achievement to the environment" [p. 25]. Would it be totally inept to interpret the trend of the doctrine as an attempt to achieve, through the intervention of the environment, what man cannot achieve through his own initiative or effort? If this interpretation is at least partially warranted, we must conclude that Skinner knows what is good—and the emphasis is to be laid on knowing. The reason for that emphasis lies in Skinner's own presentation of values. Let us consider what he says on this very topic: the most frequent concept used by him in his discussion of values [pp. 101ff] is the concept of "feel": ". . . to raise questions not about facts but how men feel about facts, not about what man *can* do, but about what he *ought* to do" [p. 102]. Is it really so? Are values *felt*? Obviously, they are not recognized, as facts are in the simple sense of the word *fact*, like the hardness of the table; but they are not theoretical entities like electrons; and they are not known because of having been methodologically, and thus deliberately, introduced into the discourse.

Values are acknowledged, and this is a different sort of intentionality involving neither feelings nor knowledge proper. Indeed, knowledge is implied here for the simple reason that there is a difference between things that are valuable in themselves and things that are valuable in relation to norms. Skinner says that "the social contingencies, or the behavior they generate, are the 'ideas' of a culture; the reinforcers that appear in the contingencies are its 'values'" [p. 128]. Further, "telling the truth . . . is the right thing to do, and telling lies is bad and wrong. The 'norm' is simply a statement of the contingencies" [p. 115]. This would mean that a norm corresponds to ideas and not to values, and that the principle of truth would be an idea and not a value—and the distinction is rather vague. But just the same "goods are reinforcers" [p. 145], which means that Skinner adheres to a view that goods are of an instrumental significance. Were it not for this interpretation, he would not be in a position to say that "survival is the only value according to which a culture is eventually to be judged, and any practice that furthers survival has survival value by definition" [p. 136]. Now, suppose that this value of survival (incidentally, *value* appears here without the usual quotation marks) is the only value of a culture: why do human individuals subscribe to this value or acknowledge it? After all, if this is a value of a culture, it has a transpersonal position. Even if it reinforces the individual, the individual has to take into account a culture that goes beyond him and survives his individual existence. Even when a value has an instrumental validity in terms of a culture, it has to be acknowledged by the individual for the sake of the culture. Along with the reinforcement, a kind of foregoing would take place; or perhaps, to call a spade a spade, a sort of self-sacrifice for the sake of cultural survival. Even when we assume the goodness of the harmony between mankind and the environment, it does not follow that every individual composing mankind achieves that harmony in his own individual orbit. The awareness of the norm or the value of the culture is not only an abstract awareness in the sense that something distant is evaluated; it also has an additional connotation in terms of abstractness. It abstracts from the individual. With all the emphasis laid on reinforcement, the conclusion cannot be escaped that Skinner presents a kind of social ethics: the reinforced individual is an instrument of, or an agent for, society. And here Skinner's criticisms of mentalism, autonomy, and such concepts as inner agent cease to have a methodical connotation and become substantive issues, and important ones.

Before going into some of the unavoidable political or social consequences of this doctrine, we must recognize the far-reaching relativism that goes along with the theory of values that Skinner explicates or implicitly suggests. Evans (1968, p. 55) quotes Skinner as saying that "the Nazis made good use of the social sciences, even though they had driven out most of the good people. It was 'good' from their point of view, of course; dangerous from ours." I am aware of my special sensitivity to this issue, but just the same it seems to me that it is more than bias that leads me to ask some rather pertinent questions:

1) What is "good use"? Is it effective use, efficient use, consistent use up to the extremity of destroying human beings?

2) In what sense can "use" be good and people be "good"? Isn't there an implicit understanding that use can be good when it serves a purpose efficiently, even if the purpose be that of driving some human beings outside the boundaries of humanity and using them as raw material? And because the Nazis decided who was a human being and who was not, didn't all those they classified as human belong to the category of good people?

3) Was the Nazi's application of the social sciences only dangerous from our point of view, or was it just simply bad? Does not our awareness of the danger follow our awareness of the badness?

Now perhaps the expressions used lack precision. But, comparing *Beyond Freedom and Dignity* to the Evans quotation and noticing the tendency so clearly visible in the book to see a relation between values and feelings—and, further, seeing as the only absolute value (if this expression is permitted for didactical reasons) the value of survival— I wonder whether the relativistic consequences are not only a memento of the consequences but also of the doctrine as a whole.

Skinner indicates some human or political consequences. But, as so often happens, the consequences he indicates call for some reservations, to say the least, about his whole doctrine:

1) "What we need is a technology of behavior" [p. 5]. After all, we know by now that technology engenders its own problems. Why are we to be naive about one kind of technology, that of behavior, when we are experienced, skeptical, and know full well that technology, in solving a problem, creates new ones. Who can promise us that there will be no pollution of the technology of behavior?

2) It may be that we won't have to wait to see the pollution coming. The pollution is already present in the model. "As to technology, we have made immense strides in controlling the physical and biological worlds, but our practices in government, education, and much of economics, though adapted to very different conditions, have not

greatly improved" [p. 6]. There is an implied imposition of one model, that of technological control, on different areas of human behavior or "practices," as it is called in the present context. There is a fundamental difference between the technological enterprise run by experts and the educational process. The educational process is directed toward every human individual. When man lands on the moon, mankind lands on the moon. Any technological achievement is a vicarious achievement for everybody within the human realm, even for those who themselves benefit from the fruits of the achievement. One can benefit from the fruits without understanding the tree. But this is not so in education proper. There is no vicarious education. Education addresses itself to every human individual, relies on his potentialities, attempts to increase them, helps to shape him by letting him shape himself. The fact that there has been a Socrates does not make mankind Socratic or educated. The level has to be achieved. Moreover, the fact that Socrates did what he did creates a post-factum continuity; every deed appears individually, even atomically. There is no guarantee that a person who has done a good deed once will do it again, even when we attribute to the person what is called a character—that is, a kind of consistency. Skinner, by suggesting a technology of behavior, suggests eradicating the differences between levels of human existence and what is called *die Sachlogik* of these different provinces. Supposedly we know not only what is perfect but also that the perfect is uniform.

3) "The problem is to free men, not from control, but from certain kinds of control, and it can be solved only if our analysis takes all the consequences into account" [p. 41]. Who knows all the consequences? Will those in control of human behavior be a sort of sociopolitical elite (the only ones who will know with all the concomitants of the cognitive activity, while the others will not know but will be subject to control)? And who will control the controllers? (It sounds like a restatement of Marx's famous question: "Who will educate the educators?") After all, the technology of behavior is grounded in a certain view of human nature and in certain skills mastered by human beings. The assumption that they will know all the consequences has to be rejected from the beginning: who knows the consequences of the consequences? But what is humanly and politically even more important is the question of government. Governments control human beings; the criterion of the legitimacy of control by a government is related to the question of whether or not the government allows humans, physically and in terms of the climate of opinion, to criticize its control. The criticism could be directed at control in general (because of convictions related to a sort of anarchism) or at the direction the control takes; it could try to change the

control fundamentally or piecemeal. Skinner says that "a permissive government is a government that leaves control to other sources" [p. 97]. Whether or not the term "permissive" is the most suitable one in the context is not very relevant; more important is the point that a legitimate government is a government that controls without prohibiting changes in its control. The technology of behavior does not provide any built-in device to maintain that possibility, because it addresses itself not to behavior but to dignity and freedom and formulates a view whereby there can only be behavior that does not call for awareness of norms, cognitive activity, and ascription of ideas and deeds. But there is a vicious circle here—to control behavior is to shift the human being from his inner forum to the commonplace of behavior. To do this, one has to eradicate the inner forum, or to control behavior to such an extent that the inner forum eventually becomes a replica of overt modes of behavior.

The last sentence of Skinner's book reads: "We have not yet seen what man can make of man" [p. 215]. It sounds like Nietzsche, not in terms of superman driven by the dionysian élan but in terms of man controlling man. There is a paradoxical pride in being man, though it is not clear whether the pride is taken in being man as a controlling man or in being man as subject to control. The pride in being a controlling man brings us back to freedom and dignity. The pride in being man as subject to control leads us to behaving well without knowing why or for what purpose. What kind of justification is possible for this kind of pride, unless we assume that somehow convictions will follow? And, if we make this assumption, we find ourselves back at the point of departure.

17

Is He Really a Grand Inquisitor?

Michael Novak

Michael Novak, a professor of religion at the State University of New York at Old Westbury, is the author of several books, including The Experience of Nothingness *(1970) and* Ascent of the Mountain, Flight of the Dove *(1971).*

Here, the professional theologian wrestles against behaviorism. In the end, however, Novak is not disparaging of Skinner's work. The reaction against Beyond Freedom and Dignity, *Novak points out, is "religious in its intensity"; yet he acknowledges that a remarkable number of Christian theologians praise the book. Novak suggests and analyzes three reasons why this should be so. The reason he stresses most emphatically is that "Skinner's sense of reality, the story he believes the universe to be living out (he calls his view 'the scientific picture'), reaches back in time to make contact with a more ancient vision. It is as if the Enlightenment were, . . . in its philosophical 'picture,' a temporary aberration. . . ."*

Novak also takes up, as his title implies, the relation between the doctrines of free will and Skinnerism.

A remarkable number of Christian theologians are praising B. F. Skinner's *Beyond Freedom and Dignity*. A number of others believe his work incompatible with Christianity. Both may be wrong.

Professor Skinner would be the last person to claim autonomous credit for *Beyond Freedom and Dignity*. It was not he, it was the environment that controlled the book's coming into being. And if we suppose that Skinner is a latter-day Thomas Aquinas, we might well imagine on his lips the echoes of an ancient outlook: "It was not owing to anything in me; everything was gift. Yes, I set hand to paper, but only through God's grace sweetly disposing all things. . . ." We recall the countless unsigned medieval masterpieces, the anonymous achievements of Chartres, and that now lost social and cultural sense that did not attach much significance to whomever it was who expressed best the artistic genius of the age. It was enough, in those days, that the people, the culture, flowered. So remembering, we recover more fully the shock of the sudden birth of ego: the Renaissance, the Enlightenment, and the Age of the Individual.

If we suppose, with Whitehead, that science flourished in the West because of centuries of habituation in the confidence that every single historical phenomenon springs from one intelligible source—no lily blooms, no sparrow falls, no hair on a single head is lost, save God knows of it—then we may trace a fairly direct line from the Logos that is identified with the God of Abraham, Isaac, and Jacob to the Logos of whom Freud wrote so affectionately in *The Future of an Illusion*: that Logos no longer personal, no longer God, but effectively exhibiting interconnectedness even in slips of the tongue, in dreams, in seemingly "irrational" aspects of behavior of all sorts.

We may say (with a roughness appropriate to brevity) that, from belief in a single intelligent Creator of all things, inseparable twins were spawned. The first was confidence in the autonomy of every individual will (which Kant identified as the essence of Enlightenment) and the second, confidence in the rational, experimental procedures of scientific method. And we may further say that, as the children rebelled from the parent, so now, with Skinner, the second twin devours the first.

For Skinner demythologizes autonomy, the individual, freedom, and dignity in conscious parody of an earlier demythologizing of the Creator and Redeemer. As God died, so now must the autonomous individual. It is not surprising that the reaction against his work is religious in its intensity.

But why on earth would theologians see merit in what Skinner is up to? There are at least three reasons. I would like to analyze them, to raise questions about problems of translation from a Christian to a Skinnerian world view, and to raise some political and institutional issues.

Humans Are Social Animals

There is a widespread belief, in this Protestant nation, that Christianity is a religion of individualism, each man his own priest and pope, each conscience inviolable, each person a potential source of autonomy and dissent. "The Protestant principle," Paul Tillich was wont to boast, lies at the heart of the modern period and overlaps with the principle of the Enlightenment—it is the principle of the free, autonomous conscience. What Christianity adds to Enlightenment is chiefly the conviction that human autonomy is God's presence in man: whoever acts autonomously is acted in by God. Theologians influenced by Heidegger and the existentialists "demythologized" the New Testament, to show that what Jesus demanded was authenticity, engagement, decisive acts: an exercise of genuine autonomy.

Classical theologians and broad popular movements in American Christianity both stress the importance of the individual and his "decision." The New England Puritans and the Southern and Southwestern populists have been at one in their fierce attachment to categories and rhetorical devices that accent the individual. (One of the bitter lessons that Catholic immigrants from Southern and Eastern Europe had to learn, in order to be "Americanized," was to pursue loneliness and laissez faire: "You're on your own," "It's up to you," "Each man for himself"—a rhetoric, and some little reality, of individual opportunity, dissolving such native social solidarity as their families once had known.)

Three critical factors tell against the model of Christianity as individualism: the teachings of the Scriptures; the practice of early Christianity; and the actualities of Christian life. The reaction against an exaggerated and errant, although in some ways helpful, emphasis on individualism has been well underway for several decades. It culminated, for example, in "the Social Gospel"; in the Constitution on the church agreed upon by the Second Vatican Council; in many initiatives of the World Council of Churches; in ecumenism; in liturgical revivals; and in the acquisition of social modes of thinking on the part of individual theologians. Reinhold Niebuhr's career, for example, may be viewed as a struggle to break free from merely individualistic categories to a larger, social conception of man—and it is a very long voyage, in this respect, from his early books, such as *Moral Man and Immoral Society*, to *Man's Nature and his Communities*. And surely nothing is more obvious to the sociologically tutored eye than the social character of actual religious attitudes and practices today.

Professor Skinner's emphasis upon the social character of human existence is thus, from a theological point of view, confirmatory of a well-established trend. For Christian theologians, one of the more influential books in recent years has been *The Social Construction of Reality*, by Peter Berger and Thomas Luckmann. The sociological viewpoint of Parsons, Bellah, and others has contributed to "systemic" analysis; and the recent disaffection with liberal WASP "superculture" (with its misleading appeals to individualism) have convinced many that social factors are central to an accurate grasp of human reality.

A second reason why many theologians find Skinner's position congenial concerns Christian images of Providence and grace. To speak merely from a Thomist standpoint [most thoroughly elucidated by Bernard Lonergan in *Grace and Freedom* (Lonergan, 1971)], nothing of good that a human does is deserving of credit; everything is grace. (The damnable thing about Aquinas, Chesterton once observed, is that he leaves nothing for a man to boast of.) Man's freedom, in this view, is thoroughly conditioned: (1) no one chooses his parents, economic situation, childhood setting, nation of origin, or historical era; (2) no one chooses his natural (we would say, genetic) endowment; (3) no one chooses the networks of circumstance in which he finds himself, or the laws or contingencies governing their behavior; and (4) no one chooses the insights, aspirations, or inspirations that emerge in his or her consciousness.

Aquinas notes that one can resist or "turn away from" creative inner lights and urgings, given by grace or graced nature. One can "turn away," for the world still belongs to "the father of lies." He defines sin as *aversio*—a turning away from those possibilities that attract one toward self-realization (that is, total knowing and total loving), a turning away, that is to say, from the God within. Thus, to be good is to align oneself with creative, life-giving tendencies; to be evil is to subtract oneself from them consciously and willingly.

All humans can take "credit" for is *aversio*. When they promote community, increase understanding and intellect, develop their talents, achieve authenticity and *caritas*, all this has been sweetly disposed on their behalf by God through—striking linguistic echo—"operant grace." When other conditions enable them to do so, but they (from past habit or inclination) turn away, *they* are responsible—they prefer familiar reinforcers to more difficult, weaker ones. Their "sin," of course, is not merely personal; the entire social order is flawed and damaging to all. At no historical time was the cultural tissue of human life solely supportive of humane, creative acts; the reinforcers often bring out the worst: the "sin" is original, the sickness—the plague—is inescapable.

Skinner would perhaps find this one-way relation to reinforcers unfair: no credit if you do, damned if you don't. But there is at least a certain plausibility in the notion that the reinforcers of the spirit are weak—they are not, for example, tangible, immediate, or sensually competitive. And, interestingly enough, in the medieval imagination, "blame" is slight for those to whom the reinforcements of the flesh are stronger than those of charity but severe for those guilty of "spiritual pride"—those who manifest an exaggerated notion of their own autonomy and importance.

In this respect, the Thomist human is, like the Skinnerian human, entirely conditioned. Far from depriving the individual of liberty, however, these cumulative networks of antecedent conditions (for Aquinas) *enable* him—and, in particular, enable him to gain insight *or* to avert his "eyes" ("to sin against the light"), enable him to extend himself to others *or* to withdraw. The range of man's possibilities includes loving his neighbor (acting truly toward him) and also murdering him.

Professor Skinner, to be sure, seems to have a stronger notion still. Not only do environment and its many reinforcers "enable," they also "control." Later in this paper, we must note the amplitude and the ambiguities in Skinner's use of "control"; it is not a word Aquinas uses of God. For our purposes, it suffices to note that, in Aquinas, because no person can act without being "enabled," both by "outer" and "inner" conditions, at no point is man's autonomy such that he may take credit for it. Such as it is, it has been given him, both in its abiding tendencies and in its actual exercise. It is "grace" or "gift," rather than his own creation. Hence, "theonomy," rather than "autonomy," is a more accurate name for the human reality. The emphasis of *autos* upon the atomic individual is not appropriate to the Skinnerian or the Thomist functioning of the self. "Autonomy" is an exaggeration. It suggests that humans in their intimate constitution are less social, less embedded in the world, than they are.

In *The Experience of Nothingness*, for example, I was constrained to argue against the sense of reality that pictures within each of us an "autonomous self." Influenced by T. S. Eliot's "Tradition and the Individual Talent," by Lasswell's work on the effect of capitalist–democratic political symbols on the self-image of individuals, by Schütz's demonstration of the social character of perception, by Lonergan's metaphor of "horizon," by skeptical observation, and, no doubt, as well by religious traditions nonverbally absorbed into my sensibility, I wished to speak of the human not as a "self" but as a "worldself," a horizon, a two-poled organism in which world and self mutually constitute each other, in which neither world nor self is ever isolable in a pure state. *I Am an Impure Thinker*, Rosenstock-Huessy entitles his meditation on a similar theme. The rejection of the sense of reality in which there figures an autonomous, separate self is not, in a word, peculiar to Skinner; and it has connections to Oriental views, which see the Western conception of self as illusory.

Skinner is aware of the parallelism between his theoretical construct and those of ancient arguments about predestination, grace, faith, works, and free will. One can imagine him, indeed, rebelling in a fairly systematic way, first against the dominance of a Calvinist view of the world, and then against an Enlightenment–Individualist view of the world. Against Calvinism, he wants to eliminate the "magic" of appeal to unseen and unverifiable actions on God's part. Against the Enlightenment, he wants to eliminate the "magic" of appeal to unseen and unverifiable actions by an autonomous self. He writes, for example, that "being good to someone for no reason at all, treating him affectionately whether he is good or bad, does have Biblical support: grace must not be contingent upon works or it is no longer grace. But there are behavioral processes to be taken into account" [p. 99].[1]

At such points, the intellectual structure of Skinner's world view—with God left out—is rather more like that of Aquinas than like that of Luther or Calvin. For Aquinas, grace operates (except in the rarest cases) through the ordinary contingencies and processes of nature, through "secondary causes"—there are always "behavioral processes to be taken into account." The whole environment, the whole "schedule of contingencies" that constitutes history, is graced. (Skinner merely believes it to be melioristic.) Simply by being what it is, it manifests God's presence, slowly building brotherliness and tutoring humans through suffering, irrationality, and pain. Were Skinner God, no doubt, the design of the universe would be less faulty, less wasteful, more economical. But it would operate no less through "secondary causes."

What I want most emphatically to stress is that Skinner's sense of reality, the story he believes the universe to be living out (he calls his view "the scientific picture"), reaches back in time to make contact with a more ancient vision. It is as if the Enlightenment were, not in its political gains but in its philosophical "picture," a temporary aberberation—a necessary stage, perhaps, but a magnificent exaggeration. Skinner concludes his book by saying:

> Science has probably never demanded a more sweeping change in the traditional [let us rather say, "recent"] way of thinking about a subject, nor has there ever been a more important subject. In the traditional picture a person perceives the world around him, selects features to be perceived, discriminates among them, judges them good or bad, changes them to make them better (or, if he is careless, worse), and may be held responsible for his action and justly rewarded or punished for its consequences. In the scientific picture a person is a member of a species shaped by evolutionary

---

[1]Throughout this paper, page numbers in square brackets refer to pages in Skinner's *Beyond Freedom and Dignity* (Alfred A. Knopf, 1971).

contingencies of survival, displaying behavioral processes which bring him
under the control of the environment in which he lives, and largely under
the control of a social environment which he and millions of others like
him have constructed and maintained during the evolution of a culture.
The direction of the controlling relation is reversed: a person does not act
upon the world, the world acts upon him [p. 211].

It is undesirable, as well as impossible, merely to go backwards
intellectually. Whereas, in the ancient West, men could say "There is
nothing new under the sun," we have, in our age, seen marvels of
invention almost annually. The astonishing fact is that inventions and
discoveries that were intended to glorify humans in their individual
autonomy have returned us so rapidly, and so unexpectedly, to an
almost tribal and surely communal image of our identity.

Once it was the Leibnitzian *monad* that gave primary shape to western
liberal perception: the whole world was viewed through the lens of the
atomic individual. Now the metaphor "spaceship Earth" directs our
perception to our common dilemmas, our common fate, our common
interconnectedness. The feeling John Stuart Mill seemed to have, that
feeling of independence attainable at least by rural landowners, has been
replaced by a new awareness. Each human is implicated in the racism,
poverty, pollution, and other diseases of his world.

Skinner cannot imagine the individual pure, free, autonomous, and
healthy: in the very center of his being resides his whole environment.
His "autonomy" is a function of social conditions, in which he is
thoroughly implicated. Whereas the metaphors that fired the hearts of
many in the Liberal era were "breakthrough," "liberation," and "be
yourself," we are entering an era in which we recognize that, for the
individual, there is no escape from the species, no breaking through the
tissues of a common environment, no uninvolved, impermeable, un-
implicated self. There is no place to hide. This social and communal
awareness is congenial to Christianity.

But the third theme that Christians may find attractive in Skinner's
work is his emphasis on earthy, bodily, environmental supports. Christianity is an incarnational religion. The dominant symbol through which
it shapes perception is that God does not appear as God (pure, dazzling,
overpowering, and inescapable) but as flesh. The godly way is not by
way of escape from flesh, but through the flesh. Hence, there are sacra-
ments, church buildings, bells, incense, music, paintings, processions,
dramatic representations; there are holy days, ashes, external acts of
penance, purple vestments for penance and white for days of joy; at
prayer, one kneels or faces eastward or extends the arms. Monastic
life, for example, is full of "reinforcers," designed so that one begins
the practices even before one has the appropriate feelings—and, indeed,

the feelings are held by some masters of the "interior" life to be irrelevant. *The Dark Night of the Soul* is a journey past feelings, memories, images, and other accustomed reinforcers. In a powerful way, the wisdom of the Benedictines—who have successfully been building and multiplying utopian communities since the sixth century—is a sort of Skinnerism in advance. *Ora et Labora*: prayer and labor are not acts solely of some autonomous self but acts of an embodied social animal. Work in the fields is social, and so is the chanting of the liturgy. And, ironically, this high social emphasis on "reinforcers" produces not uniformity but a highly developed individuality, as anyone who has known the angularity of individual Benedictines can attest.

Some Sources of Uneasiness

Still, Professor Skinner's polemic against individualism seems more successful than what he would put in its place. I note, for example, that arguments against Skinner tend not to center upon his scientific *theory* but upon his *world view*. Few question the technical validity of his laboratory work, or even the technically expressed theory interpreting it. Many do question Professor Skinner's extrapolation therefrom. They question the depth, range, and precision of his insights into the actual, concrete behavior of individuals, especially in its more complicated phases; and they question his social and political sophistication, his understanding of group or institutional behavior. Sometimes, it is true, critics also question his motives—not necessarily his conscious ones, but his unconscious ones. For it can scarcely escape attention that, in his future world, behavioral experts like himself will acquire a power rather greater than they have at present. Inasmuch as humans are, from a theological point of view, habitually and normally deceived by their own motives, the questioning of one another's motives is seldom fruitful. So we may confine our attention to the two chief sources of uneasiness: the complex phases of individual behavior and institutional behavior as Skinner portrays them.

It is a great achievement to accomplish original laboratory work with intelligence and even brilliance. It is still greater to derive, from such work, successful applications in several areas of animal and human behavior: in dealing with retardates, alcoholics, mental patients, prisoners, and even certain features of child rearing and education. As befits a young science, the field Skinner has helped launch is most successful at elementary problems, at the lower end of a scale of complexity, and most successful, so far, in elements of individual, rather than group, behavior. This is to be expected.

But Skinner has found his theorems—and more than his theorems, his approach and perspective—so instructive that he thinks he sees clues to an extension of such theorems throughout the full range of human behavior. He sees the whole field of human behavior reduced to a science and, more than a science, to a technology. Unavoidably, such a vision is, as yet, an act of faith, a project rather than an accomplishment. To accept it, one must suspend deeply reinforced traditions, well-confirmed practices, and even, indeed, the patterns of common speech.

To argue against someone else's entire world view is a most arduous sort of argument. Those within world view *A* have a way of handling virtually every difficulty that comes their way; and when absolutely necessary, they make adjustments in order to preserve their scheme. Those who perceive and act through world view *B* cannot voice objections entirely in the language and with the images familiar to them. For the two systems, world view *A* and world view *B* seldom lie, so to speak, on the same plane or along the same axis. It is extremely difficult to "translate" from the language of the one to the language of the other. The hermeneutical problems are severe.

Consequently, we tend to try new world views on for size—at first, they hardly ever fit. Usually, we return, reinforced, to our familiar world. Often, we do not "learn" much from our critics. They seem to us to miss the point. Almost necessarily so.

In reading Skinner as a Christian philosopher and as a person of political curiosity, I found myself undergoing a number of changes. My profession encourages me to suspend my own world view and to try to enter into the sense of reality, basic stories, and important symbols in which others live. In Skinner's case, however, several additional problems arose. I had to hold in check my resentment at—it seemed to me—almost deliberately insulting shortcomings in his argument. A professional critic of world views can hardly help resenting poachers on "his" terrain. If a theologian were to write as sweepingly of scientific theories as Skinner does of theories in the humanities (he calls his last two chapters "What Is Man?" and "The Design of Cultures"), the offense would be unmistakable. But the artificial boundaries of professionalism do not ordinarily operate for me as taboos; what troubled me was harder, at first, to diagnose. I had again and again to overcome my sense that, in fairly clear ways, Skinner does not really understand what he is doing once he wanders onto the new terrain. His sentences become a mixture of the astute and the naive, the precise and the gross. I felt myself alternating between sympathy and anger, admiration (he was often better than I expected) and revulsion. And the text itself alternates between a kind of *hubris* and a winning modesty, a set of pure intentions and outbreaks of arrogance. The verbal behavior of Skinner himself is a study in ambiguity and complexity; it is the work of an unintegrated, at least dual, sensibility.

For one thing, when Skinner asks "What Is Man?" he is not talking about laboratory specimens but about *me*—and everyone else. Why, then, does he not tread more carefully? There is, no doubt, a sharp difference between discourse in the humanities and discourse in the sciences. In the sciences, one expects neutral, objective, impersonal discourse. All who approach scientific measurements, procedures, and carefully controlled realms of discourse are expected to be impressed rather univocally by the "evidence." In the humanities, by contrast, one expects a certain degree of variety—and of the courtesy, dispassionate analysis, fair and due sympathy, and other painstaking efforts required to comprehend a viewpoint not one's own. Humanists specialize in the *diversity* of world views accessible to human beings. They expect the question "What Is Man" to be addressed in countless different ways; and they expect a certain sophistication in rendering viewpoints not one's own, a certain sense for nuance, a certain hesitance.

By lumping together hundreds of diverse and mutually contradictory viewpoints in the phrase, "the literature of freedom and dignity," Skinner ought certainly to have expected an angry outcry from professionals in such fields. How could he have been, as he claims, surprised by it? On some points, all would agree with him; on others, some; on yet others, perhaps no one. But precise discussion was short-circuited. A bright electric explosion resulted: a public controversy that might not otherwise have happened. All opponents felt herded into the same camp, that of "the literature of freedom and dignity." Skinner, meanwhile, asks to not be judged for the mistakes made by other behaviorists. He seems to be asking for treatment for himself as an individual, while treating grossly, even if unintentionally so, those who might disagree with him.

To a certain extent, then, Skinner manifested a naiveté one hadn't expected, a certain innocence about other fields and how they work. Philosophical discussions of "good" and "value" that are sympahtetic to his own intention, and that derive from a similar world view, he does not clearly draw upon. Much in Bertrand Russell, A. J. Ayer, Stevenson, and Ryle might have been aptly borrowed, for the sake of precision. A philosopher or a theologian would not properly take such liberties in Skinner's profession as he takes in theirs.

Still, once the feathers of ruffled professionalism have been duly calmed, there remain serious difficulties with Skinner's provocative thesis. Jean-Paul Sartre once remarked that, more than any other nation, America is a fertile soil for behavioralism. I imagine the reason for this predisposition to be twofold. First, nowhere else does the national sense of reality so deeply anticipate continual progress through science. The American religion is not so much Protestant as social Darwinist, melio-ristic, and deferential to white-coated experts. Secondly, Americans are psychically prepared for personal mobility. They change rather easily even their profound personal convictions. They have often discovered that inherited or personally acquired views turn out to have been erro-neous. David Riesman long ago described this different address to reality on the part of our national psyche as "other-directed."

In two short years of massive advertising, for example, the percentage of Americans who hold that abortion is a form of murder dropped from something like 85 percent to less than 50 percent. It is difficult to believe that the American "conscience" is not malleable. The prag-matism often acclaimed as our national philosophy may, in its theory, be high-minded, but in its practice—by Nixon, for example—it accepts signals from its environment rather uncritically. Our Horatio Algers are less "men of principle" than "men of flexibility." They are less men of a profound, stubborn, autonomous "interior" life than men alert to changes in trends external to themselves. They are plastic and adaptable. There is a sense in which Skinner merely codifies one-half of our national working practice.

And he does not really neglect, although he treats in a lower key, the other half. For example, liberals in America have, for some time, tried to emphasize the social and environmental factors "responsible for" crime. They tend to be identified with planning, control, deference to experts, and spreading bureaucracies. But liberals are also very em-phatic about defending civil liberties, academic freedom, and the rights of individuals. Conservatives, on the other hand, although often strong on teamwork, corporate responsibility, and loyalty, love to appeal to the rugged individual, his sense of responsibility, his will to succeed, his uniqueness, and his resistance to planning and bureaucratization. With half their soul, then, whether they are liberals or conservatives, Americans tend to believe devoutly in personal uniqueness, originality, fulfillment, and rights. Skinner affirms this American sense of reality, even while placing it in a social context:

> A culture has no existence apart from the behavior of the indivuals who maintain its practices. It is always an individual who behaves, who acts up-on the environment and is changed by the consequences of his action, and who maintains the social contingencies which *are* a culture. The individual is the carrier of both his species and his culture. Cultural practices, like genetic traits, are transmitted from individual to individual. A new practice, like a new genetic trait, appears first in an individual and tends to be trans-mitted if it contributes to his survival as an individual.
>
> Yet, the individual is at best a locus in which many lines of development

come together in a unique set. His individuality is unquestioned. Every cell in his body is a unique genetic product, as unique as that classic mark of individuality, the fingerprint. And even within the most regimented culture every personal history is unique. No intentional culture can destroy that uniqueness, and, as we have seen, any effort to do so would be bad design [p. 209].

Thus, Skinner defends individuality in theory. He also defends it in practice. By all reports, he is an idiosyncratic man, a highly developed individual, a dissenter from conventional wisdom, a man who goes his own way. He has not lived in a commune, a utopian community, or a closely controlled environment, and probably would not tolerate it. And he likes to see highly individualized traits developed in others. He wants to see a culture so designed that it will encourage variety and so that each individual will develop up to his or her entire inimitable capacity. He does not want to see conformity, drabness, or sameness; he wants to see diversity.

Why, then, does the actual conduct of his argument make many uneasy? For one thing, the images and symbols of science no longer sound salvific. God has died (it is said), the individual has died (Skinner says), but science, too, has died; it has lost its purity and its credibility. What the church is to Christianity, technology is to science, and by their fruits both have been harshly judged. The appeal that the cure for *bad* design is *good* design is on a homiletic par with the claim that "the only thing wrong with Christianity is that men have never tried it."

Again, never has the behavior of a younger generation been so thoroughly studied and controlled as during the past fifteen years in the United States. Never has American education been so thoroughly designed by experts. And now there is an almost universal revulsion against experts, controls, and scientific designing. The spokesmen for "progress" have led us into pollution. The actual practice of technology had made of science a revolting, plastic cheapness. Thus, a scientist who has trained pigeons and rats, and even had some success (through his disciples) with retardates, alcoholics, prisoners, and the mentally ill, can hardly expect a triumphal entry into Jerusalem. There is more than a faint sense that "we have heard all this before."

Skinner miscalculated enormously by employing words, images, and symbols that—despite his explicit disclaimers and despite his own noble intentions—called to mind Hitler's scientist, Goebbels' techniques of information control, Chinese brainwashing, Stalinist "confessions," American police "crowd control," and other memories too fresh not to be enflamed. The central symbol of his book—the word "control"—functions as a specimen of aversive conditioning. It is not a reinforcer apt to draw converts through its beauty and attractiveness. One who would give us a science of behavior, and yet not recognize the symbolic weight of his own language, diminishes our confidence in his leadership.

The Words "Control" and "Environment"

It is a standard practice of humanistic scholarship to note the various "influences" upon persons of genius, upon practices of liberty, and upon conceptions of dignity. I know of no one who supposes that the autonomous self operates wholly in a vacuum. Perhaps Kant's discussion of the autonomous will acting solely for the categorical good is as high an expression of individual autonomy as appears in our literature; but critics who note the social origins of Kant's intuitions on that point are not wanting. As for the extreme individualism of the early Jean-Paul Sartre—the Sartre who said that "for man there are never excuses" and that "man is condemned to freedom," the Sartre of the breathtaking apostrophe to freedom under total German occupation in the early 1940s—the later Sartre of the *Critique de la raison dialectique* struggles in a more dense and complicated way than Skinner to replace the self with the group and the environment.

Thus, were Skinner to argue that, in every instance of purported acts of freedom, contingencies of reinforcement are at work, who would argue? We all know that our freedom is learned from the look in the eyes of others, raised eyebrows, words, images of heroism and of compromise, training of the instincts of honesty and courage, education, honors, embarrassments, social punishments, hunger, torture, sleeplessness, anxieties, and troubles. We try hard to educate our children to be brave, truthful, honest. We speak of peoples who "have not developed the social preconditions" for western conceptions of liberty. On this point, defenders of Skinner, like John Platt, point out that there are unnecessary misunderstandings between Skinner and various humanists and social scientists; but the fundamental argument is not based on misunderstandings, merely.

Nevertheless, two sources of misunderstanding need to be clarified. One is the sweeping use that Skinner makes of "control," the other his sweeping use of "environment." When words are employed in an unusual way, or when they are used over an extraordinary range, they require special examination.

The word "control," in ordinary English, comes from a family of words and phrases like "dominate," "impose one's will upon," "guide" (in the way rails guide), "manipulate," "use as an instrument," "govern the movements of," and so on. Skinner, however, intends to call our attention to a scientific, technical point—namely, that behavior is *a function of* variables. Technically speaking, this is what he means by "control." Such functional language has a certain utility. Borrowed as it is, however, from the realm of machines, it suggests an imaginative context in which many will hesitate to speak of human beings. It seems like a faulty perspective from which to launch a study of behavior.

Even leaving these objections aside, and tentatively accepting a viewpoint that requires looking at human behavior as if it were amenable to a functional language, we cannot help noticing that human behavior "is a function of" a great many variables *of various kinds*. Variables "controlling" human behavior are brought to bear from at least three significantly different directions: the physical environment, the social environment, and the individual human organism itself. Thus, men on the moon must take oxygen with them. A raised eyebrow, a legal sanction, a silence, an argument, an insult may affect behavior. Finally, the organism's genetic endowment, its acquired skills and tendencies, and its history may limit its present options. Under each of these headings, a wide array of "reinforcers" or "contingencies" may be discerned. How complex the interactions of these sources of "control" are may be seen in artistic achievement.

A good sculptor allows his fingertips to be "controlled" by the qualities of the stone on which he works. Thus, every art, requiring enormous respect for its material, induces a remarkable docility in the artist. On the other hand, only persons of a certain endowment and a certain apprenticeship have skills sufficient to follow the subtle "signals" of the material. And besides these skills developed in the artist's past history, the artist requires, as well, a kind of "vision," an inventive capacity, a capacity for evoking, through his work, symbolic echoes in the perceptions of others. For we regularly distinguish between expert craftsmen of technical cunning and artists who "touch our souls"— that is, artists who evoke the symbolic materials of our own history.

In a certain perspective, a great artist is "controlled" by all these expectations. He is "controlled" even by the further expectation that he "surprise" us. In another perspective, artistic achievement furnishes the classic instance of what we mean by "free."

First, the artist practices an activity that serves no other function but that of expressiveness. Second, he expresses, with his material, that communion of his own symbolic world (and ours as well) to which his own instincts lead him. All of these instincts are, no doubt, genetically and socially derived. But, third, they also represent his own individuality brought—not least by mastery of long social traditions of technique and symbol—to its unique fulfillment and signature.

The social conditions under which the arts flourish are, of course, not always attained. It would help us to know what they are and to realize them. The paradox is that to "design a culture" in which the arts might flourish is, at one and the same time, (1) to "control" and (2) to maximize "individual freedom."

It is this paradox upon which Professor Skinner regularly plays. Because most persons in our culture stress the second pole, his very heavy emphasis upon the first generates resistance. Many artists and other defenders of "individual freedom" tend to believe that the methods of behavioral control *already* introduced by technology are obliterating the instincts of craftsmanship, vision, individuality, and even personhood from the repertoire of huge majorities. "The people" are becoming "a mass." Such critics see a homogenization, impersonality, and blunting of differences flowing from what has been called scientific "progress." Thus, when Skinner calls for still more efficient, less wasteful, and more thoroughly designed controls, they are loathe to trust still one more proposal on the part of scientists promising "progress," even when those scientists say that they, too, desire to promote individual fulfillment, artistic diversity, and personal vision. Experts are necessarily specialists; when acting upon complex societies, they quite literally don't know what they are doing. Too often they destroy what they would save. One doesn't trust experts, even those who come fresh from scientific laboratories.

One source of misunderstanding, therefore, lies in the aversive symbolic reverberations given off by the words that Skinner finds so attractive: "control," "technology," "progress," "experts," "perceptions tutored by work in the laboratory," and so on. Common, ordinary experiences of daily life suggest to many of us that the more the new technologies multiply among us—automobiles, television sets, assembly lines—the more sloppy and unreliable grows the craftsmenship around us. New clothes come apart at the seams, machines constantly malfunction, fewer and fewer people seem to love what they are doing. These tangible experiences provide the context in which many listen to the new cry of salvation through behavior control. Naturally, Skinner's disciples promise to do better, learning from previous mistakes.

In the interim, a second misunderstanding surrounds the other favorite Skinnerian word. Professor Skinner's use of the word "environment" is as sweeping as his use of the word "control." He seems to include, under its very large umbrella, *any* variable that may influence behavior. Thus, the entire universe is my environment; so is the more narrow ecosystem of Earth; so are my geographical surroundings here and now, and the lamp over my desk; so are ball-point pen, paper, and newsprint; so is the history of my cultural community until now, my family history, my personal memory, and the traces upon my organism of every past experience; so are those others whose views and values are significant to me, as well as my opponents, imaginary and real; so is the language I speak; so are the ideals, images, and symbols that move me. There is no doubt that all that I have and own has been given to me. "Environment" is a very large name for my benefactor, indeed.

And yet there is also a unique, individual organism, with a distinctive and inimitable history, called by a proper name, and endowed with a consciousness only more or less in tune with the organism itself: my organism in its individuality. This conscious organism seems to be, in William James' phrase, a source of "resistance" to *some* features of its surrounding environment. (Perhaps it resists even its own endowment). It seems to be the subject of actions that have an individual signature, significance, and symbolic meaning. No doubt, every aspect of its uniqueness is attributable to some interchange or other with some part of its environment. It is a "worldself," and not merely an autonomous particle of self.

The statement, then, that all human behavior is "controlled" by the "environment" may be translated in several different ways. One may decide that an appeal to an "autonomous self," subject to "magic" or "miracles" of initiative, self-origination, or responsibility, is no longer required for scientific explanation. On the contrary, one may decide that a scheme of scientific explanation in terms of variables of control will—if widely adopted—soon induce a self-image in its employers that will undercut their own capacity for creativity, self-development, and self-expression. As a third alternative, one may suggest that much more precise conceptual tools are required for speaking of human behavior, in the light of the relativization of the world's cultures, through their increasing knowledge of one another. It is possible that Skinner's language, speaking so familiarly of a "technology of behavior" and of "progress," is a western bias—an illusion, perhaps even specifically WASP in its aspiration. He pictures, no doubt, an orderly, clean, economical world not familiar to the imagination of any other culture.

Some gain in conceptual precision is made if we notice that, whatever the variables of human behavior, some are weightier than others. The state of the weather may "control" some decisions of mine at some times; at other times, it may count hardly at all. Opposition from professional scholars may, at times, lead me to abandon an hypothesis; at other times, even without the support of a single other, I may obstinately but conscientiously hold firm. At one time, a loaded pistol may move me as a convincing "persuader"; at another, not even a pistol can "control" me. Is it possible, then, that, once we have accepted an ideal as part of our symbolic reality, we can resist other features of the environment—prison or torture—unto death? On one occasion, a rational argument may lead me to a sweeping change of mind; on another, even though defeated in argument, I continue to think my position correct and only my defense faulty. If "environment" covers every such feature, what light does it shed?

If Skinner did not claim so much for his technology of behavior, we might be willing to concede him more. So complex is "environment," so variable are the "controls," that, in assenting to the fundamental Skinnerian principle that environment controls behavior, we do not know what we are agreeing to. Whatever the preliminary successes in elementary, rudimentary behavior, the fascinating complications of human behavior—not yet exhausted even in song and fiction—have hardly yet been addressed by science. Shall a science of behavior arrive before the Parousia, the "end of time"? To trust in it requires great faith.

In these respects, Skinner's work is more like theology than like science. The burgeoning of such speculation, if it continues, may well bring about, from an unexpected direction, that rebirth of metaphysics that accompanies each new cultural age.

18

A Quiver of Queries

Joseph J. Schwab

*Joseph J. Schwab, professor of education and of the biological
sciences at the University of Chicago, is the author of several books,
including* Biology Teacher's Handbook *and* The Teaching of Science
as Inquiry.

*With this chapter, we present a cogent summary—analyses of the
debate Skinner has stimulated throughout the intellectual world.
In the course of the conference on Skinnerism at the Center, the need
for a synthesis of the stands taken by the various speakers became
apparent. Schwab undertook this task and, in executing it, developed
this summary of questions that had been raised about behaviorist
theories. He also categorizes the various opinions expressed by
conference participants so that, in this one paper, one can review the
favorable and unfavorable comments made on Skinner's work. It
prepares the way for Skinner's own concluding response, with which
this book ends.*

I shall summarize those of the critical papers on Skinner that are available to me.[1] I shall summarize by way of two schemes that are roughly

---

[1]Those examined are by Max Black, Alexander Comfort, Arthur Jensen, Chaim
Perelman, Dennis Pirages, Lord Ritchie-Calder, Robert Rosen, Arnold Toynbee, and
L. A. Zadeh.

orthogonal to one another. The first scheme is concerned with those facets of the text, of the argument as such, that are questioned by the critics. The second scheme is concerned with those assertions by Skinner that are called into question by virtue of the critics' doubts about the argument.

Scheme 1

The span of Skinner's argument rests, on one side,[2] on a series of premises concerning the nature of science or, at least, the nature of the best and most reliable science. First, for Skinner, a science must treat its subject matter in its own terms. In his case, behavior itself must be examined. A study of the substrate of behavior (neurons, synapses, the organization of the brain, hormones) will not do. A study of some larger encompassing subject matter of which individual behavior is a part (society, culture, institutional structure, the flow of history) will not do. Second, a science must seek to establish "laws" and limit itself to such laws, statements of predictable uniformities of observable behavior. It must disavow conceptual structures (momentum, energy) inaccessible to observation. It must go beyond description, however exact and extensive.

Given these premises, Skinner can assert his own mode of scientific enquiry as a privileged one. In the light of its conclusions, deviant conclusions from other sources that have used other modes of enquiry (personality theory, social psychology, sociology) can be rejected or submitted to the dominance of Skinner's law-seeking and law-stating science of visible behavior as such.

The criticism of these premises is, in general, that the matters dealt with here are issues of principle and not of fact. They are not issues of fact, inasmuch as the choice of the level of enquiry, and the choice of the form that the account of enquiry should take, determine what facts are relevant to enquiry. It follows, then, that an argument that one level of enquiry is better or more appropriate than others can be matched by equally strong arguments for enquiry at other levels. Arguments and facts stressing the rightness of descriptive laws as the proper outcome of enquiry can be matched by arguments and facts stressing the rightness of coherent conceptual structures or even of meticulous running description.

This is to say that an investigator concerned with individual behavior

---

[2]The other side rests on Skinner's scientific work. No critic questions it. Some do not out of ignorance of it; others, because they know it and recognize its high quality.

may, as Skinner has done, choose an originating enquiry that treats such behaviors in their own terms. He may also, however, choose originating enquiries that treat these behaviors in terms of the enveloping context in which they occur; or he may seek the basis of his account in the underlying substrate of behavior. There are no prior principles, agreed upon by all, that establish one order in which these researches should be done, nor any arguments, acceptable to all, that establish one as better than the others.

What holds for the level at which enquiry should be pursued holds also for the form that the account of the enquiry may take. It may be a statement of uniform antecedent–consequent chains of events. It may be the construction of a complex equation in which only a few of the terms can be referred directly to visible, measurable constants and variable quantities.

I hasten to add that these criticisms do not constitute a mere relativism. There is better and worse research in the eyes of these critics (and Skinner's ranks among the best), but the criteria of better and worse concern the soundness with which the work that is required by a choice of principles of enquiry is carried out, and do not concern the choices of these principles.

Criticisms aimed at this part of Skinner's argument are made, suggested, or illustrated by Black, Ritchie-Calder, Rosen, and Zadeh. Black asserts, for example, that the question of the appropriate mode of enquiry poses problems that are difficult and complex, that the pattern of enquiry pursued by Skinner is entirely defensible—but not defensible as excluding others. Rosen points to the possibility of multiple universes of discourse. Zadeh illustrates what might be done by pursuing a pattern of enquiry vastly remote from Skinner's: construction of a mathematical model that deliberately uses "fuzzy" (that is, loosely defined) variables. Ritchie-Calder points to the roles of chance, uncertainty, and indeterminacy in modern physics to counter Skinner's insistence on predictable uniformity as the proper outcome of scientific investigation.

The second most common concern among the critics in question is for factors affecting behavior that they feel Skinner, by virtue of his exclusivist premises, has dismissed, displaced, or underemphasized.

Comfort, for example, names four factors, each of which may preempt some part of the field of behavior and thus reduce, to an extent as yet undetermined, the potency of Skinner's operant conditioning. Comfort points, first, to the clear existence of behaviors laid down during embryogenesis of the nervous system, and, as we shall see, this is much more than a statement of the existence of some discrete "instinctual" behaviors (for example, patterns of sheep herding in certain varieties of shepherd dogs). Second, he points to the possibility that some of the conditionable spaces in this genetic program of behavior may have shapes of their own—that is, that some new behaviors may be inducible, and others may not. Third, he suggests that Skinner, in rejecting unobservables, may well have thrown away a few too many, especially the identity sense, the experience of "me," which (it is implied, though not stated) may be the beginning of a process of self-chosen and self-executed conditioning (freedom). His fourth point is an outright statement of part of what is implied in the third—the possibility of a considerable amount of wholly endogenous conditioning. In general, Comfort points out that what we know from biology forbids our treating any organism—and especially man—as clay in the hands of the potter-conditioner. Organisms—and especially man—have a say in the process. They engage in a complex dialogue with the environment.

To his numbered four, Comfort adds a frightening fifth: the existence of a variety of men who are inveterate and unalterable seekers and users of power. If this is true, the countercontrols invoked by Skinner as the means by which his proposed program is to avoid dictatorship may be far less powerful than he conceives them to be.

Jensen and Pirages similarly draw attention to factors minimized in Skinner's treatment. Jensen is concerned with the extent to which our genetic endowment sets limits and determines directions for conditioning. Pirages raises a possibility inherent in the Durkheimian origination of sociology—that there are social facts (facts about the structure of society) that are quite distinct from facts about individuals, and that these social facts exhibit aspects of human behavior that are not mere aggregates of behaviors of individuals taken singly. If this is true, a program of operant conditioning developed for the modification of individual behavior will encounter problems it does not anticipate. It will need, as supplement, a program based upon knowledge of institutions and communities as such.

Black is especially concerned with Skinner's sweeping discard of "mentalistic" terms, especially the terms "intention," "(deliberate) action," "motive," and terms that refer to feelings (love, rage, shame, guilt)—the terms directly concerned with freedom and responsibility (dignity?). Black's concern, moreover, is not grounded in a sense of philosophical proprietorship in such matters, nor in a doctrinaire philosophy. It rises out of the substantial and surprisingly rigorous body of analysis of such terms, undertaken by philosophers in the last ten years, as the terms are used, both in common language utterances and by well-trained experts concerned with such matters. This body of philosophical analysis—which is a far cry from the doctrinaire stance commonly associated with "philosophy"—has disclosed a surprisingly large burden of defensible meaning and effectiveness in such terms.

Jensen's concern with omissions partly overlaps Comfort's. He raises the desirability of bringing into the account of behavior a concern for the ways in which genetic factors may not only reduce the scope of behaviors amenable to operant conditioning but also determine those moments in the development of an organism when conditioning can occur and those periods when conditioning cannot be effective.

The third aspect of Skinner's treatment seriously questioned by his critics concerns his use of language in the intermediate steps of his argument. These criticisms, by no means *ad hominem*, point to ambiguities (ambiguities that Rosen gently calls "broad semantic fields") in such key words in Skinner's argument as "control," "responsible," and "environment." The ambiguities are seen as permitting numerous equivocations and occasional beggings of the question. By "equivocation," the critics mean that, in a series of propositions that constitute the steps of an apparent argument, a key word, such as the word that stands in the position of the subject of each of the series of propositions, changes its meaning from proposition to proposition. The word is a "hat check" for one "hat" in one proposition, and a check for quite a different one in a later proposition of the sreies. Hence, the series, which appears to lead to an inference concerning the first referent of the word, ends with a conclusion about something else. By question begging, the critics mean that a question is so phrased that it foredooms the answer: the answer is inherent in the question.

Black is especially concerned with equivocation on "responsibility," seeing it used, at one moment, in the sense of deserving of praise or blame, and seeing it used later to mean no more than "being the source of a determiner." He is concerned with similar shifts in the meaning of "environment" and "control." Toynbee is concerned with equivocations in the passages in which Skinner claims to translate from the language of mentalism to the language of behavior, equivocations that lead to Skinner's denial of the existence of freedom. Perelman is concerned with equivocations in those passages that translate value statements to reinforcement statements—translations that purport to show, that is, that utterances of value statements are merely symptoms of effective conditioning. And Ritchie-Calder, like Black, is concerned with equivocations on "environment."

The fourth aspect of the argument to which criticism is addressed is that crucial interface at which Skinner passes from scientific knowledge to exhortations concerning choice and action. This criticism points out the extent to which the discursive and inductive logics of science are not, as a rule, applicable to problems that concern the concrete and particular (as against the abstract and generalized subject matters of scientific statements). Unfortunately, neither scientists nor logicians yet know very much about the processes of deliberation that carry us from knowledge to defensible decision about concrete and particular action. We are especially ignorant about the ways in which scientific knowledge is modified and brought to bear in the process of making decisions. We are sure that scientific knowledge does not, by itself, dictate policy; we are equally sure that it is germane to the making of policy; we are not at all clear as to the transformations that lie somewhere between these two, except that what some call values and others call conditioning are somehow involved.

Scheme 2

I turn now to the targets, those conclusions of Skinner's that suffer most from these criticisms. (Some repetition, unfortunately, is unavoidable.)

Standing first in frequency of criticism is Skinner's estimate of the efficacy of reinforcement techniques. It is a crucial target, because the whole argument toward policy and action stands or falls on the extent to which reinforcements will determine human behavior. It is, however, an uncertain criticism, because (in my scrutiny, at least) the text of *Beyond Freedom and Dignity* nowhere makes an unequivocal claim concerning this efficacy. The critics, therefore, enjoy a certain freedom in assigning claims to criticize. (In Skinner's oral statements at the seminars held at the Center for the Study of Democratic Institutions, the claims were modest and marked by the qualifications proper to the scientific habit; in the uncertain statements in the published work, there is ground for reading any claim from the extreme of universal application downward.)

At any rate, Comfort points out, as earlier indicated, that the scope apparently claimed is variously foreclosed in some unknown degree by imprinting, endogenous programming, inveterate and recalcitrant power-seeking proclivities, and genetic programs laid down in the nervous system.

Rosen demonstrates, by construction of a well-based mathematical model, that one behavior may be conditionable, an alternative not. He develops a second well-based model illustrative of the possibility that some operant conditionings, once successfully established, can be irreversible. Rosen proceeds, then, to develop models after the Turing machine, both a specific one and a universal one, that exhibit two matters of great importance. First, he shows that it may not be possible, in a reasonable time—or even, perhaps, in a finite time—to discover, by random trial, the key by which the internal state of the organism can be placed in susceptibility to a specific conditioning. (Thus, Rosen raises, once more, the question of whether the one mode of enquiry commended by Skinner suffices, because the alternative to random search for the key to readiness is knowledge of the substrate, of the inner system of the organism.) Rosen proceeds, finally, to point out that, although it is possible to conceive of the existence of a collection of Turing machines such that there is one that can solve any *class* of nameable problems, a well-established theorem demonstrates that, nevertheless, there are some specific problems that the machines cannot solve. Consequently, Rosen suggests, there may be some social and political behaviors, perhaps crucial ones, that are unconditionable.

As a coda, Rosen also raises the problem involved in the very large scale of conditioning activity required for its sociopolitical use. He points out that, if there is grave difficulty in finding the appropriate initial state of any one universal Turing machine, it is a problem *a fortiori* for a great many, each in an unknown and probably different initial state.

Pirages points out that the numbers of men who would be involved in political-social scaled conditioning are more than numbers of men, that they constitute structures and substructures (societies, bureaus, institutions) that may be subservient to laws of their own, over and above the laws of conditioning discovered by Skinner. (Again, this is the matter of levels of enquiry.)

The second target of criticism is Skinner's elimination of freedom. Toynbee argues, for example, that the work we are considering, *Beyond Freedom and Dignity*, is itself a plea for a new policy and a departure from the past and, therefore, is itself an instancing of freedom. He also points out that historians record, with considerable authenticity, the existence of a substantial number of conspicuous social deviants (rebels and saints) who appear to have escaped the net of conditionings of their culture.

Ritchie-Calder points out that indeterminacy, chance, and uncertainty, legitimate conceptions in some sciences, will, if taken into account in a science of behavior, provide scope for the discovery that freedom may, indeed, exist in some degree.

Others argue to similar purpose. Black finds the argument *against* freedom vitiated by equivocations. Perelman points out that, to the extent that *Beyond Freedom and Dignity* fails to persuade, its failure is a failure of the reinforcement process. (Perelman's own expertise concerns rhetoric—persuasion—and is committed to action undertaken as the measure of a persuasion's success.)

The third target is Skinner's cavalier treatment of the problem of reciprocal control of the controllers (his defense against the charge of fascism). Three critics—Perelman, Black, and Comfort—each differing from the others in training and expertise—are agreed, to a surprising extent, on the existence and obdurateness of a variety of men bent on the exercise of power over other men. They hold, in consequence, that countercontrol will not control. The controllers will.

I close with one comment of my own.

The source of many of Skinner's difficulties lies in *the passage* from his scientific work to the book under discussion, not in the book itself. The difficulty is a biological classic: the extrapolation from knowledge of things *in vitro* to conclusions about things *in vivo*, from the glassware of the laboratory to "life."

In the typical instance, the biologist excises an organ or bit of tissue from a living body, places the living part, thus isolated, in the experimental situation dictated by his problem, and observes and reports the behavior of the isolated part truly and well. Then he asserts, with or without qualification, that the doings and undergoings of the organ in the laboratory glass will characterize those of the organ in its place as one organ among many in the complex system called the organism.

The unvoiced premise is that the organ beneighbored is the same as the organ alone; that the factors permitted by the experimenter to react with the organ in its laboratory setting adequately represent the factors operative in and on the organism as a whole.

The experimenter may have made every effort to make this premise true. But whether he has succeeded or not depends on the completeness of his knowledge of the organism intact. That his knowledge is *not* complete is evidence by the very fact that the experiment *in vitro* was performed.[3]

An indubitable parallel exists in the case of Skinner. He and his cohorts may have made every effort to include, in their "experimental space," all the factors that operate in human life. Individual differences in genetic background may have been included. Organisms that interact and form a social structure may have been employed. Subgroups of

---

[3]For the purposes of scientific enquiry, a questionable transition from laboratory to life is not an error but a difficulty to be overcome. For experiment *in vitro* gives leads for observations *in vivo*. Further, assertion of sufficient congruency of the two provokes enquiries to resolve the question of whether they are sufficiently congruent or not. In *Beyond Freedom and Dignity*, Skinner makes it clear that he is aware of both these points. Indeed, he remarked more than three decades ago (Skinner, 1938) that "it is presumably not possible to show that behavior as a whole is a function of the stimulating environment as a whole. A relation between terms as complex as these does not easily submit to analysis and may perhaps never be demonstrated."

organisms with widely different histories of earlier training may have constituted the experimental group. Effort may have been made to note, record, and report differences in response to reinforcement efforts to shape behavior. It remains true, however, that neither Skinner nor anyone else knows enough about human behavior, human culture, and human society to be sure that an experimental space so designed duplicates all the complex facts of human life.

What, then, can be concluded about human behavior *in vivo*, taking account of the results obtained by Skinner in his experimental space? Certainly, that much behavior of many men is the consequence of operant conditioning—by parents, sibs, peer groups, and significant adults beyond the family, by usages of ethnic groups and social classes, and by the laws. We may even conclude *à la* Ivory Soap, that 99.44 percent of the behavior of 99.44 percent of men is so determined. But the 0.56 percent remains and, with it, the possibility of freedom and dignity.

19

Answers for My Critics

B. F. Skinner

B. F. Skinner, the author of Beyond Freedom and Dignity, *is regarded by many as the most influential and controversial living behavioral psychologist. Harvard professor Skinner is the author of* The Behavior of Organisms, Walden Two (*a novel*), Science and Human Behavior, Verbal Behavior, Cumulative Record, The Technology of Teaching *and* Contingencies of Reinforcement. *Skinner, who was present throughout the conference, delivered his response after the presentation by Schwab. This chapter provides Skinner's most complete response to his critics.*

The preparation of this chapter was supported by the National Institutes of Mental Health, grant no. K6-MH-21, 775-01.

Beyond Freedom and Dignity is based on nearly forty years of research on the behavior of organisms. I have long been concerned with its implications, and my first paper on that theme was published seventeen years ago. I spent three years on the present version. It comes as something of a surprise, therefore, to have the book described as a "melange of amateurish metaphysics, self-advertising technology, and illiberal social policy." I feel that there must be some mistake.

And indeed there is. Most of my critics have shown a surprising misunderstanding of the science on which the book is based and of the nature of my treatment of the subject. The almost inevitable comment of my friends is, "But that is not what you were saying!" The fault, of course, may be mine. For many readers, I have obviously not developed my position logically or presented it clearly. I may claim some exoneration, however. I am touching a sore spot. No one who values a democratic way of life can be very happy about what is happening in its name today, and any critique of its basic principles is therefore likely to evoke an angry response. There *must* be something wrong with the book, and the easiest way to find something wrong is to misunderstand it. Paraphrase certain premises inaccurately, draw some absurd conclusions, and you may then rush on to call what I am saying nonsense or gibberish. This headlong dash to dismiss the book without dealing with its argument is fortunately not conspicuous in the present papers. Nevertheless, there are misunderstandings which call for comment.

The argument of the book rests on the existence, or at least the imminence, of a science of behavior. I believe that such a science exists, but I made no effort to prove it. I assumed that my readers would either look up the references at the end of the book or take my word for it for the sake of argument. But that was not what happened. Instead, one finds frequent allusions to the "science of behavior" that prevailed half a century ago, with its rats in mazes, its dogs and dinner bells, and its formulation of behavior as a bundle of reflexes. Then, human behavior seemed, indeed, not unlike the behavior of a robot or a marionette.

What has come to be called the experimental analysis of behavior is a highly advanced science, as rigorous as any part of biology dealing with the organism as a whole. In hundreds of laboratories throughout the world, complex environments are arranged, to which organisms from a fairly wide range of species, including man, are exposed. The research is not statistical or actuarial; it is almost always the behavior of a single organism that is being analyzed. Yet the results are highly reproducible from laboratory to laboratory. Certain measures are taken to simplify the design of such experiments, but the situations under analysis are far from simple. It is difficult, if not impossible, to discover what is happening in a typical experiment through casual observation alone.

This is perhaps only a small part of what could be called "behavioral science," but it is particularly relevant to our problem. The analysis differs from reflexology by emphasizing the consequences of behavior, the significance of which will appear later. The word "operant" is used to emphasize the fact that behavior operates upon the environment to produce consequences, certain kinds of which "reinforce" the behavior they are contingent upon, in the sense that they make it more likely to occur again. So-called contingencies of reinforcement represent subtle and complex relations among three things: the setting or occasion upon which behavior occurs, the behavior itself, and its reinforcing consequences. Suitable contingencies generate behavior which, in man, is said to show the operation of higher mental processes. Consider, for example, the cognitive process of attention. Why do we not respond to all the stimuli impinging upon us at any given time? It is easy to say that we act upon the environment selectively, as if some Maxwell's demon opens and closes a gate, allowing some stimuli to enter and keeping others out. But how are we to explain the demon? An internal gate keeper is a fiction. All we know is that we respond to some stimuli and not to others, and we can explain that fact by looking at the contingencies. An experiment will demonstrate.

In an experimental space, a hungry pigeon pecks at a small disk on the wall, and when it does so, food occasionally appears from a dispenser. As a result, the pigeon is more likely to peck the disk again. There is a complication, however. The disk may be either red or green and it may have a triangle or a square projected upon it. If food appears only when the pigeon pecks a disk which bears a given set of these properties, the pigeon will come to peck only that set. For example, if we reinforce pecking a green disk but never a red, the pigeon will stop pecking the red disk and continue to peck the green. If we reinforce pecking triangles but not squares, the pigeon will peck triangles and stop pecking squares. If we reinforce pecking only a green square or a red triangle, it will stop pecking the green triangle and the red square. But now a further complication: we slowly weaken the stimuli—washing out the color by adding white light and putting the pattern out of focus. The pigeon finds it more and more difficult to make the discriminations. But suppose we provide two other disks which, if pecked by the pigeon, will cause the color to improve or the figure to clarify. Under these conditions, the pigeon will keep relevant properties clear. If color is essential for the discrimination, it will peck the disk which keeps the color strong. If the pattern is essential, it will peck the disk which keeps it in focus. If both are needed (if only the red square and the green triangle are reinforced, for example), the pigeon will keep both form and color clear. In other words, the contingencies induce the pigeon to maintain just that condition of the stimuli under which it behaves successfully. The pigeon "looks at" the form and not the color, or at the color and not the form, or at both, depending upon the contingencies of reinforcement. This is very much like what we do when we observe stimuli, although the behavior through which we control their properties is by no means so conspicuous. Other contingencies can be arranged to produce behavior which could be said to show self-knowledge or self-management.

As our knowledge of the effects of contingencies of reinforcement increases, we can more often predict what an organism will do by observing the contingencies; and by arranging contingencies, we can increase the probability that an organism will behave in a given way. In the latter case, we may be said to "control" its behavior. The term does not mean forcible coercion or the triggering of a jack-in-the-box kind of reflex action. The biologist who "controls" a disease does not wrestle with it physically. He simply changes some of the conditions under which the disease flourishes. Human behavior is controlled not by physical manipulation but by changing the environmental conditions of which it is a function. The control is probabilistic. The organism is not forced to behave in a given way; it is simply made more likely to do so.

It is dangerous and foolish to deny the existence of a science of behavior in order to avoid its implications. It is equally dangerous to dismiss its technological uses. Many of these may be seen in other experiments on behavior. A pigeon, for example, can be induced to behave in ways which, if the subject were human, would be said to report its sensations or perceptions. Special techniques make it possible to "ask a pigeon whether or not it sees a faint spot of light," and, with them, the spectral sensitivity of the pigeon has been determined with almost as much precision as that of man. Psychopharmocology, experimental psychiatry, and neurophysiology have also made extensive use of operant techniques.

In the world at large, the most impressive results have been obtained in certain relatively closed systems, as in the management of institutionalized psychotics, in the care of retardates and autistic children, and in training schools for juvenile delinquents. But more and more is being done in open systems, such as in the care of children in the home and in day-care centers, in classroom management, in the design of instructional materials, and in incentive systems in industry. Much of this still has a long way to go, and some of the reasons why we are not taking greater advantage of the technological power of a scientific analysis are discussed in my book. Certainly, it will not do to dismiss the implications by saying that the promise of a behavioral technology is a mere bluff and that we have nothing to fear. (That contention, incidentally, is effectively counterbalanced by some critics' predictions of a tyrannical or totalitarian misuse of control.)

The analysis shifts to the environment a causal role previously assigned to a person's feelings, states of mind, purposes, or other attributes. But what about the subjective evidence? Are we not aware of the feelings which prompt us to act, or the ideas we eventually express in words, or the intentions or purposes we later carry out? Can we not say that this evidence is ignored by any analysis which assigns causality to the environment?

Behaviorists do not "ignore" consciousness. On the contrary, they have developed reasonably successful ways of talking about it. A small part of the universe is enclosed within the skin of each of us, and we can observe some of this as we observe the world around us. But in spite of their teeming intimacy, we do not discriminate successfully among the states or aspects of our own bodies. The reason is expressed in the old philosophical notion that nothing is different until it makes a difference. When a person turns a handspring, he responds to various stimuli coming from his body, and he could not turn a handspring successfully without them, but he does not *know* these stimuli simply because he responds to them. Knowing arises from a different kind of contingency. We teach a child to "know his colors" by reinforcing verbal responses in the presence of colors. We show him red, and if he says "Green," we say No," and if he says "Red," we say "Yes." The result is different from such a practical response as picking a red apple instead of a green one; it might be said to show the possession of "abstract knowlegde." We cannot follow the same procedure in teaching a child about his internal states. We cannot show him diffidence, for example, and correct him if he says, "Embarrassment." No matter how closely he may be in contact with his own body, we are not in contact with it to anything like the same degree and, hence, cannot set up good discriminative repertoires.

Even though our knowledge of our own bodies is defective, the stimuli we receive from them are salient, and, at any given moment, they may be stronger than what we can recall of the personal histories which were responsible for them. Moreover, they seem to be in the right temporal position to function as causes. If I say that I came to this meeting because I felt like coming, I may seem to give some sort of explanation. But can I explain why I felt like coming? If I try to do so by pointing to what has happened in my life with respect to similar meetings, then I must ask whether that explains why I felt like coming or the fact that I actually came. Will not certain past circumstances explain both why I came and why I felt like coming? It is a reasonable view that both self-knowledge and self-management must be derived from society, because contingencies which give rise to them require a verbal environment. When, therefore, an experimental analysis shifts the emphasis from an autonomous man to the environment, no subjective evidence can stand in its way.

Beyond Freedom and Dignity does not use a scientific analysis of behavior for purposes of prediction or control. The science lies behind the book rather than in it. It is used merely for purposes of interpretation. Other sciences interpret nature without attracting attention. When a physicist gives a quick explanation of what is happening when a tennis ball behaves strangely during a game, he can be challenged; he doesn't have the facts. But his account is more likely to be correct than that of someone who is not familiar with trajectories, air friction, Venturi forces, and so on, under the controlled conditions of the laboratory. Interpretation is a substantial part of many fields of science, including geology, astronomy, subatomic physics, and evolution. When phenomena are out of reach in time or space, or too large or small to be directly manipulated, we must talk about them with less than a complete account of relevant conditions. What has been learned under more favorable conditions is then invaluable.

As I have pointed out, casual observation is seldom enough to explain what is going on in an operant laboratory, even when the organism under analysis is as "simple" as a pigeon. Looking into an experimental space, one sees stimuli appear and disappear, responses being made, and reinforcers occasionally appearing and being consumed. But in a modern experiment, the interrelations among these three events may be very hard to detect. Additional information is to be found in the log of the experiment, which tells us something about the genetics of the subject and its environmental history; in a visual display, such as the standard cumulative record, which shows, at a glance, changes in rate of responding over a period of time; and, above all, in an inspection of the apparatus which arranges the prevailing contingencies of reinforcement. An observer who has had experience in the use of such additional information is much more likely to interpret correctly what he sees when he looks into an experimental space for the first time.

My *Verbal Behavior* was an exercise in interpretation. In it, I pointed to similarities between the contingencies of reinforcement which generate verbal behavior and the contingencies which have been analyzed with much greater precision in the laboratory. The account is, I believe, more plausible than those proposed, without benefit of laboratory experience, by linguists and psycholinguists when they are dealing with the same kinds of facts. *Beyond Freedom and Dignity* is also an exercise in interpretation. It is not science as such, but it is not metaphysics, either. It analyzes certain behavioral processes which have played a part in the struggle for freedom and dignity. When I question the supposed residual freedom of autonomous man, I am not debating the issue of free will. I am simply describing the slow demise of a prescientific explanatory device. Autonomous behavior is treated simply as uncaused behavior. The argument is, I believe, quite similar to that against vital forces in biology. Until biochemistry could account for all bodily processes, a prescientific agent was said to be operative. It was not a matter of disproving the reality of vital forces through metaphysical disputation which made the concept unneccessary; it was, rather, a matter of making steady advances in biochemistry.

My discussion of values is also not metaphysical. It is a behavioral analysis of the things people call good, for reasons to be found in the evolution of the species and in the practices of a social environment. Of special importance are the "goods" which arise when a culture contrives immediate reinforcers which generate behavior having certain deferred consequences. The culture "makes the future important" by analyzing contingencies, by extracting rules from them, by reinforcing people when they follow the rules, and so on.

It would be absurd to claim that such an interpretation is now fully adequate, but the objections most often raised are not always cogent. The translation of traditional terms into what is often contemptuously called "behaviorese" may still be awkward. Traditional terms have acquired many meanings, and the reader who takes a given translation to stand for more than one may complain of equivocation. A word like "contingency" is conspicuous, and its repeated use may lead to complaints of unnecessary repetition, but my book is about contingencies, and it would be costly to introduce synonyms simply for the sake of variety. Again, operant behavior is, as I have pointed out elsewhere, the field of purpose, but although we may repeat the word "purpose" with impunity, to repeat such an expression as "reinforcing consequences" is to run a considerable stylistic risk. Such risks must be accepted, if we are to get on with the analysis.

My treatment of freedom can be summarized briefly. (It is said that I do not sufficiently identify the authors of the literature of freedom; I mention some of them—Voltaire, Diderot, Rousseau, J. S. Mill, and a few moderns—but I do not "review the literature"; I am concerned with certain kinds of statements, such as were, or might have been, part of the literature, and those who have insisted that "no one talks that way any more" and that I am attacking straw men have, in fact, supplied many other examples.) Through certain processes of escape and avoidance, extensively analyzed in the laboratory, we respond to those who treat us aversively either by moving away from them or attacking and weakening them. We may then "feel free," and say that we can now do only what we want to do. But the experimental analysis of behavior has clarified the process of positive reinforcement which induces us to do what we feel like doing. It is particularly dangerous to dismiss this evidence, because the control exercised through positive reinforcement has no built-in source of countercontrol.

The argument with respect to dignity appeals to the same kind of evidence. We give a person credit for his achievements when we can see no other explanation of his behavior, but a scientific analysis reveals unsuspected contributions from the environment which naturally diminish the role supposedly played by the person himself.

These are not academic issues. The literatures of freedom and dignity have strongly defended and aggrandized the individual, and he fights doggedly to protect his supposed prerogatives. I have pointed to two unfortunate consequences. One is the support of punitive practices. If we simply punish bad behavior, we can give the individual credit for behaving well; but if we build a world in which he naturally behaves well, the world must get the credit. He is being automatically good; he is exhibiting no inner goodness or virtue. It is said that the nations of the world are spending two hundred billion dollars every year in the name of defense, all in the form of potential punishments to be used if other people behave badly. Possibly as much is spent in maintaining domestic order. Yet, in spite of this staggering waste, the suggestion that we should direct ourselves to the construction of a world in which people will be "naturally" good will be rejected by most defenders of freedom and dignity. When we turn to nonpunitive measures, we permit ourselves to use only the least effective, because we thus leave something for which the individual can take credit, something which testifies to his freedom of choice.

I simply ask my reader to consider the possibility that human behavior is always controlled, and by conditions which we are slowly coming to understand. As I have noted, control does not mean physical restraint or manipulation in the etymological sense. The behavioral scientist simply changes the environment in such a way that behavior is changed. The literatures of freedom and dignity have not been concerned with freeing man from control but merely with changing the kind of control. We still have a long way to go to get the best results.

But that, of course, raises a basic issue. What *are* the best results? Who is to use the practices derived from a scientific analysis of behavior, and to what end? I have tried to answer those questions, not by giving names or specifying values, but by applying a behavioral analysis to what has happened and is likely to happen in the evolution of cultures. It will not be any person or any kind of person, benevolent or compassionate, who will determine the use to be made of a behavioral technology. To look for assurance to a kind of *person* is to make the same old mistake. We should look instead to the culture of which such a person's behavior will be a function, switching again from a supposedly originating individual to a controlling, largely social environment. In the past, individuals have emerged to seize power and use it to advance their own interests. They have done so because the culture has permitted them (indeed, induced them) to do so. In a different culture, power will be used in a different way. What way is a question to be answered by looking at the consequences.

It is a difficult kind of answer, and I have obviously failed to make it clear to many of my readers, who have offered a different answer—namely, that a science of behavior and its technology can lead only to a totalitarian despotism—and, as usual, have implied that a Cassandran prediction needs none of the factual support demanded of anyone who prophesies a better world. Selection by consequences raises the question of how the future can figure in the "decisions" which affect it. Somehow or other, living things have circumvented the rule against final causes. It is the future of a mutation which "decides" whether it is good or bad. Genetics and ecology point to the mechanisms which make this possible in natural selection. In the field of behavior, it is the reinforcing consequences which alter the probability that an organism will subsequently behave in a given way. The physiological mechanisms which make this possible (themselves a product of natural selection) are not yet known. Presumably, the consequences must, to some extent, overlap ongoing behavior, but reinforcers may be conditioned to permit the shaping and maintaining of behavior under circumstances in which relevant consequences are long deferred. The social environment we call a culture plays an important part in mediating deferred consequences for the individual.

Both in natural selection and in operant conditioning, consequences take over a role previously assigned to an antecedent creative mind. Before Darwin, the word was spelled with a capital M, and it was supposed to have produced the millions of diverse creatures found on the surface of the earth. In operant conditioning, the selective action of consequences generates behavior traditionally attributed to another creative mind. Both in natural selection and in operant conditioning, the purpose or design attributed to a creative agent also changes place. As I have pointed out elsewhere, the field of operant behavior is the field of purpose.

The question of who is to control, and to what end, must be answered by still another process of selection—in the evolution of cultures. New cultural practices are like mutations. A practice which contributes to the survival of those who practice it survives when they survive. This third circumvention of the rule against final causes becomes possible when, by virtue of the two other circumventions, a species reaches the point at which it builds a culture. The human species has obviously reached such a point, but it has not been necessary that anyone plan or design a culture in advance, because the notion of selection dispenses with the need for design. No one designed the anatomy and physiology of the human species and no one designs the behavior which emerges under natural contingencies of reinforcement. Similarly, no one need design a given stage in the evolution of a culture.

At some point, however, design becomes possible at all three levels. Changes can be made either by changing the conditions of selection or by introducing new mutations. Breeding practices have changed contingencies of survival and have modified the evolution of various species. Geneticists are now talking about the possibility of introducing mutations to speed evolution or change its course. In operant conditioning, it has long been possible to change the topography of behavior by changing contingencies of reinforcement, and we may produce novel forms of behavior by changing the provenance of the behavior which undergoes selection. Similarly, the evolution of a culture may be affected by changing the contingencies of survival (for example, by making it possible for less effective practices to satisfy contingencies) or by introducing new practices as mutations.

In the evolution of a culture, up to the point at which design becomes feasible, new practices may arise for reasons which have no bearing on their survival value, and this may be true even when practices are "deliberately" designed for the sake of future consequences. The survival of a practice may have no connection with the consequences responsible for its introduction. It is only when the survival of the culture is taken into account that a special kind of design emerges, a design in which the contingencies of that survival shape and maintain the behavior of the members of what Harvey Wheeler has called a new profession.

Up to the point of explicit cultural design, a social system emerges as a compromise between would-be controllers and those they would control. Some kind of uneasy equilibrium is maintained between nation and nation, nation and citizen, capital and labor, therapist and patient, teacher and student, or parent and child. Control and countercontrol explain the behavior of the parties involved—although, traditionally, such behavior has been mistakenly attributed to personal traits, such as compassion or benevolence. We make the same mistake when we look to personal traits for assurance that the power of a technology of behavior will not be misused. I have argued elsewhere that certain classical examples of mistreatment—in homes for young children or the aged, in prisons, in hospitals for psychotics, and in homes for retardates—arise not because those who run such institutions lack compassion but rather because those who live there cannot exert countercontrol.

Some balancing of control and countercontrol may be a first step in the design of an effective culture, and a successful result may be said to yield the greatest good of the greatest number. But such a design will not necessarily have survival value, and those who are concerned for the future of a culture must go beyond the countercontrolling pattern. The good of the culture may be quite unrelated to the personal goods of controller and controllee (although this is not likely to be the case, because the culture depends ultimately upon the strength of its members). We might say that the person who designs entirely for the good of the culture should be untouched by personal goods—but this is impossible, because the good of the culture can act only when it has been converted into personal goods. Nevertheless, some sacrifice of personal goods may be needed, and, in the extreme case, the sacrifice may be total. The soldier who gives his life for the good of his country or to make the world safe for democracy or communism is under the control of a particular kind of social environment, and religious martyrdom shows a similar pattern. It is not too difficult to show how such environments arise or why they are likely to survive. But can we escape from the jingoistic devices which, although they make for survival, suggest some kind of social Darwinism? Where are we to find the conditioned reinforcers which will work for the future of mankind?

It may be, as it has been so often in the past, that we must look to aversive contingencies. Almost everything now being said about our global problems is designed to strengthen behavior having the form of escape or aviodance: we must save mankind from an overpopulated, impoverished, and polluted earth and from nuclear destruction. The cultural designer who proposes measures clearly designed to *save* mankind is not likely to be challenged. But should we overlook the possibility that we can move toward a world in which people will be not only safe and in possession of the goods they need but more likely to show the kinds of creative achievements of which the human species is capable?

If we are to make sure that no individual or small group will emerge to use despotically the power conferred by a science of behavior, we must design a culture in which no one *can* emerge in such a position. A system of control and countercontrol is a primitive device which may contain depotism, and it is supported by powerful contingencies affecting all parties, but it must be supplemented by practices which bring people under the control of a more remote future. This is not a choice to be made; it is a matter of selection. If despotic rule is bad, immoral, or unethical, then it is the sign of a bad culture, and another kind of culture will be more likely to survive—if it can get its chance. Such a chance could conceivably arise by accident, but we have reached the point at which it may come from explicit design. Those who have been induced by our culture to be concerned for its future have the opportunity to change the evolution of that culture in a most important way.

References

Ayllon, T., and H. H. Azrin, 1968. *The Token Economy: A Motivational System for Rehabilitation and Therapy*. New York: Appleton-Century-Crofts.

———, and J. Michael, 1959, The psychiatric nurse as a behavioral engineer. *Journal of the Experimental Analysis of Behavior*, 2:323–334.

Azrin, N. H., and W. C. Holz, 1966. Punishment. *In* W. K. Honig, ed., *Operant Behavior: Areas of Research and Application*. New York: Appleton-Century-Crofts.

Baer, D. M., and M. M. Wolf, 1970. The entry into natural communities of reinforcement. *In* R. Ulrich, T. Stachnik, and J. Mabry, eds., *Control of Human Behavior* Glenview, Ill.: Scott, Foresman.

Bandura, A., 1971. *Social Learning Theory*. New York: General Learning Press.

Barnet, Richard, 1971. The game of nations. *Harper's Magazine*, 243(1458):53–59.

Bellman, R. E., and L. A. Zadeh, 1970. Decision-making in a fuzzy environment. *Management Science*, 17:B-141–B-164.

Blau, Peter, 1964. *Exchange and Power in Social Life*. New York: John Wiley & Sons.

Boakes, R. A., and M. S. Halliday, 1970. The Skinnerian analysis of behavior. *In* R. Borger and F. Cioffi, eds., *Explanation in the Behavioral Sciences*. Cambridge: Cambridge University Press.

Boggs, L. J., and V. V. Rozynko, 1972. Effects of the reduction in magnitude of monetary reinforcement with an alcoholic population. Paper presented at the Western Psychological Association Conference, Portland, Oregon, April 1972.

Bohm, D., 1965. *The Special Theory of Relativity*, Appendix: physics and perception, pp. 185–230. New York: W. A. Benjamin.

Bower, G. H., 1970. Organizational factors in memory. *Cognitive Psychology*, 1:18–46.

Bower, T. G. R., 1966. The visual world of infants. *Scientific American*, 215(6): 80–92. (Available as *Scientific American* Offprint 502.)

Bracht, G. H., 1970. Experimental factors related to aptitude–treatment interactions. *Review of Educational Research*, 40:627–645.

Brener, J., and D. Hothersall, 1966. Heart rate control under conditions of augmented sensory feedback. *Psychophysiology*, 3:23–28.

———, and R. A. Kleinman, 1971. Learned control of decreases in systolic blood pressure. *In* Theodore X. Barber et al., eds., *Biofeedback and Self-control 1970: An Aldine Annual on the Regulation of Bodily Processes and Consciousness*. Chicago: Aldine-Atherton.

Bridgman, P. W., 1959. *The Way Things Are*. Cambridge, Mass.: Harvard University Press.

Bucher, B., and O. I. Lovaas, 1968. Use of aversive stimulation in behavior modification. *In* Marshall R. Jones, ed., *Miami Symposium on the Prediction of Behavior, 1967: Aversive Stimulation*. Coral Gables, Fla.: University of Miami Press.

Buckley, N. K., and H. M. Walker, 1970. *Modifying Classroom Behavior*. Champaign, Ill.: Research Press.

Budzynski, T., J. Stoyva, and C. Adler, 1969. Feedback-induced muscle relaxation: application to tension headache. Paper presented at the ninth annual meeting of the Society for Psychophysiological Research, Monterey, California, October 1969.

Burgess, R. L., R. N. Clark, and J. C. Hendee, 1971. An experimental analysis of anti-litter procedures. *Journal of Applied Behavior Analysis*, 4:71–75.

Chomsky, N., 1957. *Syntactic Structures*. The Hague: Mouton and Co.

———, 1971. The case against B. F. Skinner. *New York Review of Books*, December 30, 1971, pp. 18–24.

Cohen, H. L., I. Goldiamond, et al., 1968. *Training Professionals in Procedures for Educational Environments*. Washington, D. C.: Educational Facilities Press–IBR.

Crider, A., D. Shapiro, and B. Tursky, 1966. Reinforcement of spontaneous electrodermal activity. *Journal of Comparative and Physiological Psychology*, 61:20–27.

Daly, Herman, 1973. *Toward a Steady-State Economy*. San Francisco: W. H. Freeman and Company.

Darlington, C. D., 1969. *The Evolution of Man and Society*. New York: Simon and Schuster.

Davis, K., 1947. Final note on a case of extreme isolation. *American Journal of Sociology*, 57:432–457.

———, 1966. Sociological aspects of genetic control. *In* J. D. Roslansky, ed., *Genetics and the Future of Man*, pp. 173–204. New York: Appleton-Century-Crofts.

DiCara, L. V., and N. E. Miller, 1968. Instrumental learning of vasomotor responses by rats: learning to respond differentially in the two ears. *Science*, 159:1485–1486.

Douglas, R. J., and K. H. Pribram, 1969. Distraction and habituation in monkeys with limbic lesions. *Journal of Comparative and Physiological Psychology*, 69:473–480.

Ehrlich, Paul R., and Anne H. Ehrlich, 1972. *Population, Resources, Environment: Issues in Human Ecology* (2nd ed.). San Francisco: W. H. Freeman and Company.

Engel, B. T., and R. A Chism, 1967. Operant conditioning of heart rate speeding. *Psychophysiology*, 3:418–426.

———, and S. P. Hansen, 1966. Operant conditioning of heart rate slowing. *Psychophysiology*, 3:176–187.

Erickson, C. W., and J. L. Kuethe, 1956. Avoidance conditioning of verbal behavior without awareness: a paradigm of repression. *Journal of Abnormal and Social Psychology*, 53:203–209.

Estes, W. K., 1959. The statistical approach to learning theory. *In* S. Kock, ed., *Psychology: A Study of a Science*, vol. 2. New York: McGraw-Hill.

Evans, R. I., 1968. *B. F. Skinner: The Man and His Ideas*. New York: E. P. Dutton.

Feinberg, Gerald, 1969. *The Prometheus Project*. New York: Doubleday.

Fenichel, Otto, 1945. *The Psychoanalytic Theory of Neurosis*. New York: Norton.

Fetz, E. E., and D. V. Finocchio, 1971. Operant conditioning of specific patterns. *Science*, 174:431–435.

Forrester, Jay Wright, 1971a. Counterintuitive behavior of social systems. *Technology Review*, January 1971.

———, 1971b. *World Dynamics*. Cambridge, Mass.: Wright-Allen.

Frank, Jerome, 1966. Galloping technology, a new social disease. *Journal of Social Issues*, 22(4):1–14.

Fuller, P. R., 1949. Operant conditioning of a vegetative human organism. *American Journal of Psychology*, 62:587–590.

Gardner, John W., 1969. A failure of leadership—a time to act. Address delivered before the National Press Club, Washington, D. C., December 9, 1969.

Gardner, R. A., and B. T. Gardner, 1969. Teaching sign language to a chimpanzee. *Science*, 165:664–672.

Garfield, Z. H., J. F. McBrearty, and M. Dichter, 1969. A case of impotence successfully treated with desensitization combined with in vivo operant training and thought substitution. *In* Richard D. Rubin and Cyril M. Franks, eds., *Advances in Behavior Therapy*. New York: Academic Press.

Goldiamond, I., 1965. Stuttering and fluency as manipulatable operant response classes. *In* L. Krasner and L. P. Ullman, eds., *Research in Behavior Modification: New Developments and Implications*, pp. 106–156. New York: Holt, Rinehart and Winston.

Greenspoon, J., 1955. The reinforcing effect of two spoken sounds on the frequency of two responses. *American Journal of Psychology*, 68:409–416.

Guiton, P., and D. G. M. Wood-Gush, 1962. The sexual behavior of domestic birds in relation to early experience. *Proceedings of the Twelfth World Poultry Congress, Sydney*, pp. 516–518.

Hamilton, W. D., 1970. Selfish and spiteful behavior in an evolutionary model. *Nature*, 228:1218–1220.

Hardin, G., 1968. The tragedy of the commons. *Science*, 162:1243–1248.

Harman, Willis, 1971. Planning amid forces and instutitional change. Paper presented at the symposium Planning in the Seventies, Washington, D. C., May 3–4, 1971.

Harlow, H. F., and M. K. Harlow, 1962. Social deprivation in monkeys. *Scientific American*, 207(5):137–146. (Available as *Scientific American* Offprint 473.)

Harrison, G. A., J. S. Weiner, J. M. Tanner, and N. A. Barnicot, 1964. *Human Biology: An Introduction to Human Evolution, Variation, and Growth.* London: Oxford University Press.

Held, Richard, 1965. Plasticity in sensory-motor systems. *Scientific American*, 213(5):84–94. (Available as *Scientific American* Offprint 494.)

——, and A. Hein, 1963. Movement-produced stimulation in the development of visually guided behavior. *Journal of Comparative and Physiological Psychology*, 56:872–876.

Hogan, R. A. 1968. The implosive technique. *Behavior Research and Therapy*, 6:423–431.

Holden, C., 1971. Psychologists beset by feelings of futility. *Science*, 173:1111.

Holland, J. G., and B. F. Skinner, 1961. *The Analysis of Behavior.* New York: McGraw-Hill.

Homme, L., et al., 1970. *How to Use Contingency Contracting in the Classroom.* Champaign, Ill.: Research Press.

Huxley, Aldous, 1932. *Brave New World.* Garden City, N. J.: Sun Dial Press.

Jacobsen, E., 1938. *Progressive Relaxation.* Chicago: University of Chicago Press.

James, W., 1931. *Pragmatism: A New Name for Some Old Ways of Thinking.* New York: Longmans. (Originally published in 1907.)

Kamiya, J., 1969. Operant control of the EEG alpha rhythm and some of its reported effects on consciousness. *In* Charles T. Tart, ed., *Altered States of Consciousness.* New York: John Wiley & Sons.

Kant, Immanuel, 1755. No dilucidatio. . . . *In* E. Cassirer, ed., 1912–1920. *Immanuel Kant's Werke*, vol. 1. Berlin.

Kapostins, E. E., 1963. The effects of drl schedules on some characteristics of word utterance. *Journal of the Experimental Analysis of Behavior*, 6:281–290.

Koestler, A., 1968. *The Ghost in the Machine.* New York: Macmillan.

Kraft, T., and I. Al Issa, 1967. Behavior therapy and the treatment of frigidity. *American Journal of Psychotherapy*, 21:116–120.

Krasner, L., and L. P. Ullman, 1965. *Research in Behavior Modification.* New York: Holt, Rinehart and Winston.

Kuhn, Thomas S., 1962. *The Structure of Scientific Revolutions.* Chicago: University of Chicago Press.

Lacey, J. I., D. E. Bateman, and R. Van Lehn, 1953. Autonomic response specificity: an experimental study. *Psychosomatic Medicine*, 15:8–21.

Lenneberg, E. H., 1967. *Biological Foundations of Language.* New York: John Wiley & Sons.

——, 1969. On explaining language. *Science*, 164:635–643.

Lerner, Daniel, ed., 1958. *The Passing of Traditional Society.* New York: The Free Press.

Lifton, Jay, 1968. Protean man. *Partisan Review*, 35:13–27.

Lindsley, D. B., 1961. The reticular activating system and perceptual integration. *In* D. E. Sheer, ed., *Electrical Stimulation of the Brain*. Austin: University of Texas Press.

Lonergan, Bernard J., 1971. *Grace and Freedom* (edited by J. Paout Burns). New York: Herder and Herder.

Lovaas, O. I., G. Freitag, V. J. Gold, and I. C. Kassorka, 1965. Experimental studies in childhood schizophrenia: analysis of self-destructive behavior. *Journal of Experimental Child Psychology*, 2:67–84.

Mach, E., 1959. *The Analysis of Sensation*. New York: Dover.

Madsen, C. H., W. C. Becker, and Don R. Thomas, 1968. Rules, praise, and ignoring: elements of elementary classroom control. *Journal of Applied Behavior Analysis*, 1:139–150.

Marcuse, Herbert, 1964. *One Dimensional Man*. Boston: Beacon Press,

Meichenbaum, D. H., 1971. Cognitive factors in behavior modification: modifying what clients say to themselves. *American Psychological Association Journal Supplement Abstract Service Research Report* (25).

Miller, G., E. Galanter, and K. Pribram, 1960. *Plans and the Structure of Behavior*. New York: Henry Holt.

Miller, N. E., 1969. Learning of visceral and glandular responses. *Science*, 163:434–445.

———, and L. V. DiCara, 1967. Instrumental learning of heart-rate changes in curarized rats: shaping and specificity to discriminative stimulus. *Journal of Comparative and Physiological Psychology*, 63:12.

Newell, A., J. C. Shaw, and H. A. Simon, 1958. Elements of a theory of human problem solving. *Psychological Review*, 65:151–166.

Ophuls, William, 1971. Leviathan or oblivion. Mimeographed paper, Department of Political Science, Yale University.

Orwell, George, 1949. *Nineteen Eighty-four*. London: Secker and Warburg.

Osborne, J. G., 1970. Free-time as a reinforcer in the management of classroom behavior. *In* R. Ulrich, T. Stanchik, and J. Mabry, eds., *Control of Human Behavior*, vol. 2. Glenview, Ill.: Scott, Foresman.

Pico della Mirandola, Giovanni, 1486. Oration on the dignity of man [translated by Elizabeth Livermoore Forces]. *In* E. Cassirer et al., eds., 1948. *The Renaissance Philosophy of Man*. Chicago: University of Chicago Press.

Pirages, Dennis, 1972. *Modernization and Political Tension Management: A Socialist Society in Perspective*. New York: Praeger.

Platt, J. R., 1966. *The Step to Man*. New York: John Wiley & Sons.

———, 1970. Hierarchical restructuring. *General Systems*, 15:49–54.

———, 1971. How men can shape their future. *Futures*, 3:32–47.

Premack, D., 1959. Toward empirical behavioral laws. *Psychological Review*, 66:219–233.

———, 1962. Reversibility of the reinforcement relation. *Science*, 136:255–257.

———, 1965. Reinforcement theory. *In* D. Levine, ed., *Nebraska Symposium on Motivation*. Lincoln: University of Nebraska Press.

Pribam, K. H., 1962. Interrelations of psychology and the neurological disciplines. *In* S. Koch, ed., *Psychology: A Study of a Science*, vol. 4. New York: McGraw-Hill.

———, 1969. DADTA III: computer control of the experimental analysis of behavior. *Perceptual and Motor Skills*, 29:599–608.

———, 1970. Comment on "The Skinnerian Analysis of Behavior." *In* R. A. Boakes and M. S. Halliday, eds., *Explanations in the Behavioral Sciences*. Cambridge: Cambridge University Press.

———, 1971a. The realization of the mind. *Synthese*, 22:313–322.

———, 1971b. *Languages of the Brain*. Englewood Cliffs, N. J.: Prentice-Hall.

———, K. W. Gardner, G. L. Pressman, and M. Bagshaw, 1963. Automated analysis of multiple choice behavior. *Journal of the Experimental Analysis of Behavior*, 6:123–124.

Pryor, K., 1969. Behavior modification: the porpoise caper. *Psychology Today*, 3(7):46–47, 64–65.

Pumroy, D. K., and Shirley S. Pumroy, 1965. Systematic observation and reinforcement technique in toilet training. *Psychological Reports*, 16:467–471.

Rapoport, A., 1957. Scientific approach to ethics. *Science*, 125:796–798.

———, 1966. *Two-Person Game Theory: The Essential Ideas*. Ann Arbor: University of Michigan Press.

Rozynko, V. V., K. D. Swift, and Josephine Swift, 1972. *Alternatives to Punishment*. Documentary film, Profile Films.

Salk, L., 1966. Thoughts on the concept of imprinting and its place in early human development. *Canadian Psychiatric Association Journal*, 11:S296–S305.

Sasmor, R. M., 1966. Operant conditioning of a small scale muscle response. *Journal of the Experimental Analysis of Behavior*, 9:69–85.

Schrödinger, E., 1945. *What is Life?* Epilogue, p. 87. Cambridge: Cambridge University Press.

Schultz, J. H., and W. Luthe, 1959. *Autogenic Training*. New York: Grune and Stratton.

Semb, G., and J. A. Nevin, 1971. Letters: understanding man's behavior. *Science*, 174:891–892.

Sennet, R., 1971. "Beyond Freedom and Dignity," on problems of society and conditioning of behavior. *New York Times Book Review Magazine*, 24 October 1971, pp. 1, 16.

Serber, M., A. Goldstein, G. W. Piaget, and F. Kort, 1969. The use of implosive-expressive therapy in anxiety reactions. *In* R. D. Rubin and C. M. Franks, eds., *Advances in Behavior Therapy*. New York: Academic Press.

Sidman, M., 1966. Avoidance behavior. *In* W. Honig, ed., *Operant Behavior*. New York: Appleton-Century-Crofts.

Skinner, B. F., 1938. *The Behavior of Organisms*. New York: Appleton-Century-Crofts.

———, 1948. *Walden Two*. New York: Macmillan.

———, 1953. *Science and Human Behavior*. New York: Macmillan.

———, 1957. *Verbal Behavior*. New York: Appleton-Century-Crofts.

———, 1958. Reinforcement today. *American Psychologist*, 13(3).

———, 1959. *Cumulative Record*. New York: Appleton-Century-Crofts.

———, 1966. The phylogeny and ontogeny of behavior. *Science*, 153:1205–1213.

———, 1968a. *The Technology of Teaching*. New York: Appleton-Century-Crofts.

————, 1968b. Paper presented at UNESCO Symposium on Brain Research and Human Behavior, UNESCO House, Paris, March 1968.

————, 1969. *Contingencies of Reinforcement: A Theoretical Analysis.* New York: Appleton-Century-Crofts.

————, 1971. *Beyond Freedom and Dignity.* New York: Alfred A. Knopf.

————, and R. Sennet, 1971. [Skinner's comments on Sennet (1971); Sennet's reply]. *New York Times Book Review Magazine,* 21 November 1971, pp. 36, 50.

Spevack, A. A., and K. H. Pribram, in press. A decisional analysis of the effects of limbic lesions on learning in monkeys. *Journal of Comparative and Physiological Psychology.*

Staats, A. W., C. K. Staats, R. E. Schutz, and M. Wolfe, 1962. The conditioning of textual responses utilizing "extrinsic" reinforcers. *Journal of the Experimental Analysis of Behavior,* 5:33–40.

Stern, R. M., 1970. Operant modification of electrodermal responses and/or voluntary control of GSR. Paper presented at meetings of the Society for Psychophysiolgical Research, November 1970.

Stewart, J., W. H. Krebs, and E. Kaczender, 1967. State-dependent learning produced with steroids. *Nature,* 216:1223–1224.

Stuart, R. B., 1970. *Trick or Treatment.* Champaign, Ill.: Research Press.

————, and B. Davis, 1970. *Behavioral Control of Overeating.* Champaign, Ill.: Research Press.

Terrace, H. S., 1963a. Discrimination learning with and without "errors." *Journal of the Experimental Analysis of Behavior,* 6:1–27.

————, 1963b, Errorless transfer of a discrimination across two continua. *Journal of the Experimental Analysis of Behavior,* 6:223–232.

Tharp, R. G., and R. J. Wetzel, 1969. *Behavior Modification in the Natural Environment.* New York: Academic Press.

Tiger, L., 1969. *Men in Groups.* London: Nelson.

Tribus, Myron, and Edward C. McIrvine, 1971. Energy and information. *Scientific American,* 224(3):179–188. (Available as *Scientific American* Offprint 670.)

Truax, C. B., 1966. Reinforcement and non-reinforcement in Rogerian psychotherapy. *Journal of Abnormal Psychology,* 71:1–9.

Tugwell, Rexford G., 1970. *A Model Constitution for the United Republics of America.* Santa Barbara: Center for the Study of Democratic Institutions.

Ulrich, R., T. Stachnik, and J. Mabry, 1966. *Control of Human Behavior.* Glenview, Ill.: Scott, Foresman.

U.S. Bureau of the Census, 1970. *Statistical Abstract of the United States, 1969,* p. 148. Washington, D. C.: Government Printing Office.

————, 1971. *Statistical Abstract of the United States, 1970,* p. 227. Washington, D. C.: Government Printing Office.

Waddington, C. H., 1967. *The Ethical Animal.* Chicago: University of Chicago Press.

Walter, W. Grey, 1950. An imitation of life. *Scientific American,* 182(5):42–45.

Whaley, D. L., and R. W. Malott, 1971. *Elementary Principles of Behavior.* New York: Appleton-Century-Crofts.

Wolpe, J., 1958. *Psychotherapy by Reciprocal Inhibition*. Stanford, Calif.: Stanford University Press.

————, and A. A. Lazarus, 1967. *Behavior Therapy Techniques*. New York: Pergamon Press.

Zadeh, L. A., 1971. Toward a theory of fuzzy systems. *In* N. DeClaris and R. Kalman, eds., *Aspects of Network and System Theory*. New York: Holt, Rinehart and Winston.

————, 1973. Outline of a new approach to the analysis of complex systems and decision processes. *IEEE Transactions on Systems, Man, and Cybernetics*, SMC-3:28–44.